# PERSPECTIVES™ ON
# BRANDING

**THE AGENCY PERSPECTIVE**
**JASON I. MILETSKY**

**THE BRAND PERSPECTIVE**
**GENEVIEVE SMITH**

# COURSE TECHNOLOGY
## CENGAGE Learning™

**Perspectives on Branding**
**Jason I. Miletsky and**
**Genevieve Smith**

**Publisher and General Manager, Course Technology PTR:** Stacy L. Hiquet

**Associate Director of Marketing:** Sarah Panella

**Manager of Editorial Services:** Heather Talbot

**Marketing Manager:** Mark Hughes

**Acquisitions Editor:** Mitzi Koontz

**Series Editor:** Jason I. Miletsky

**Project Editor:** Kate Shoup

**Editorial Services Coordinator:** Jen Blaney

**Copy Editor:** Kate Shoup

**Interior Layout:** Shawn Morningstar

**Cover Designer:** Mike Tanamachi

**Indexer:** Larry Sweazy

**Proofreader:** Heather Urschel

For product information and technology assistance, contact us at
**Cengage Learning Customer and Sales Support, 1-800-354-9706.**

For permission to use material from this text or product, submit all requests online at **cengage.com/permissions.**

Further permissions questions can be e-mailed to **permissionrequest@cengage.com.**

Library of Congress Control Number: 2008935083
ISBN-13: 978-1-59863-872-1
ISBN-10: 1-59863-872-6

**Course Technology, a part of Cengage Learning**
20 Channel Center Street
Boston, MA 02210
USA

Cengage Learning is a leading provider of customized learning solutions with office locations around the globe, including Singapore, the United Kingdom, Australia, Mexico, Brazil, and Japan. Locate your local office at: **international.cengage.com/region.**

Cengage Learning products are represented in Canada by Nelson Education, Ltd.

For your lifelong learning solutions, visit **courseptr.com.**
Visit our corporate Web site at **cengage.com.**

Printed in Canada
1 2 3 4 5 6 7 11 10 09

*I'd like to dedicate this book to my mom, Donna Miletsky,*
*and everyone on the Benrubi side of the family.*
*My dad and I each have our names on book covers,*
*so this at least puts her name in the spotlight, as well.*
*Love ya, Mom!*

—JASON MILETSKY

*Dedicated to my colleagues at WaMu.*
*I am proud of our accomplishments and*
*appreciate the opportunity to have worked with you.*

—GENEVIEVE SMITH

# ACKNOWLEDGMENTS

First, I'd like to thank everyone at Cengage Learning, including Mitzi Koontz, Mark Hughes, and my editor, Kate Shoup, who really did an outstanding job. I'd especially like to thank Stacy Hiquet, who worked with me to make the entire *Perspectives* series a reality. While I'm at it, I'd also like to thank everyone at Cengage Learning who worked with me on my earlier book, *Principles of Internet Marketing*. I know I became a lot harder to work with once *Perspectives* got under way, and I appreciate you all putting up with me!

Thanks, too, to Genevieve Smith, my counterpart in this book and one of the all-time great brand-builders. First came Radio Yes!, now *Perspectives on Branding*. Hopefully we'll have more chances to work together in the future.

Of course, I couldn't have done any of this without some of the great cast of clients I've worked with over the years, the team at PFS, and especially my business partner and the best damned PR guru I know, Deirdre Breakenridge.

As in all of my books, I want to thank everyone and anyone who's given me encouragement, believed in me, or even just been patient when work and writing have kept me from seeing them as often as I might have wanted to. This includes my parents; assorted uncles, aunts, and cousins; Cindi; Jackie; Chris; and everyone I've promised to stay in better touch with but haven't. Lastly, thanks to everyone at Eros Café in Rutherford, NJ, and the café in the Barnes & Noble in Clifton, NJ, who let me sit there for endless hours and kept me jacked up on Diet Pepsi while I wrote this.

—JASON MILETSKY

First and foremost, I'd like to acknowledge my family for their support during the writing of this book. Thanks, too, to my co-author, Jason Miletsky, for his limitless enthusiasm and insights. Thanks to Kate Shoup, our editor, who's been my rock, and to the entire team at Cengage Learning, including Stacy Hiquet, Mitzi Koontz, Mark Hughes, and everyone else who brought this book to life. Finally, many thanks to Steve Rotella for providing me with the opportunity to work and for his confidence in me.

—GENEVIEVE SMITH

# About the Authors

**Jason Miletsky** is CEO and executive creative director at PFS Marketwyse, a leading New Jersey agency specializing in helping mid- to large-sized companies bridge the gap between traditional and Internet marketing. An industry veteran, Jason heads up a creative team of marketing professionals focused on developing brands and generating awareness through traditional, online, and integrated efforts. His marketing work has included successful consultation and campaigns for companies including Hershey's, AmerisourceBergen, Emerson Electric, JVC, and The Michael C. Fina Company. Jason has authored eight books, including *Perspectives on Marketing* and *Perspectives on Branding*, as well as his new college textbook, *Principles of Internet Marketing*. Jason speaks publicly at seminars, companies, and universities on topics including marketing, brand-building, and various Internet-related topics. He has been a featured speaker for the Institute of International Research (IIR), National Association of Broadcasters (NAB), Strategic Research Institute (SRI), New Jersey Institute of Technology (NJIT), Pratt, and others. Jason is a graduate of Brandeis University (1994), and currently lives in Nutley, NJ.

**Genevieve Smith,** who now works as a consultant, was the chief marketing officer at Washington Mutual, where her broad responsibilities included brand management, advertising, customer optimization, e-commerce, line of business, and corporate marketing. As CMO, Smith was the driving force in building the company's strong consumer-friendly brand and differentiating WaMu as a bank that is fun, friendly, and "unbank-like." Smith previously served as the executive vice president of WaMu's customer optimization and e-commerce groups; before that, she was executive vice president of marketing for WaMu's home loans and insurance services group. Together with her marketing teams, Smith has earned numerous communications-industry awards, including the 2003 Cannes International Festival Silver Lion, the AMA Gold Effie, and a Clio, and the *AdWeek* 1st Place Out of Home Award. *Advertising Age* magazine named her among the Top 50 Marketers of 2006, making Smith the only CMO of a bank to be included in the prestigious list. Smith has more than 20 years of experience in financial-services marketing. Before joining WaMu, she held a broad range of senior-marketing and sales-management positions with American Savings Bank, which WaMu acquired in 1996. She also served as vice president and director of Empire Savings and Loan and as a partner at Northern Financial Services. Smith has also served on the Fannie Mae Advisory Board, a company that works to make it possible for low- and middle-income families to buy homes of their own. Smith received her bachelor's degree in business administration and anthropology from Antioch University and studied dance and anthropology at Universidád de las Américas in México.

# TABLE OF CONTENTS

# Part Two
# Operationalizing the Brand 101

# Part Four
# Brand Evaluation and Evolution                                    **199**

## Part Five
## Just for Fun                                                   241

## Closing Remarks                                                 263

## Index                                                           265

# INTRODUCTION

W alk down the aisles of any bookstore or library and you're bound to see plenty of books written by two or more authors. But sit down and read through it, and it's doubtful you'll be able to tell which author has contributed which information. They've collaborated, shared notes, and have ultimately written the book from a single voice.

But is that the best way to learn about a given topic? Sure, the authors are usually recognized experts in their field and can draw from some unique experiences and insights, but each book only takes into consideration a single viewpoint—one perspective that the reader is supposed to accept as true. That might make for an interesting read, but it only tells half the story. The importance, value, and methodology of brand-building, for example, may look dramatically different when seen through the eyes of a representative of a brand than through the eyes of a representative of a marketing agency. Each may be an expert when it comes to the art of brand-building, but their approach—and even their fundamental beliefs— could be quite opposite, simply because they work on different sides of the fence.

That's what makes the books in the *Perspectives* series so different from any other books on the shelves. Each offers a true 360-degree learning experience that gives you the opportunity to learn by providing two distinct and often opposing viewpoints. It's a rare chance to get both sides of the story so that you, the reader, can get a more complete understanding of the given topic.

In order to make a series like this work, though, the authors for each book need the freedom to write in their own voice and provide their own opinion, even at the risk of conflicting with their co-author. Therefore, it's important to note that **the authors of this book have not collaborated on their work during the course of their writing.** In fact, neither author will even have a chance to read their co-author's submissions until after the book has been completed. This is what makes *Perspectives* books such a unique concept, and a true opportunity to get both sides of the story.

In *Perspectives on Branding*, Jason I. Miletsky represents the agency perspective, while Genevieve Smith speaks on behalf of the brand. Through a total of 90 questions divided into five distinct parts, Jason and Genevieve give their expert opinions on important topics including understanding the brand, operationalizing the brand, marketing it, evaluating success, and measuring ROI. Part how-to book, part philosophical debate, *Perspectives on Branding* covers all the topics that anyone involved in brand-building would need in order to vastly improve their knowledgebase and skill set.

We hope you have as much fun reading *Perspectives on Branding* as we had working on it. Sometimes the authors whole-heartedly agreed with each other. In other instances, they couldn't have been more different. There's no question, however, that it's eye-opening to see the different perspective each author provided. But the perspectives don't end in this book. We want to hear your point of view, as well. Visit the blog site for this book at PerspectivesOnBranding.com to comment on select content, read questions and answers that don't appear in this book, and let us know whose perspective you agree with more.

# OPENING REMARKS

**JASON MILETSKY**

You really have to love an entire industry built on vague generalities. "Branding" and "brand-building" remain common buzzwords among agencies and companies, but while everyone seems to agree that they're necessary, not everyone really understands what it all means. It's like there's this brand fog that exists in the center of the marketing universe—dense, thick, maybe even a little foreboding, clearly there but hardly defined. We all reference it with awe (the more seasoned marketers even feign a little wisdom) when we set our strategies, but few people are ready to answer the real, hard questions —the ones that require firm answers.

Branding isn't just an exercise we go through to keep ourselves busy or make our jobs seem more complicated than they really are. It's a necessary part of increasing market share, generating ROI, and building a fan base. In short, in a skeptical world, branding is the development of trust, and trust is a conduit to revenue.

This trust doesn't just apply to the consumer. True marketers understand that the brand needs to take on a life of its own. It needs to be lived through every pore of a company, product, and service—internally and externally. But if marketers are Dr. Frankenstein, then brands are our monsters—and the larger they are, the tougher they can be to control. Will the monster become reckless and be run out of town by the villagers? Or will it be trustworthy and loved by all? That all depends on how well the brand is built and, more importantly, how well it's understood.

One of the reasons I was so excited to write this book was that it forced me to think—I mean, *really* think—about the right answer to each question. Not just the canned answers agencies like to give because they make us sound smarter, but what I actually believe—the truth, *my* truth, beyond the typical crap that sounds nice but doesn't mean much. I'm hoping that in this book, I'll be able to provide some of the firm answers that marketers really need to know about what a brand really is, why it's important, how to properly market it, and how to know if the efforts you're taking are actually working.

Can I really speak on behalf of all agencies? Probably not. With so many different belief systems out there when it comes to branding, it's doubtful that every agency exec will completely agree with my thoughts on the topic. But I'll draw from my own experiences and my own studies, and hopefully, if nothing else, I can provide some hard-hitting, useful information, free from the vague generalities that so many marketers have gotten used to.

This opportunity to share my experiences and perspectives on branding came at an unusual time in my career. The very week I agreed to write this book, the bank that employed me as CMO, WaMu, was seized by the FDIC and sold to JP Morgan Chase. This was the result of declining consumer and investor confidence in the midst of the global financial crisis.

Earlier in the year, according to an annual study of consumers by research firm Brand Keys, WaMu topped the list of bank brands "best able to engage consumers and create loyal customers," beating out Bank of America, JP Morgan Chase, Wells Fargo, and Citi. As well, WaMu was named the leader in industry-reputation rankings for the second consecutive year according to a national study of corporate reputations by the Reputation Institute. According to U.S. consumers surveyed, WaMu's reputation score (64.04) was the highest among U.S. banking industry companies, ahead of Wachovia (61.22), Wells Fargo (57.38), and Bank of America (50.94). The previous year, WaMu received the 2007 Customer Service Champs Award (*Business Week*); was deemed Top Retail Bank in Customer Satisfaction in the West and Midwest regions (*JD Power & Associates*); and ranked number one in customer satisfaction among the top five online banks, with 78 percent of customers reporting they were "highly satisfied" (*ComScore*).

We'd built a differentiated brand that drove business and was an efficient tool for acquiring and keeping customers, and that delivered on its promise. According to Millward Brown's Brand and Ad Monitor, WaMu enjoyed the highest consideration score among major banks in the USA in 2008. Yet, with all of that, the company did not survive the economic crisis. Did the brand fail the business or did the business fail the brand? We've debated this quite a bit, and have discovered there really is no definitive answer to that question.

I've had the unusual opportunity to work on shutting down the WaMu brand and to be involved with the new owners as they re-brand the company. This is not something your average CMO expects to wake up one morning and find herself doing; it's been a fascinating experience. Through all the highs and lows, I've had the chance to work with some of the best brand professionals through our great agencies, work with people who are passionate brand zealots, and to experience the exhilaration of riding the wave of a brand on the move.

Writing this book has offered me a tremendous opportunity to reflect on what it really takes to build a brand, as well as what I've experienced that's good and what's maybe not so good. I've shared those with you as I see them, drawing from my experiences. I don't consider myself an "expert" by any means, but I've seen a lot and am passionate on the topic of branding. I trust some of my real-life experiences and observations will be useful to the reader.

# PART ONE
# Understanding the Brand

# Q: HOW WOULD YOU DEFINE A BRAND?

**JASON MILETSKY**
**THE AGENCY PERSPECTIVE**

Here it is: The first—and possibly most important—question of this book. I gotta set the tone. More urgently, I have to get the answer right to avoid turning you off before you've even had a chance to read this—for free—in the Barnes and Noble café whilst spilling your venti mochaccino all over the cover.

The problem is, I'm guessing that Vegas oddsmakers would say it's more likely that physicists will come up with a unified theory of everything before marketers will agree on a single definition of what a "brand" actually is. One definition I can quickly dispel, though, is the popular (and irritating) assumption that a brand is just a logo. (Hint to anybody who comes to my agency looking for a job: Defining the brand as a logo is a sure-fire way to keep the interview short.)

That's not to say I don't have an opinion as to the definition of a brand, of course. Indeed, my definition is probably one that most marketing types either believe or use as the foundation for their own unique spin. Drum roll please:

> **brand:** The sum total of all user experiences with a particular product or service, building both reputation and future expectations of benefit.

Let's break this down by looking at real-life examples:

You've got clients coming in from out of town and you want to put them up in a really lush, comfortable hotel. Are you going to make reservations at Motel 6? Of course not, because you know that Motel 6 is a low-cost, low-frills, low-comfort chain meant more for convenience and cost-savings than for comfort and amenities.

While traveling out of state, you pass a Pizza Hut right around dinner time. Do you need to wonder what to expect? No, because the Pizza Hut interior design, menu offerings, portions, and taste are pretty much exactly the same in every restaurant in every state.

In each case, you instinctively know what you can expect—even if you've never actually visited a Pizza Hut or Motel 6. Their reputation is such that consumers know what to expect from each, and know that their experience will be the same regardless of geography. That reputation is the brand.

So where does the logo come in, and why do so many people mistake it for being the brand itself? I'll go into that in more detail later on, but for now, I can tell you that the logo—along with other visual and audio elements such as colors, fonts, taglines, and even musical affiliations (think "by Mennen")—is the tangible (for lack of a better word) element that provides recognition of the brand. It *represents* the brand. As soon as consumers see a logo, they can reach into their mental filing cabinets containing every brand they've ever come in direct (or indirect) contact with, and establish an immediate expectation upon which to base a purchasing decision.

Of course, it's not as easy as simply being consistent in whatever product or service is being provided. Reputations and expectations must be based on *something* if consumers are going to put their trust in a brand. The elements that make up the brand and work toward building this trust include the following:

- **The promise:** Although this isn't always expressly stated, it's one of the key factors in branding. What is being promised to the consumer? Nike doesn't just make sneakers. Anyone with rubber and laces can do that. Nike is promising a better athletic and fashionable experience through use of their product. They're promising a lifestyle, where their buyers will be part of an in crowd that includes sports and music stars. Do they ever come out and say that? Not that I've heard…but the promise is clearly there.

- **The personality:** Like people, brands have their own personalities. Some are quirky (think Volkswagen); others are refined (think Jaguar); and still others can range from downright silly and approachable to corporate and wise. The brand's personality creates that emotional connection that draws in a target market. That doesn't mean the brand's personality is strictly a part of the marketing process (although it's always important to market with the personality in mind). Rather, the brand's personality is something consumers come to rely on. Part of a brand's enduring reputation is how true they stay to that personality.

- **The USP (unique selling proposition):** This is the single element that makes any company, product, or service different from any other company, product, or service. It could be a distinctive recipe for ranch dressing or special quilting that makes a paper towel more absorbent. Whatever it is, every brand needs to provide at least one quality that makes it unique on the market.

As mentioned in my definition, a brand is "the sum total of all user experiences." This sum total is in constant flux, with additions and subtractions made with each consumer interaction. This is why brand-building—the process of making those interactions more positive than negative—is so important. In building their reputation, brands need to not only be aware of these elements—the promise, the personality, and the UPS—but consistently fulfill each one. Any time the promise is broken, a dent is made in how the brand is perceived by the public. Any time the brand is not true to its personality, it takes another step away from its customers and further diminishes its viability.

GENEVIEVE SMITH
THE BRAND PERSPECTIVE

 The classic definition of a brand would probably go something like this:

> A brand is a unique and identifiable symbol, association, name, or trademark that serves to differentiate competing products or services. It is both a physical and an emotional trigger to create a relationship between consumers and the products or services being offered.

An easier way to say this could be:

> A brand is the relationship a customer has with a company and/or its products and services. It's more than just the logo; it's the total experience that acts as the emotional trigger.

These definitions focus on the consumer's relationship with the brand, but there are other facets to consider (which we will talk about in more detail later): the thinking that a brand can be both a strategic and financial asset, managed for profit, and that a brand can create loyalty among employees, making it easier to recruit high-caliber talent.

## BRANDS AS EMOTIONAL TRIGGERS

Since we are talking about the consumer, let's take a minute to explore the notion of brand as an emotional trigger. Brands can be hated, like Enron, because of that company's perceived lack of ethics and its poor treatment of employees. Then there are brands we know about but really don't feel much connection to one way or the other. MasterCard and Visa are often thought of in this way; you hardly notice them. There are other brands that we like; they put a smile on our face—think BMW or Godiva chocolates. Finally, there are brands people absolutely love—a loyalist wouldn't even consider any other brand in its category. Apple and Harley Davidson are good examples here; people love these brands. They are passionate about them, and eagerly encourage others to buy them because they themselves have a deep emotional connection to the brand.

# Q: WHAT ROLE DOES BRAND-BUILDING PLAY IN BUILDING A MARKET?

**JASON MILETSKY**
**THE AGENCY PERSPECTIVE**

Recently, I had a 40-minute layover at a train station in Philadelphia and decided to hit the food court rather than sit alone on an empty train. I got in line at the Cosi counter, because I've always liked Cosi, and hadn't had it in awhile. (If you ever get the chance, try their turkey and brie. Best sandwich ever.) But while I was waiting, I noticed a local, independent sandwich stand with a hand-printed sign that said "Cheese Steak Larry's: Best Chese Stakes in Philly." (Yes, the words "cheese" and "steaks" were misspelled.) Even though I had my doubts that it was the *best* in the city, I figured, I'm in the city that's known for its cheese-steak sandwiches, so I really couldn't go wrong. Two bites of Cheese Steak Larry's unhappy-looking sandwich and soggy fries (on a semi-clean tray) and one more line later, I was happily eating the Cosi turkey and brie sandwich I knew and loved.

My point (and I do have one) is that this got me thinking about the power and necessity of brand-building. (Yes, I am that much of a nerd that bad excuses for food can launch me into spontaneous thoughts on branding.) The city of Philadelphia had done such a great job building its brand as *the* premier spot for cheese steaks that I had abandoned my place in line for a meal I knew I would like to get a sandwich from a food vendor I had never heard of. Philadelphia has built its market. It has claimed ownership of the cheese-steak sandwich, and in doing so, has built a market for them.

Cheese Steak Larry, however, doesn't need to build a market. By virtue of being in Philadelphia, he's got one built in—and it's mostly a transient one. (Nobody who lives in Philly is going to go out of their way to eat in the train station.) So Larry just doesn't need to worry about impressing customers with his cooking prowess, because we're all just passing through. We can't offer him repeat business or much in the way of word-of-mouth marketing, so why bother spending extra money on quality ingredients?

But while the Cosi vendor might not have any more repeat business than Cheese Steak Larry does, Cosi *does* have a reason to provide quality food and service: The experience consumers have at this location will influence their decisions to eat at Cosi locations in New York, Los Angeles, or any other city. The Cosi reputation (its brand) precedes it.

Through brand-building—managing and monitoring the elements of the brand and marketing and communicating its message and reputation—brands can effectively build their markets, creating loyal customers who buy purposely rather than randomly. Randomness and situation-based consumer purchasing may generate a few dollars for vendors like Larry, but it's not sustainable and can't be counted on. With brands, there is a constant need to communicate the promise and personality, generate awareness of a positive reputation, cushion the blow of negative consumer experiences, and ensure that the visual elements like the logo have recognition in the marketplace. Companies must make sure that their brand fulfills its promise to the market—and it's the act of brand-building (whether handled internally or through an agency) that communicates that promise. Brand building helps develop a relationship with consumers where decision-making is at least partly based on emotion and where there is reasonable hope for future purchases.

GENEVIEVE SMITH
THE BRAND PERSPECTIVE

⌐ The brand can play an integral role in driving both short-term revenue gains (through superior customer experience, which drives preference) and long-term shareholder value. For example, a vital brand can drive the following:

- Consideration and preference for products and services

- Price premium protection

- Loyalty among employees and customers

When a company is focused on building their brand, they are by extension building a market at the same time. In fact, those companies that develop and build brands with deep resonance for consumers have the best prospects for growth. We will discuss this in many ways throughout the book; in my opinion the direct linkage between the brand and a company's success is what makes the topic of branding so important.

# Q: IS THERE A DIFFERENCE BETWEEN A BRAND AND A COMPANY? WHAT ABOUT BETWEEN A BRAND AND A PRODUCT?

JASON MILETSKY
THE AGENCY PERSPECTIVE

There is definitely a difference, although in everyday writing and conversation (due, I think, to limitations in the English language), "brand" is often used interchangeably with "company" and "product." But while people—including yours truly—may substitute the word "brand" for the word "company" in their everyday writing or conversation, it's important to understand the conceptual difference. Anyone with $50 can register an LLC and, in less than a week, be the owner of his or her own company. Notice that I said company—not brand. A company is legal paperwork, shares of stock, permits, infrastructure. It's an entity organized for the purposes of taking action. The same goes for products. Products are materials, ingredients—they are physical items that can be sold and transferred from one entity to another. But that's no more a brand than a company is.

Where it gets fuzzy is in the naming, because a single name can refer to all of the above. Take Pepsi, for example. Few people ever refer to the company by its proper name, PepsiCo. Instead, for most people, "Pepsi" interchangeably refers to the company (the entity that manufactures and sells the product), the product (the cola drink made up of carbonated water, sugar, and syrup), and the brand (the reputation for being a consistently refreshing beverage with a distinct taste that's connected to a younger generation). An interesting illustration of the difference can be seen at their respective Web sites: As of this writing, the PepsiCo Web site (http://www.pepsico.com) is a staid, corporate, boring site that gives information but hardly promotes a distinct personality or design style. Compare this to the brand site located at http://www.pepsi.com. Notice I call it a "brand" site, not a "product site"; that's because information about the product is actually not that easy to find, at least compared to images and information related to music, sports, environmental issues, clothing—cultural touch points that Pepsi uses to lock its brand into its target market and create an emotional connection.

In everyday usage, it's inevitable that everyone will confuse company, product, and brand with each other—and that's okay. The truth is that while yes, there is a difference, and no, the brand is neither the company nor the product (nor the logo, for that matter), it really doesn't matter. As long as marketers understand that building and promoting the brand is vital to growth and necessary for building consumer trust, I can't see any reason why a distinction has to be made outside of strictly academic circles.

GENEVIEVE SMITH
THE BRAND PERSPECTIVE

I don't believe there is a difference between the brand and the company. In my opinion, they are one and the same. The practices that are internal to a firm, such as operations, human resources, or its economics (just to name a few), are what inform things like products, services, practices, and even brand marketing and expressions. Ultimately, who a company is will be reflected in the interactions that company has with the consumer, both tangible and intangible.

Products are not a brand. They are a bundle of attributes or features, functions, benefits, and uses that can be exchanged in either tangible or intangible forms. Ideally, however, the brand should inform product development. Your products represent your brand in a really powerful way—i.e., they are literally what are for sale. Products are also where most firms allocate their communications investments, so the quality and believability of a firm's products are intrinsic to the success of the brand.

A good brand will challenge product development to create category-killer products. (A recent example of a category-killer product is the iPod. How many times have you heard someone say, "I want to create the iPod of my industry?") Here are some key points to keep in mind when thinking about product development:

- **Don't give away the farm:** Create products based on consumer demand, and you won't have to compete on price alone.

- **Design products to work better together if they share the same brand:** Again, use consumer demand to create product bundles.

- **Don't be afraid to tip a few cows:** You can bust perceived category barriers because frequently, consumers don't think like people inside your company or category.

- **Position your products against a mindset, not a category description:** Create products out of a consumer mindset in order to differentiate your products—and hence, your brand.

# Q: • IS A BRAND SIMPLY A LOGO?
# • WHY OR WHY NOT?

**JASON MILETSKY**
**THE AGENCY PERSPECTIVE**

 NO! (I hope that wasn't too subtle.)

I made my views on this clear in my very first answer in this book and I mention it in other appropriate areas because it's a topic I could rant against over and over. The brand is not simply a logo. Period.

The real debate isn't with general consumers, who will generally never make the distinction between a brand and a logo (and they don't need to—branding will still affect them whether they know it or not). The real debate is with the scant few marketing professionals who hold on to the belief that the brand is the logo, and it's no more complicated than that.

In *Perspectives on Marketing*, a book I wrote with Michael Hand, part of my answer to the question "What is the best way to define a brand?" went something like this:

> Visit any cattle farm and you'll see herds of cows with letters or icons burnt into their butts with a branding iron. This practice of marking animals is at the very root of branding. Because cows pretty much all look alike (I've always wondered how a bull knows which cow is his wife…), farmers needed a way to tell which cows belong to which farmer. To solve this problem, farmers started to burn a mark on their cattle to distinguish which cows belong to which farm should herds ever become intermingled. The mark (brand) helps to tell one cow (product) from another. Therefore, one definition of a brand is:

> **brand:** An icon or mark (logo) that helps distinguish one product from another.

I go on to explain, though, that while this may in fact represent the birth of modern-day branding, it's not a fair apples-to-apples comparison:

> There is a slight disconnect with the previous definition. Let's revisit the farmer. The farmer brands his cows to prove ownership—not so that you, the consumer, can pick out his cows from those of another farmer. By the time his cow ends up on your plate, you are thinking far less about which farm it came from than you are about whether you will still have room for dessert afterward. That's a very different scenario than the one in which a consumer is choosing to drink Pepsi instead of Coke.

So if you're a farmer, then yes—a brand is a logo. Get out the irons and start searing some beef. If you're not a farmer, then drill this into your head: The brand is not the logo. The logo *represents* the brand. It's an iconic means of conveying a message and a means for promoting recognition among the target audience, but it is not interchangeable with the brand itself.

GENEVIEVE SMITH
THE BRAND PERSPECTIVE

⮎ The logo is an important element of the brand expression, but people who believe the brand is simply a logo are incorrect. The logo can be thought of as the brand signature. That said, there are brands whose logos are so well associated with the brand that it has become shorthand for expressing everything the brand stands for. You can see this in categories such as sports, fashion, automotive, green, political movements, and many others; people wear/drive/carry logo-branded merchandise because of what it says about them. This is not necessarily because the logo itself is particularly cool or artful, but rather because of what the brand associated with the logo stands for—and, by association, the consumer's own personal brand or beliefs.

So while an iconic brand logo may carry tons of equity in the market, the logo itself is merely visual shorthand for the brand—a visual demonstration of the brand in communications. You can look at the logo like a badge—and you'd like people to wear it with pride because of what it stands for.

Consistency and management of the logo is vital to the effectiveness of the brand because of their close association—which is why people may joke about "logo police." But if you don't maintain and protect the integrity of the logo, you just never know where it might show up!

# Q: IS THE BRAND PROMISE EVER STATED DIRECTLY IN MARKETING? OR IS IT MORE OF AN INTANGIBLE CONCEPT?

JASON MILETSKY

THE AGENCY PERSPECTIVE

This question really relates to the larger concept of what a brand promise really is, how it's conveyed, and what importance it holds. Simply stated, the brand promise is the benefit the brand will deliver to consumers—and keeping that promise is one of the most important things a company can do. The brand promise can be expressed directly, made crystal clear, or it can be subtle and unspoken; either way, a promise is a promise and needs to be kept.

Suppose you're planning a vacation. You visit a Web site that promises to provide more comprehensive information on remote destinations than any other travel site on the Internet. While using the site for research, you notice that it speaks highly of the island of St. Maarten in the Caribbean, detailing an exciting night life, a championship golf course, and award-winning restaurants. You're sold! You book your flight, pack your bags, and head out, anxious to play a round of golf and dance the night away. There's only one problem: the Web site neglected to mention that a hurricane hit the island a few years back and destroyed the golf course, which was never rebuilt. It also left out the fact that the night life consists of bars and clubs that are open only during specific months of the year —read: not when you're there. So much for "comprehensive information!" the bottom line: The site did not deliver what it promised. It promised comprehensive information, but the information it actually provided was old and incomplete. The next time you are planning a trip, it's highly doubtful you'll return to the site for information.

While trust can be difficult to build, losing it can be a much quicker process. Keeping the brand promise is key to building trust in a brand. Initially, the consumer can only go by what the brand promises and assume that the promise will be kept. If the promise is kept, then the brand is strengthened. A positive reputation has been maintained, and the expectation of positive future experiences with the brand is increased, making it more likely that the consumer will use that brand again. If the promise is broken, the brand is breached, raising doubt and diminishing trust—and regaining consumers' trust is often impossible.

Do consumers really give a brand only one chance to fail? It depends on the brand. How much leeway a company has in breaking its promise will largely depend on its longevity and history—or, put another way, how much trust equity the brand has built up. The more trust consumers have in a brand, the more likely they'll be to forgive broken promises—to a point.

Take Nike, for example. Nike makes sneakers—the sneakers are their product. Their brand reputation is delivering high-quality, stylish products that will enhance athletic performance. When a consumer purchases a pair of Nikes, the expectation is that the shoes will be comfortable and last a long time, even after aggressive use. For decades, Nike has kept that brand promise and met consumer expectations, even though (to my best recollection) that promise has never been expressly stated. Now suppose a consumer purchases a new pair of Nikes and they fall apart in the middle of a basketball game just two days later. That consumer will be annoyed, but his confidence in the Nike brand won't have taken too much of a hit. Because Nike has built enough trust equity to overcome a single bad experience, chances are the customer will assume it was just one bad pair of sneakers off the assembly line, and will obtain a new pair. But now suppose that a few days later, the consumer's ankles start to hurt during his weekly tennis game because the sneakers aren't providing the proper support. Will this consumer buy *another* pair of Nikes? Maybe, but his trust in the brand will have been shaken—and he just may look at a pair of Reeboks the next time around. Sure, after enough time has passed, the consumer might write off these negative experiences and buy the Nike brand again, but there is no question that on some level, damage will have been done. And of course, most brands don't have the time, money, or exposure that Nike has to overcome isolated negative experiences. Brands must take care to keep their promises each and every time in order to develop the trust necessary for gaining and retaining consumer loyalty.

While the brand promise often has to do with the quality of a product or service, that's not always the case. McDonald's doesn't claim that eating there is akin to dining in a five-star restaurant. Their promise is to provide you a quick meal that is inexpensive and tastes good. Women don't buy sweatshirts from Juicy Couture because of their promised high quality. The subtle promise is that if you own Juicy products, you will be part of an elite, fashionable crowd. The promise in this case involves lifestyle factors rather than product-related factors, such as speed or quality.

As brand builders, marketers must manage how the promise is expressed and how consumers understand it to make sure they're not inadvertently promising something they can't deliver. That's one of the most challenging things about marketing: The brand understands the promise and the agency understands the promise, but does the audience? Building a brand involves using tangibles (Web sites, advertisements, etc.) to communicate intangible concepts such as a promise or personality in a way that makes sense, is perceived as desirable by consumers, and on which the brand can realistically follow through.

**Genevieve Smith**

**The Brand Perspective**

If all the stars were perfectly aligned, then perhaps—and only perhaps—your brand promise would be suitable for translation into customer communications. Why is it hard to state the brand promise in marketing? Because the brand promise is not a marketing message. It is a reflection of internal operations and of the company's position in the minds of consumers that is then translated into customer communications.

For example, we developed an internal brand promise for WaMu called Simpler Banking and More Smiles. We urged all employees to ask themselves two questions about the work they do:

- Does it make things simpler for the customer?
- Will it make them smile?

The theory was, if every employee could answer these two questions positively day in and day out, the brand promise would succeed. This was a naturally disruptive brand in a very stodgy category: banking. Banks typically fall into the category of "disliked" or "not really relevant," but WaMu was attempting to position itself as a bank people love.

Many people fell in love with the statement "Simpler Banking and More Smiles," and we explored using it in one form or another in external communications as a tagline of sorts. This just didn't work for consumer marketing, however, because in testing, the word "simple" equated to starter bank, or a bank that cannot serve all the customer's needs. And "smile"—well, everyone likes that, but the intent is to actually *create* the smile, not say we are going to do it. The job of marketing and customer communications was to capture the emotional benefit and ultimately the feeling of banking with WaMu—but the words "Simpler Banking and More Smiles" did not do the job externally.

I do believe that the brand promise is more of an intangible concept; it's aspirational and acts as a "true north" for much more than simply marketing. It has to motivate internally and must be a bellwether against which many actions are judged. For example, is a new product aligned with the brand promise? What about a policy change or price structure?

# Q: DOES A COMPANY'S MISSION STATEMENT HELP DEFINE THE BRAND?

**JASON MILETSKY**
**THE AGENCY PERSPECTIVE**

Personally, I think mission statements are pure crap. At least, I've never seen one that makes sense to me or rings even remotely true. Most of them don't say anything meaningful at all, and just use standard marketing buzzwords that could just as easily relate to any company.

Take this charmer from Aflac:

> *To combine aggressive strategic marketing with quality products and services at competitive prices to provide the best insurance value for consumers.*

What? Are they serious? What's the point of that? All they did was take a bunch of the most important words in marketing—"quality," "products," "services," "prices," "best," and "value"—and string them together in a sentence. It doesn't say anything useful to anybody, doesn't make any bit of difference to how they do business, and, if the word "insurance" were removed, could just as easily apply to any other company regardless of size or industry. Plus—and I don't want to argue semantics, but I will—that's not really their mission anyway. Corporations aren't that altruistic. Their mission is to make money. Look at this mission statement for AGCO, a leading agricultural equipment manufacturer:

> *Profitable growth through superior customer service, innovation, quality and commitment.*

At least that's honest! Their mission is to achieve profitable growth. Everything after the word "growth" simply states the means by which they plan to generate that growth.

But I still don't really see the point in having the mission statement. The AGCO mission statement might be honest, but does it say anything? Okay, they want to generate profitable growth. What company doesn't? And, okay, they'll do it by providing superior customer service, innovation, quality, and commitment.

15

Does any legitimate company go into business with the intention of providing sub-par customer service, out-of-date ideas, useless crap, and indifference? Not likely.

So no, I don't think the mission statement does squat to help define the brand. I don't think it helps to promote the brand, direct the brand—I don't think it has anything to do with the brand. Now, the brand promise, on the other hand, is a different story. Where the mission statement is some ambiguous line meant more for internal purposes (I guess), the brand promise is the stated or implied benefit that the brand will provide to its customers—and it's one of the most important elements of the brand. For more on the brand promise, refer to Question #5, "Is the Brand Promise Ever Stated Directly in Marketing? Or Is It More of an Intangible Concept?"

**GENEVIEVE SMITH**
**THE BRAND PERSPECTIVE**

↳ The mission statement is an expression of the company's history, managerial style, concerns, resources, and competencies. It is used to guide the company's decision-making process with respect to what the company's business is, who it serves, etc. A mission statement is expected for investors and other key constituents and employees, and frequently reflects the company's charter and what the company's founders and executives think about the business. Similarly, a successful brand will be a reflection of the sum of parts of the business operations, employees, and customer segments; it cannot be at odds with or inherently different from the company's stated mission.

My preference would be to see linkage between the internal brand promise, external expressions, and mission statement. I will admit, however, that although we were able to weave elements of the mission statement into the WaMu brand promise to align them, I was supremely *un*successful in rewriting and consolidating the company's various statements—mission statement, vision statement, values statement, and brand promise—into the Simpler Banking and More Smiles platform at WaMu. The fact was, how all these statement were linked together and how they guided internal and external customer interactions was about as clear as mud. I decided that in the grand scheme of things, this was not a battle I wanted to fight—but given more time, I would have, because I think it's important for every employee to be able to articulate a few things—ideally, the mission statement and brand promise—really well.

# Q: • DOES EVERY BRAND HAVE TO HAVE • A UNIQUE SELLING PROPOSITION?

JASON MILETSKY
THE AGENCY PERSPECTIVE

Yes, but let's be clear about what it means to be "unique" and determine how unique a quality has to be before it really makes a difference to the consumer.

To my knowledge (and some scientist somewhere could possibly prove me wrong), no two things can be 100-percent identical. Geography alone would make each of them unique, in that two entities can't occupy the same exact space at the same exact time. Even if you clone a dog, with the original and the copy completely the same from a genetic standpoint, the dogs would still be unique based on the fact that at any given time, they would each stand in different places.

The same is true for companies. Take two competing comic-book stores in neighboring towns, for example. As chance has it, both are run by nice guys who are very passionate about comic books, both have exactly the same inventory of comic books, both present each comic book in the same way, and both charge the exact same price for each book. For all intents and purposes, both stores are the same. Their only real difference is geography, so it stands to reason that consumers will simply shop at whichever store is closer to them. Proximity to the consumer makes each store unique enough.

But now let's place those stores across the street from each other. Now, even geography doesn't make a difference. They're competing for the same pool of customers. The natural tendency of each store owner would be to take some action—lower prices, offer a comic-book–delivery service, hold in-store comic-book–art workshops, or what have you—that makes his or her store unique so that consumers will have a reason to choose his or her shop over the other.

So what happens when geography isn't a factor? The same basic principle holds true. Take competing brands of soap. All manufacturers ship to the same supermarkets, so it doesn't matter to the consumer where their offices, factories, or distribution centers are located. The competing products are on the shelf next to each other. If all these bars of soap were exactly the same, then the total market would simply be divided equally among them. But again, the natural tendency of competing companies is to try to stand out among their competition in order to draw in a larger audience, and to build a brand based on their unique qualities.

So the answer to the question "Does every brand have to have a unique selling proposition" is yes, they do. Without one, the company might survive, but not the brand. But what *really* matters is the relevancy of this unique quality. In the case of soap, if one company simply decides to carve an X into the center of each bar, it may make those bars unique, but not in a way that consumers will care about—so it won't help build the brand. Instead, these manufacturers must instill unique qualities that are more relevant to the market—scent, size, price, shape, or something else along those lines.

GENEVIEVE SMITH

THE BRAND PERSPECTIVE

If you want consumers to pick your brand when faced with vast choices, there needs to be a unique selling proposition. The unique selling proposition is what separates your product or offering from another. It can be feature based, price based, or maybe even just that magic something that makes it cooler than a similar product.

Suppose you are in the soup aisle at your local supermarket and you'd like to buy a can of tomato soup. Have you ever counted the number of brands and varieties of tomato soup that are available? I have—and I lost track at 40. In the face of such a selection, what is going to make you pick one over the other? Price? Quality? Value? Reliability? Familiarity? Do you pick the soup your mom always made? Do you choose one because it's microwaveable? Do you select one with an easy-open can? Do you choose the one that is heart healthy, low fat, low cholesterol, no salt, low salt, or organic? Or do you just pick one whose packaging you like? These features combine to create a unique selling proposition for each soup brand.

You can look at the unique selling proposition as the company or product point of difference from other similar offerings. Without the USP or point of difference, what makes the brand relevant? *Sans* differentiation, the product won't stick around for long.

# Q: How Would You Describe "Brand Personality"?

**Jason Miletsky**
**The Agency Perspective**

⮑ Think about the people you run into on a daily basis. Some are super funny. Some are great listeners. Some tend to be more serious. Some are terrific conversationalists or are deeply philosophical. Some are obnoxious. Some are shy or depressing, and others are upbeat. Chances are, the people you gravitate toward are people with whom you share similar personality traits.

Likewise, you'll probably gravitate toward brands with personalities similar to your own. Like people, brands have their own personalities, and they use that personality to relate to a market that shares similar traits. The M&Ms brand, for example, comes off as fun and irreverent, while Godiva comes off as serious and elegant. Each brand has developed a personality meant to attract a specific audience. Consumers' belief that a brand understands them and their lifestyle, and will provide products and services with that understanding in mind, helps forge a lasting bond and strengthens brand loyalty.

Often, people use first impressions to judge personalities—usually based on aesthetic presentation. Don't believe me? Go to any crowded place that attracts all different types of people, such as a mall. Find a bench, sit back, relax, and observe. Watch the people walking by. See the woman with the heavy make-up, pink hat, and loud pink pants? What do you think her personality is like? What about that guy with the comb-over, wearing the sweater vest and walking timidly behind his wife, his head down and his hands deep in his pockets? How about the teenager walking up the down escalator, with the black Metallica T-shirt, baggy jeans, and half of his hair shaved off? Right or wrong, people often make an immediate assumption about others' personalities just by the way they look—the colors they wear, the style of clothes they choose, and other visual elements.

Brands are no different. Brand personalities are often immediately judged by how they present themselves to the public through visual elements and marketing efforts. To create this emotional connection, a brand must carefully balance how it looks and acts (how it's marketed) so that everything is in sync. Think back to the guy with the comb-over and sweater vest, walking dejectedly behind his wife in the mall. What did you assume about him from how he looked and acted? How would your image of him change if he veered off into a music store and started jamming away on an electric guitar? What if you saw the kid in the black Metallica T-shirt sipping a cappuccino while expounding on the economic ramifications of further European Union expansion? Most likely, your assumptions about their personalities would change. Indeed, you might not know *what* to think, because their image and actions contrast with each other. When it comes to judging people, this type of contrast may be little more than a mild curiosity. When it comes to brands, however, any disconnect between aesthetics and action can be the difference between brand loyalty and brand indifference.

GENEVIEVE SMITH
THE BRAND PERSPECTIVE

Brand personality is the brand image (i.e., what's currently in the mind of consumers) expressed in terms of human characteristics. These are distinguishing and identifiable characteristics that offer consistent, enduring, and predictable messages and perceptions. You want the brand expression to translate into the emotional connection we spoke about earlier, engaging the consumer with the brand in a similar fashion to engaging with a person or personality.

Think of it like buying a gift for someone. In the course of choosing the gift, you typically contemplate whether it "fits" with the recipient's personality. A brand is recognized in the same way. You can't really fake the brand personality. If the consumer reacts to some form of marketing by saying, "Huh—that doesn't sound or look or feel or smell like brand xyz," it means the brand is trying to do something not inherent in its personality.

# Q: SHOULD THE PERSONALITY OF THE BRAND REFLECT THE COMPANY FOUNDERS AND EXECUTIVES, THE TARGET MARKET, OR SOMETHING ELSE?

JASON MILETSKY
THE AGENCY PERSPECTIVE

This answer isn't clear-cut. This issue can be tricky, because the truth is that the brand personality needs to take many variables into consideration. On the one hand, because the personality of a brand is the key to creating an emotional connection with the audience, it would be reasonable to conclude that the personality should reflect the market. On the other hand, however, a brand needs to be comfortable in its own skin in order to consistently maintain its personality—and very often, there can be a conflict between what the market wants and what the brand can actually maintain.

It's too easy to say that the personality of the brand need not reflect the personalities of the company's founders or executives. I think their personalities will absolutely play at least some role in how the brand's personality is developed. I can't say for sure, but I have to think that the key executives behind the popular video-game developer EA, for example, are at least a little edgy and fun. I'd be shocked to find out they all wear three-piece suits to work every day, where they smoke cigars while discussing the moral decline of modern society. But how influential the personalities of key execs are to the brand may be somewhat minimal, and may instead depend more on the product being sold and the market being reached. That is, it's pretty safe to assume that the key execs behind Barbie aren't eight-year-old girls.

The real answer is that the personality of the brand isn't reflective of any one entity in particular, but a balance of all of them. There's no point in the brand personality for a gaming company being stuffy and serious simply because that's the personality of the key execs, because it'll turn off the market they're trying to reach. At the same time, there's no point in that same gaming company presenting itself as wild, crazy, and edgy simply because that's what the market wants.

If the decision-makers aren't comfortable in that skin, they won't be able to sustain that brand personality. Every brand needs to find a balance between what the market will respond to and what it can reasonably be expected to consistently present. The point where these two needs meet is the starting point for developing the brand's personality.

**GENEVIEVE SMITH**
**THE BRAND PERSPECTIVE**

The brand personality, in its purest sense, is a reflection of the relationship between consumers and the company's products and services—and as such, it absolutely must reflect or inspire the target audience. As mentioned, the brand is also a reflection of the company itself, including its management, practices, and operations. As such, it is inescapable that the brand will also reflect the company's history, people, and operations.

It is worth noting that in some highly successful brands, like Apple, Wal-Mart, Virgin, and many more, the personality of the most senior leader (Steve Jobs, Sam Walton, and Richard Branson, respectively) is tremendously influential on the brand personality. These types of leaders are so influential that in many cases, their personalities stand for their brand in a way not generally seen in commerce. In other words, the individual develops a community of followers who see the company's leader and its products as interchangeable.

# Q: • ARE TAGLINES IMPORTANT?
# • WHY OR WHY NOT?

JASON MILETSKY

THE AGENCY PERSPECTIVE

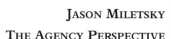 I suppose brands can get along fine without taglines, though personally, I'm a fan. I'm always surprised, however, by how many companies don't really understand what a tagline is or how it should be used. Most often, they seem to assume that the tagline should be long, should be bulky, and should say as much about them as they can write in one long, Kerouac-style run-on sentence. That's completely missing the point; in fact, that approach renders the tagline completely useless.

The tagline *should* be a brief statement used to send a quick message about the brand promise or a summation of a core competency. (Note the word "summation" —as in "short," or "summary.") Typically, the tagline is closely associated with the logo, and they appear together on everything from business cards and letterhead to advertising and marketing campaigns.

Because the tagline is the one line of copy that audiences will most closely associate with a brand, its importance cannot be understated—which is why developing the right tagline for a brand can be tough. Effective taglines typically serve one of six primary functions:

- **They serve as a call to action:** With just a few words, a strong tagline can inspire its audience to take some sort of action, while also telling them something important about the brand. Consider Apple's famous two-word tagline, "Think Different." The line suggests to people that they should change their way of thinking and open their minds to less traditional ideas, but it also establishes Apple as a company whose ideas, technology, and products are more innovative than their competitors'.

- **They relay the benefits of the brand:** As discussed earlier, for a brand to be successful, it must provide some benefit to the target market. It must improve or enhance their life in some way. Without this, there's virtually no reason for consumers to make a purchase. Taglines like Miller Lite's old but famous "Great Taste...Less Filling" take a direct approach, telling their market quickly and simply what benefits their brand will provide to customers.

■ **They reconfirm the promise:** The promise is one of the most important elements of a brand; it lets consumers know what they can expect from their involvement with a brand. Taglines such as Geico's "15 Minutes Could Save You 15 Percent or More" or UPS's "We Deliver for You" reinforce the promise in a succinct and memorable fashion by wrapping it into the tagline.

■ **They associate their product or service with an intangible need or idea:** These taglines tend to be more vague and less communicative, establishing the value or importance of a brand by linking it to an intangible concept. Outback Steakhouse's tagline "No Rules, Just Right" positioned the brand as serving quality meals in a fun environment.

■ **They point out the risk of not using their brand:** In order to make their product or service seem more like a necessity, brands will often use their tagline to make audiences consider the negative results of *not* using their brand. Ireland's (yes, countries are brands, too) 2008 U.S. travel campaign used the tagline "Can You Afford Not To Go?" to highlight the value packages they offered in the face of the weakening dollar.

■ **They link the tagline to their logo:** Because the tagline and the logo are usually closely associated, many taglines are written in such a way that they form a close association with the logo. Allstate Insurance's tagline "You're in Good Hands with Allstate" reinforces their logo of two open hands, while still stating a promise to take good care of their customers.

Logos tend to go through evolutions—minor or sometimes dramatic—over time. Taglines, however, get changed a bit more frequently in order to keep pace with changing times, market environments, and core competencies and to maintain a fresh, young feeling about the brand.

↳ Taglines are completely optional additions to the brand expression—*unless* you happen to land on one that becomes such an iconic part of the brand that it serves as a shortcut for consumers to identify what the brand stands for. For example, here are a few taglines; you fill in the brand:

- Just Do It
- Think Different
- The Ultimate Driving Machine

In these cases, the tagline and the logo are locked up with the brand name; because they express so clearly what the brand stands for, the taglines have become a permanent part of the brand's identity.

> Many times, advertising campaigns are developed with a tagline. In these cases, the tagline serves as a specific campaign sign-off, not as permanent tagline. A campaign tagline can live for a long time if the campaign does, but it may never become a truly iconic part of the brand expressions.

I think it's important to take a lot of care with a tagline. If you decide to go this route, the tagline, as good or bad as it is, will stick with a brand for a long time to come—you need to be SURE it is expressing exactly what you intend, and that you are committed to it for the long haul.

# Q: HOW IMPORTANT IS A BRAND GUIDE OR STYLE GUIDE TO THE DEVELOPMENT OF A BRAND?

JASON MILETSKY

THE AGENCY PERSPECTIVE

A brand guide or style guide (some people make a distinction between the two—I tend not to) is vital to development. It's the bible of the brand that helps maintain consistency among all components, media, marketers, and venues.

Brand guides become more important (and usually larger) the bigger and more extensive a brand is. As a brand grows, elements of it are more likely to be handled by an increasing number of people for a variety of purposes. Freelance designers, multiple advertising agencies, and printers are just a few of the many people and/or companies that may have a role in how the brand gets marketed. With a brand guide in hand, each of these players will have all the specs and information they need to make sure colors are spot on, font styles match, and all elements of the brand are followed exactly.

I've heard people argue that it's not really that important to be so exact in each and every detail. If the shade of blue in the logo on the Web site is a little different from the blue used on the print ad—well, what's the big deal? Who notices? Brand managers make accommodations for how elements like color are handled by different media such as print on computer monitors, and any fluctuations outside of this are absolutely a big deal. If it's easy enough to shrug off small differences between shades of color, then it's only a matter of time before the brand loses all semblance of consistency.

Maintaining consistency is key to brand-building—not just in look and feel, but for attitude, language, and personality. It's how consumers make associations between what they see and the expectations they have about interacting with a brand. Without this consistency, the consumer could become confused—or worse, could come to think of your brand as disorganized and not well established.

It often surprises me how many companies don't have a viable brand guide. Even large, multinational brands sometimes have poorly made guides that leave out a lot of detail—if they have a guide at all. When dealing with a client that has no guide, we're often forced to call or e-mail many more questions than usual; in one extreme case, we were reduced to taking screen shots of the client's Web site and using the Eyedropper tool in Photoshop to pick up colors we thought looked about right. So although it may seem at times that the brand guide is overkill, they are a valuable tool for saving time and maintaining consistency.

GENEVIEVE SMITH

THE BRAND PERSPECTIVE

One word: critical. Once you've designed the brand identity and aligned it for maximum effectiveness across all mediums and touch points, the only way to ensure it's not compromised is to implement ironclad brand standards. You must develop the brand guidelines and style guide so that the look and feel can be implemented consistently in communications.

Frequently, a company will use a variety of internal and external design resources to create its marketing, and the only way to ensure the visuals are always "in brand" is to refer to the guide, which is used to evaluate the accuracy and quality of the work being produced. The guide is also used to design the Web site, and to guide advertising and promotional materials—in fact, all visual assets. At WaMu, we insisted that the internal materials also reflect the brand style guide so that there was consistency both internally and externally.

The way a brand looks is very important to how it is perceived. In addition, its design elements act as points of differentiation in the marketplace. Absent adherence to the style guide, it doesn't take long for the brand to stray from the original design. If that happens, the brand loses its distinctive visual advantage.

When we first began the re-branding of WaMu, we conducted a visual inventory, which was absolutely fascinating. There were so many visual styles, and every one under the sun was used in one fashion or another! We created a document that showed the old inventory all together; what was stunning was that there was absolutely no company identity. It was all over the map. No surprise, as there was no style guide. Each agency or internal resource designed what they thought looked good or was the best communication. And of course, all these were done in a vacuum as the work was produced in different silos or areas of the company, absent guidelines.

# Q: WHAT ARE THE KEY COMPONENTS THAT THE BRAND GUIDE SHOULD INCLUDE?

**JASON MILETSKY**
**THE AGENCY PERSPECTIVE**

The brand guide will be larger or smaller based on the size and scope of the brand and the type and amount of marketing involved. I've seen guides that are two pages, and I've seen guides that are well over 100 pages.

As a lowest common denominator, every brand guide should have the following elements:

- **How the logo should or should not be used:** Marketers need to know where on the page the logo needs to go (if this is mandated). Can it appear over an image? Can it appear vertically as well as horizontally? Guides need to clearly explain all the rules regarding use of the logo.

- **Color breakdowns:** Primary and secondary color palettes should be provided, with information for how these colors can be created including Pantone numbers, RGB and CMYK breakdowns, and hexadecimal codes.

- **Font styles:** Preferred fonts for use in advertising and other marketing material need to be noted, as do preferred fonts for Internet marketing efforts.

- **Image types:** Brand guides should describe and show examples of the types of images they want associated with their marketing. Some brands, for example, may want everything to be certain illustration styles, while others may want only black-and-white photography.

- **Special rules:** Some brands may have special notations for their use that they feel are important in order to maintain their brand integrity. These rules, if they exist, should also be included.

Keep in mind, these are the bare-bones basics that need to be included. More fully developed (and more useful) guides will include information such as approved language (is it "e-mail," "email," or "E-Mail"?), adjectives that describe the brand personality, special logo usage for truck sides and building signs, and other such information. One piece of information that I emphatically believe should *not* be included is rules regarding how advertising should be developed. The guide should give advertising agencies the baseline for how the personality should be presented and any logo treatments, but should not define how an ad should look, feel, or sound. This is not the guide's job, and will ultimately limit the creative nature of advertising.

GENEVIEVE SMITH
THE BRAND PERSPECTIVE

↳ A brand guide should include the following:

■ A description of the brand promise and what the brand stands for, including

- Brand differentiators (i.e., what makes the brand unique)
- Key messages

■ Brand architecture, including

- Logo lockup
- Naming

■ Logo, including

- Logo usage guidelines such as position, application, colors, size
- Approved logo lockups
- Registration mark usage

■ Tone of voice, including

- Style of language (e.g., informal or formal)
- Marketing messages

■ Color, including

- Primary color palette
- Background and subhead color palette
- Text colors, grayscale, black-and-white

- Typography, including
  - Typeface
  - Typeface for screen
  - Graphic devices
  - White space
  - Justification
  - Text color for subheads, titles, and body copy
- Graphic devices
- Photography, including
  - Objective photography
  - Lifestyle photography
  - Format, e.g. full bleed, no bleed

# Q: WHAT ROLE DO COLOR, FONTS, AND IMAGES PLAY IN BRAND DEVELOPMENT?

**JASON MILETSKY**
THE AGENCY PERSPECTIVE

Colors, fonts, and images play a vital role in how your market perceives your brand. They're the emotional conduit that can make or break a brand's personality. All visual elements of the brand need to be considered carefully if they're going to have a positive impact on the market.

## COLOR

Color plays an enormous role in the decisions we make as consumers—indeed, in how we feel about everything from companies and products to colleges and sports teams. The feelings that colors elicit and the reactions they can cause are taken seriously by companies establishing and marketing their brands. (Those feelings and reactions also explain why hospitals dress nurses in light blues and pinks; patients relax more around these soothing, calming colors.) The colors used will resonate powerfully and create a strong association with the brand. The orange and green on every Crayola crayon box and the red and white on every can of Coca-Cola are standout examples of how colors play a role in consumer brand recognition. Likewise, a turquoise gift box with a white ribbon lets a person know immediately that the gift is from Tiffany & Co.

Different colors hold different power and meanings for people, and entire sciences have been dedicated to studying how colors can affect both individuals and audiences, en masse. In the U.S., for example, colors have some very definitive associations:

- **Black:** Dignified, sophisticated, powerful

- **White:** Innocent, optimistic

- **Gray:** Steady, stable, disciplined

- **Blue:** Loyal, responsible, conservative

- **Red:** Exciting, passionate, aggressive

- **Green:** Natural, balanced, healthy

- **Yellow:** Happy, warm, alert

- **Purple:** Regal, wise, celebratory

- **Orange:** Vibrant, energetic, playful

---

Blue is the most popular color for brands, and can be considered a relatively safe choice.

---

That said, colors need to be selected carefully, because they can be interpreted differently depending on the audience's culture, class, age, gender, and other demographic categories. For example, although the color white symbolizes purity and innocence in Western cultures, Eastern cultures associate white with death and funerals. Younger audiences are drawn to brighter colors, while muted and pastel colors are more likely to attract the attention of adults. Men tend to favor cooler colors like blues and greens, while women often appreciate warmer colors like reds and oranges.

## FONTS

Similarly, fonts are important in establishing the brand look. Fonts can help promote the brand personality. Each of the thousands of fonts available has its own unique way of evoking an emotion and can speak volumes about the brand simply by the way the letters are formed. It is important to understand the five basic styles of fonts and what feeling or mood each style evokes:

- **Serif:** Serif fonts are fonts with non-structural details or ornaments on the ends of the some letter strokes. These fonts have a pretty serious look to them, and can be used to denote strength, sophistication, and longevity.

- **Sans-serif:** Sans-serif fonts are fonts without the non-structural details found in serif fonts. Although they are not as serious as serif fonts, they are not necessarily frivolous, either. San-serif fonts are considered to be more sleek, modern, and youthful.

- **Script:** Script fonts are exactly what you would expect: variations of script. Some are simple script; others are very fancy and ornate. They can denote class and sophistication, but can be difficult to read if not used properly.

- **Handwriting:** Handwriting fonts look like handwriting. Usually these are used to convey a more casual—maybe even sloppy—feel, and can give the brand a slightly more personal edge. Children's brands are especially prone to using handwriting fonts to establish a more youthful personality.

- **Artistic**: Artistic fonts range from understated to unreadable. There is a wide variety of artistic fonts, and they can be valuable in establishing a particularly whimsical, playful, or edgy brand personality.

**Different fonts convey different things.**

There is, of course, a practical side of fonts that needs to be considered as well. Take this book, for example. I can't stand the font that's being used. To me, it doesn't go with the cover design. I wanted something a little edgier—at the very least, something sans serif. But one of my editors, Mitzi, explained to me that when it comes to books, sans-serif fonts are harder to read than serif fonts. The serifs allow the reader's eye to move from word to word more easily. All this is to say that practicality sometimes takes precedent.

The issue of practicality also comes into play with Web sites because if a person viewing the site doesn't have the font used in the site's copy installed on his or her computer, the user's computer will simply replace the missing font with a default font (usually Times or Helvetica). So wacky, wild fonts simply won't work for Web sites unless the fonts appear in graphics. Graphic copy on a site is fine for titles and headlines, but not body copy; placing body copy in an image file makes it more difficult to edit and will limit the site's chances of being picked up by search engines. A good brand developer will know what types of fonts can represent the brand personality and which are more practical for particular uses, and will regulate font usage properly between headlines and body copy; print, Web, and other media; and so on.

## IMAGES

Images are also critical to a brand. First and foremost, images must be consistent throughout all uses of the brand. In other words, don't load your brochures with funky, hand-drawn illustrations and then use photography on the Web site. Consistency in brand-building is key, and I can't think of anything that makes inconsistency more obvious than a disconnect in image style.

As with colors and fonts, the image style you choose for your brand will help consumers understand what your brand's personality is. But there's a lot more to it than that. As the saying goes, "A picture's worth a thousand words"—and all of the words expressed in a picture will affect the building, marketing, and perception of a brand.

You need to consider two main elements when it comes to images:

- **Content:** Content is fairly easy to understand—it's the subject matter being shown. Content can be conveyed in product shots from different angles, application shots of products or services being used in practical situations, location shots or even general marketing shots (like those abhorrent pictures of people shaking hands—*ugh*). What content is shown is typically less a part of the brand as it is a part of the marketing of the brand, though.

- **Style:** Style, which is very much a part of a brand and will apply universally to every image used to promote the brand, is a little trickier to grasp. Simply put, style is the artistic means by which an image is shown. There is an infinite number of styles for both photographic and illustrative work, ranging from ultra-artistic to simple and fairly generic.

When putting the early pieces of the visual brand together, be sure to avoid creating problems for yourself and the marketing team later on: Images aren't always easy to come by, and can be pretty expensive depending on the type and amount needed. Highly stylized images may require a professional photographer, which can be cost-prohibitive. The more standard and less expensive images that can be bought online from a royalty-free Web site can be unimaginative and may well appear on other companies' marketing materials. Consider the brand's long-term needs, your budget, and the time constraints you'll most likely face during the early stages of assembling images to represent your brand.

GENEVIEVE SMITH
THE BRAND PERSPECTIVE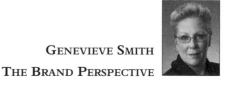

Color, font, and images are the visual language of the brand, each serving its own important purpose:

- **Color:** Color helps the brand stand out. Consistent use of color promotes recognition, clearly differentiating the brand from competitors. For example, banking brands are characterized by a monotonous sea of blue and red; to differentiate ourselves at WaMu, we developed a color palette of bright, light, optimistic, and friendly primary colors. And we didn't color-code our areas of business; rather, we applied color themes randomly across communications materials to help ensure we never became just another blue and red bank. While we found that using a lot of different colors went a long way toward helping us stand up and stand out, other brands take a different approach, committing to a single color. If you've ever visited a T Mobile store, you've seen a brand that has committed to a color, boldly applying it to every customer touch point. Their idea? Make "pink" equal "T Mobile."

- **Typeface:** Used consistently, typeface becomes a distinctive and familiar part of the brand. Typeface essentially represents the brand "voice," helping to communicate the brand personality. So if you've got a brand that is approachable, modern, and friendly, you would pick a unique typeface that conveys those attributes. A unique typographic identity inspires immediate recognition, communicating and presenting a unified voice to customers.

- **Images:** Images are tools that help brands establish a meaningful relationship with the audience by communicating the brand's personality in a compelling and engaging way. Put another way, brands use images—be they photographs or illustrations—to tell stories and make human connections. These images can reinforce the brand philosophy, possibly achieving a distinctive style that becomes synonymous with the brand. Brands typically use lifestyle photography (real people, places, scenarios) and object photography (everyday objects, animals, or items with a more conceptual twist) in their communication, although some commit to graphic illustrations instead of photography for their imagery. (I say "commit" because although illustrations can be unique and ownable, developing and growing an illustration library involves a significant investment.)

Developing an image library that is custom-created for the brand involves a lot of work and expense. To cut costs and time, some companies use stock photography, which can be purchased with a click of the mouse and instantly applied to communications. While this approach may be beneficial in some ways, it does pose one major problem: I've seen a stock image we used applied in a competitor's materials and, even worse, its advertising.

You absolutely must be relentless in developing these visual elements to reflect the brand; then you must take on the thankless task of policing—yes, policing—these visuals. Why? Because it is human nature to want to attempt to improve on what exists, and it is the nature of creative talent and agencies to secretly scorn a standardized approach through fear it will limit creativity—you must protect the brand standards. They must not be randomly modified.

# Q: THE BRAND GUIDE IS BUILT. NOW WHAT?

**JASON MILETSKY**
**THE AGENCY PERSPECTIVE**

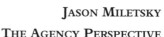

It's built? Done? Everybody's happy and we're ready to release it? Go get a drink! Or 12! Sure, there may still be a few loose ends to tie up, but you deserve a night to throw a few back. Once you sober up, you'll be ready for the *real* work.

You thought building the brand guide was tough? That's nothing compared to putting it into action! And here's the really ironic part: That new brand guide that took you an eternity to put together? It'll paint you into a creative corner. One of the best parts of developing a new brand is the near limitless latitude developers have to be creative. You're building the rules in a lawless environment. You get to start from and work with a totally clean canvas. What an amazing— and rare—opportunity! Well, don't get used to it. Once the guide is built, you'll have a lot of rules to follow—rules that *you* created. So at least some of the work you'll be doing going forward won't be nearly as fun because of the new set of rules that are now in place.

If the brand guide is for a completely new brand or the redevelopment of an existing one (as opposed to being for an established brand that just never had a guide and finally decided to put some rules for itself down on paper), the first thing you need to do is unveil the new brand to employees and get them jazzed up and excited about it. In my answer to Question #23, "Should You Get Employees' Input While the Brand Is Being Built? Or Is That Just a Nightmare Waiting to Happen?" I discuss the importance of sharing and celebrating the new brand with your employees. This celebration, however, should include a serious, no-bullshit explanation to salespeople, marketers, and anybody else who may use the brand in promotion or marketing why it's important to follow the guidelines. Take this opportunity to make sure they understand the rules you've laid out and to let them know who they should get approval from before anything gets printed and published. (Someone needs to assume the role of the brand police; this person or entity should be established at the outset and introduced during the rollout.)

At the same time, the brand needs to be communicated to existing clients so they don't feel confused, and so they understand that the new brand is a step forward that will affect them in a positive way. And finally, the new brand needs to be broadcast to the market as a whole. This is usually best done through public relations initiatives designed to generate as much attention as possible. A rebranding effort in particular can be fodder for increased media exposure.

Then comes the hands-on work. The guide-building process likely involved an inventory of all collateral work that needs to be done (or, in the case of a rebrand, redone), including brochures, catalogues, sell sheets, PowerPoints, sales videos, etc. (Notice I didn't mention Web site—the Web site is usually put together along with the brand guide so that the site and the new brand launch at the same time). Once the guide is launched, that inventory will have to be tackled, either all at once or one step at a time (usually a step at a time). Especially at the outset, this will probably require that employees work on parallel paths in order to get multiple things done at once. Every last bit of the old brand (if any) has to vanish and be replaced with the new brand. This includes exterior office signs, wall art—everything.

And then there's the marketing. Don't let the adrenaline rush that comes with completing the brand die down. Have your celebratory drink, and then cash in on the excitement and post-launch media attention to roll out marketing programs. Get some ads out there, send e-mail blasts, launch promotions to introduce consumers to the new brand look and feel. Develop a strategy and market the hell out of the new brand to get it out there into the market.

**Genevieve Smith**
**The Brand Perspective**

 Now the fun begins!

Depending on the size and complexity of your company, rebranding according to the style guide is a daunting task, and must be done over time and with a careful eye to expenses—an exercise that requires both patience and tenacity.

To ease the transition, a team should be assigned while the style guide is in development to scour the company—including all lines of business and support groups—to develop a complete inventory of existing communications materials. The ideal is that current inventory can be depleted (and has been managed during brand-guide development for minimal orders) while the new materials are created so that at re-order, the newly branded creative replaces the old look and feel.

This is not simply a find and replace exercise. Done right, you are not simply putting a new face on old materials; this is an opportunity—maybe a once-in-a-lifetime on the client side—to completely rethink how a company goes to market through their communications as seen through the lens of the new brand expressions and to ask the following:

- Why do we produce this?

- Is there a better way to communicate?

- Is this how we want to speak to customers?

- Is this an investment we need to make?

In a retail environment comprised of a distribution network—supported by a big advertising budget, an eCommerce channel, and a lot of customer communications such as statements and direct mail—you can coordinate the rebrand around the highest-impact customer touch points. These include the following:

- Merchandising and collateral systems

- Advertising

- Direct mail

- Internet user interface

While these are the obvious areas to focus on, if a company is really going to commit to the brand, then internal communications such as the intranet, signage, PowerPoint decks, e-mail, and operational materials, such as customer-notification and legal language, also must be rebranded.

At WaMu, we determined it was critical to the brand to communicate with our customers in a straightforward, clear, and simple manner, and to say it with a smile. This applied not just to marketing, but to everyday language, like that used when talking on the phone, in emails, in presentations, and in briefs. But because banking is such a heavily regulated and complex service industry, one of the biggest hurdles was working with our legal department to find a way to advise customers of what they need to know legally without being overly complex and obscure in doing so. In the end, however, we were able to develop some basic communication principles, including the following:

- **Use straightforward language:** Rather than using "bank speak"—for example, saying "Premium variable rate interest bearing account with limited checking writing"—we used a more straightforward approach: "An account that pays you interest and allows you to write up to five checks a month."

- **Be conversational:** Rather than using the formal "Dear Valued Customer, we look forward to being of continued service," We used a more conversational "Dear Mrs. Smith, thanks for banking with us."

- **Engage people:** We moved from an impersonal tone, as in "When using your check card (as we may be offering at the time), as the Prime Rate (Index) goes up or down, the new variable rate will take effect," to an engaging one: "Your check card has a variable rate of interest, which is connected to the Prime Rate. If the Prime Rate moves up or down, you should know that your rate will move too."

My advice? Go deep and broad, and be relentless in applying your brand style guide throughout the company. Realize, however, that this is a journey that never ends, as new communications materials will always be in development. For this reason, it is important to have a process for continuous review.

# Q: DOES AN AUDIENCE FIND A BRAND IT CONNECTS WITH? OR IS A BRAND BUILT WITH A SPECIFIC AUDIENCE IN MIND?

JASON MILETSKY
THE AGENCY PERSPECTIVE

I think when a brand is built with a specific audience in mind, it's destined to fail. Remember that episode of *The Brady Bunch* where Peter tried out different personalities? It's the "pork chops and apple sauce" episode. He thought he was dull, so he tested different personalities to see if he could jazz himself up. Of course, none of these manufactured personae worked, and he gave up. Depressed by the outcome, he sat dejectedly alone at his own party—until a girl came over and asked why he was by himself. Peter explained that he was dull, and the girl (who I thought was quite cute) told him that was ridiculous. Before he knew it, Peter was surrounded by a dozen cute girls, all telling him how great his personality was.

Ah, if only all of life's lessons could be learned by watching *The Brady Bunch*.

The point is, a brand is developed by a combination of many variables that come together at once—but at its core, the brand needs to stay true to itself. There's no point in a brand promising something that it can't deliver simply because it's what the market wants. The same goes for the personality of the brand—don't bother trying to relate to surfer dudes if you don't know the lingo and feel more comfortable chatting up business execs. The surfer dudes will see you as a *barney* and you'll end up *wiping out*.

Brands should start from a point that they're comfortable with and can be successful in. "Here is what we can promise you and know that we can deliver. This is our personality, and we know that we can be true to it." Consumers will gravitate toward the brand whose promise is desirable to them and whose personality most reflects their own (and whose message is most visible through marketing).

But it doesn't end there—brands are rarely carved in stone. They're living, breathing, and—most importantly—*evolving* entities that can be altered and maneuvered as needed. From a comfortable starting point, brands can look out over their market and see where opportunities exist to enhance and add to the promise (while staying within the scope of what they can realistically fulfill), or alter their personality for a wider appeal (again, within a reasonable scope of what they can actually do). Through the evolutionary process, brands can slowly change who they are without feeling like they're falling outside of their comfort zone, where they can best perform. It's better to establish yourself in the market, let the core base of consumers find your brand, and build from there than to go for an unreachable market by forcing your brand to be something it isn't.

I'll give you a practical example: Years ago, we did the marketing for the leading manufacturer of automotive lighting products—you know, those ultra-cheesy neon lights that go around license plates or make the entire underbody of a car glow. Our client was far and away the number-one brand, and for a long time, the only brand that mattered in the industry. But their target demo was males, 17–24 years old—a particularly fickle group that is notoriously hard to market to. Making it even more difficult was the psychology behind why they bought these products: These were counter-culture consumers who spent more money tricking out their cars than they spent on the cars themselves, partly because they genuinely loved the products, partly because it gave them access to an exclusive community of like-minded peers, and partly because it pissed off their parents and other adults. The second their parents went out and bought an under-car kit for the family Tahoe would be the same second the target market started uninstalling their own kits.

The fact was, our client decided what was cool in this community. If they said red was the color everyone should have, then that's the color everyone would buy. And the owner, who this market revered as a cult hero of sorts, was the standard bearer for giving the big F-U to the man. The market either overlooked or deliberately ignored the fact that he sat on top of a $50-million business— until something *really bad* happened: Our client made it onto the *Inc.* 500 list of fastest-growing companies for the fourth year in a row. One more year, and they'd be among only a handful of companies to ever make the list for five straight years. And suddenly, *that* became the owner's focus. All of a sudden, he became civilized.

I remember the day when I knew it would all go downhill. We were putting together their monthly newsletter, and he sent us a new picture of himself to use on his page. Replacing the old image of him wearing a stained T-shirt was this new one—of him in a suit. A suit?! That wasn't really him. He wasn't corporate guy; he was cool guy! We pleaded with him to use the old picture, knowing full well that this market wouldn't want to buy their counter-culture, stick-it-to-the-man, we-want-adults-to-hate-us lighting gear from someone who looked like their dad. Ultimately, we were overruled. This simple photograph started a new age for the brand in which they were no longer run by cool; they were run by corporate. In trying to be something he wasn't he ended up losing both "cool" and "corporate." He didn't make the *Inc.* 500 for the fifth year in a row, and he managed to alienate his audience to the point where their company is now barely relevant.

GENEVIEVE SMITH
THE BRAND PERSPECTIVE

From my viewpoint, the audience of consumers is constantly expanding, changing, and growing with popular culture, and they will find brands to connect with as their tastes and needs change. Nonetheless, most brands will want to manage and target their offerings with a specific audience in mind; it's more sensible than saying our audience is everyone! Branding to specific audiences involves focusing on customer segmentation and lifecycle marketing in the hopes of predicting future trends both to keep the brand relevant and connected to the audience and to keep the audience loyal to the brand.

Let's use Disney as an example. Disney's brand promise is family entertainment. When Disney expands their business through the acquisition of non-family types of entertainment products or properties, Disney does not move off its brand promise of family entertainment, nor do they expand the master Disney brand and the audience who connects through the family-entertainment platform. And in many—if not most—instances, they do not attempt to re-engineer significant acquisitions like ABC, ESPN, Touchstone, and Miramax to become family entertainment or to be branded as part of the Disney family. Why? Because those "non-Disney" entertainment products and properties are aimed at a different audience.

Of course there are innumerable instances where the audience finds a brand it connects with, without the brand targeting that audience. For example, how did Courvoisier, Tommy Hilfiger, and MAC suddenly become popular brands with urban audiences? These brands didn't target that audience, but consumers in that market connected with the brands, and the rest is history.

# Q: • How Important Is It to Test-Market
# • a Brand Before Launch?

Jason Miletsky
The Agency Perspective

I like to do at least some research before launching a new brand, but the problem is that most clients don't want to spend the time or money. I don't mean the *Fortune* 500, multinational type of clients; I mean the small- to medium-sized companies, especially in the B2B world. These companies almost always want to forgo the research process and skip right on over to development—and from there, boogie on into execution, and call it a day. If absolute speed is the thing, then chances are research won't be part of the mix, which is kind of too bad. I like going to market quickly, but I'm not a big believer that common sense is enough to base a brand on. There needs to be at least a modicum of research done prior to launch.

Research doesn't always have to be official. In an ideal world, a large brand would be put in front of an independent focus group or be subject to surveys prior to going live (the more expensive and more potentially visible a brand is likely to be, the more important these efforts are). But life's not always ideal. If official research isn't in the budget, try gauging reaction informally by asking people in another department of the company or people within the agency who aren't connected to the account for their feedback. At the very least, you'll be able to find out the following:

- Does the brand properly reflect the brand personality?
- Is it memorable?
- Will it stand out from competitors enough so that the market will notice it?
- Is the look and feel such that the brand will have some longevity without becoming dated too quickly?
- Would it make the consumer more or less likely to interact with the brand in the future?

Keep in mind, though—and this is more for readers on the client side, since all agencies already know this (and I expect plenty of fan mail from agency people for spelling this out)—that when I say "informal reaction," I am *not* talking about your barber, mailman, sister-in-law, or anybody else you happen to come across and feel like asking for their opinion, regardless of whether they understand marketing or are part of the target market you're trying to reach. Those people's opinions *do not* matter, and, it's a waste of time and money to make changes or judgments based on their feedback.

GENEVIEVE SMITH
THE BRAND PERSPECTIVE

It is very important to test a brand through all stages of development while you are building it as well to test-market the brand before it is broadly launched. If you don't, you may find yourself with a loser in market. That said, sometimes a brand is wildly successful all by itself. These brands require very little test-marketing because demand research in the concept stage clearly shows it's going to be a huge winner. It won't need significant revisions based on in-market results. Let me give you two examples—one that ended well despite the fact that we hadn't done much in the way of test-marketing and one that resulted in a decision to *not* launch a product after extensive test-marketing.

First, the story with the happy ending: At WaMu, we had become known for our free-checking product. Indeed, this product had become so closely associated with the brand, we were able to significantly outpace our competition in consideration and account generation even though we had a smaller footprint in the market. Over time, though, the competition caught up, coming on strong and encroaching on our brand's position. At the same time, many non-traditional competitors, such as ING Direct and other Internet bank players, had emerged. Both of these developments meant we had to either defend our position or give up market share.

So, how do you improve on free? By making things *freer* than free, perhaps? Actually we were able to build four new features into the product that we knew our competition would not be able to match: one free overdraft a year, free wire transfers, no ATM surcharge, and free checks for life. Our research showed that consumers responded extremely favorably to these enhancements because they were solutions to pain points that consumers themselves had identified in banking. We *also* found—and this was a bit of a surprise—that when we tested our new free checking product, it researched overwhelmingly well on ease and convenience. Consumers felt that with our product, they would spend much less time looking for fees and pain points than would otherwise be the case. Indeed, the value was so transparent, it was easy for them to just choose our product without even shopping the competition.

Because management wanted to launch the new product with national advertising with a four month lead time, there was no opportunity test-market it. We had to go with our consumer research and launch. But in this case, we had a very happy ending: The product was successful beyond anyone's expectations, resulting in 1.2 million net new checking accounts in year one. The Council on Financial Competition named it one of the top 25 great innovations, and when we launched it online, Keynote ranked us in the top three in their Ease of Use Online category. We opened up a new market for WaMu with online originations, where we quickly won and maintained the number-one market-share position. And not only was this product a sales winner, but it was also additive to the brand in all the dimensions we focused on developing and extending.

Now the story with a less-happy ending—despite our having followed a very classic path of product development, consumer research, and extensive in-market testing. As I mentioned, the WaMu brand was fairly one-dimensional, known primarily as the home of free checking. Naturally, the company wanted to expand its reach and reputation as a good place to save as well as to open a checking account. It also wanted to respond to the frighteningly low savings rate by consumers in America, building a product that would do good by encouraging Americans to save.

Our product development group built a savings product that offered a very high interest rate for one year on new deposits auto-deposited from the checking account, with a ceiling on the number of dollars that could be deposited each month. (Although the first-year interest rate was stunningly high, we put a limit on the number of deposits that could be made in order to help ensure the product's profitability.) The financials assumed that the savings would roll over after the first year into a much lower–interest-rate account and stay there.

And *wow*, did this product test off the charts in terms of consideration, demand, and brand compatibility. As an advertiser, I was frothing at the mouth to launch the product because our research showed consumer demand would be through the roof. So we choose four geographic areas in which to test-market the product. We created a name, advertising, point of sale, merchandising, and all the other marketing bells and whistles to support a market launch and sustained communications platform in the test markets. No surprise, in the test market, the product sold like hotcakes. The results were incredible, just like our research showed they would be.

And yet, we never launched the product. What happened? Consumer behavior in real life, that's what. With respect to account utilization, the consumers did not behave as we thought they would—indeed, as they *said* they would—in research. That is, they said they would commit to saving, and to rolling those savings over when the time came, but in fact were not willing to do so. The product lost money, and no matter what we did with communications, we could never prove that it would perform financially. There was an inherent flaw in the financial model in that consumers did not maintain their savings balances. But our consumer research was also flawed in that we simply could not predict with sufficient accuracy what consumer patterns would be after the initial sale.

We had invested time in product development, research, communications, sales support, and advertising, but at the end of the day we could see from the real-life results that this product would be a long-term drag on the company's financial performance, so we abandoned the national product launch and walked away from the concept. This is not a "bad" ending, per se. It's simply an example of using all the classic tools to develop and test-market a brand or product, concluding it doesn't work, and opting not to launch it—which is sometimes the way it happens, as well as why test-marketing is a good idea.

One last thought on this: Sometimes, a business may intuitively know that a brand or product is going to be a winner, and taking a classic approach—which may involve a fair amount of bureaucracy—may threaten a quick-to-market move. There is no right answer here—senior management must decide to take the risk or not. But there are proven methodologies for testing if you want to be really sure (see the next question).

# Q: • WHAT ARE THE BEST WAYS TO • TEST-MARKET A NEW BRAND?

**JASON MILETSKY**

**THE AGENCY PERSPECTIVE**

↳ You've got a new product and want to get a sense of consumer sentiment about it before you pour tons of money into production, distribution, and marketing. Good idea. Test-marketing gives you a chance to see what people think of your product before you commit. By testing, you can get an idea of whether demand will be high enough to risk the expense and determine whether any alterations need to be made before doing a major launch.

Before going into some of the test-marketing methods you could consider, I want to point out one method that you should *never* use: relying on the opinions of family, friends, and anyone else who either falls outside your target market or might be likely to give you positive feedback out of fear of hurting your feelings. These opinions might feed your ego, but they're not going to give you any real insight into whether a market is likely to buy your new brand.

There are, however, other methods that can prove more helpful:

- **Develop a prototype:** Before you can test anything, you'll need to get a prototype created. People won't be able to give you accurate feedback without being able to hold something in their hands and try it out. Drawings, photographs, and descriptions aren't bad, but they're not enough for any kind of useful test marketing.

- **Get feedback from buyers:** With the prototype in hand, get feedback from key buyers who you'll need to stock your product. Ultimately, their opinions will weigh heavily on whether your new brand makes it to market, so make sure you go to them for their thoughts. For many brands, Wal-Mart alone may be their single greatest ally—or obstacle—when it comes to getting their product in front of their audience, so Wal-Mart's opinions prior to mass production might be more necessity than luxury.

- **Work with select retailers for a limited test run:** Select a certain geography and work with local retailers or local outlets of national chains to run a limited-time test run in their stores. Make sure to give it a fair chance for success with some in-store marketing efforts that let shoppers know your new brand is available.

- **Compare your product against competing products:** Formally or informally, gather a focus group of potential consumers and ask them to judge your brand versus competitors in the marketplace. Use this opportunity to determine what makes your product unique and how it might fare against rivals when mass produced.

- **Introduce the new product at trade shows:** Trade shows can provide a great opportunity to test new products in front of an eager and honest audience. Depending on the show, your new brand could be exposed to potentially thousands or even tens of thousands of people in a single location who you can tap into for feedback.

- **Hit the streets:** Sometimes, there's nothing more effective than good, old-fashioned tactics like hitting the streets. Get a team of people to set up shop outside a mall or grocery store, in a crowded parking lot, or on street corner, or go door to door. It's crude and overly simplistic, but it can work!

GENEVIEVE SMITH
THE BRAND PERSPECTIVE

↳ At the end of the day, what you want to create with the launch of a new product or brand is demand—and, by extension, growth. So test-marketing is actually the easy part: It's marketing. But to reach the test-market phase, you have to spend a lot of time with product development and finance researching whether an idea is worth investing in performing a test market, regardless of methodology. This centers on creating demand estimates that identify which levers drive sales and profit maximization, feature importance relative to costs to provide optimal results, and modeling to provide solid sales estimates.

If you determine that the product is worthy of market testing—it's passed all the smell tests, regulatory and otherwise, and consumer research says it will sell—how do you go about actually testing? There are three primary approaches:

- You can test something in the physical market by carving out part of your distribution network that is isolated from the rest.

- You can test in a laboratory by producing product not available in the general market for use in a controlled environment.

- You can test on the Internet.

And of course, there is an infinite number of nuances and sciences associated with test-marketing depending on the industry. We see examples of this every day—for example, people being paid to participate in pharmaceutical testing, new foods being tested in supermarkets, Starbucks testing a new coffee in some stores, new auto prototypes being tested in foreign markets, etc.

> Depending on the category you are working in, the testing will be more or less difficult and rigorous. Probably the most difficult testing is for industries like the pharmaceutical industry because of various regulations and standards that require companies to prove that the product is beneficial to living beings before it can even be packaged for limited and controlled testing.

It is the job of the marketing group to package and create compelling communications to support the test. You've got to put your all into supporting this brand or product, throwing out the best you've got for the test—even knowing the product may never see the light of day beyond testing. After all, you probably don't control much else beyond how well the brand is communicated, so it's your job to rock it. At the same time, you need to remember that the marketing of the brand or product is *also* being tested, meaning your creative work and tactics will be open for examination, discussion, and evaluation, just like everything else in the test. You may, then, be tasked with delivering multiple creative executions and tactics to be tested, just as the product may be tested with various features and benefits. As such, it is important to approach the creative with the right test and control methods so as to provide a full evaluation of its effectiveness.

# Q: WHAT IS THE MOST IMPORTANT ELEMENT IN BUILDING A BRAND: TIME, MONEY, OR SOMETHING ELSE ENTIRELY?

JASON MILETSKY

THE AGENCY PERSPECTIVE

Before I get too deep into the answer, I want to make sure we're all on the same page regarding the question. As I mentioned in my answer to Question #1, "How Would You Define a Brand?" the brand is basically the reputation a company, product, or service has with its market, and the expectations consumers may develop regarding any potential interaction with the company, product, or service. Developing this requires time more than anything else—time, and the constant, continued fulfillment of the brand promise. "Building a brand" is something different. It can imply the deliberate steps taken to market the brand and communicate its message to the audience. It can also mean the act of developing the initial pieces that would go in the brand guide, like the logo, color palette, description of the brand personality, etc. I'll answer the question using both definitions with mid- to larger-sized brands in mind, starting with the development of the brand guide.

There really isn't a single correct answer, so I'll break down the three most important elements that are required:

- **Time:** Time is always going to be a factor, and there's always going to be a disparity between how long the brand will take to build and how long the company being branded would like for it to take. But it's not a fast process. The development of any brand involves a lot of complex moving parts, many of which will be subject to multiple rounds of presentations and revisions, research, testing of consumer reaction, writing, designing, and so on. When my agency rebranded WebMD into Emdeon (WebMD is now just a product owned by the Emdeon parent), we were under an extremely tight deadline, expected to create the brand in less than three months starting with a clean slate. (Except the name—the Emdeon name was developed by another agency, but we were responsible for everything else.) It took a team of professionals more than 2,900 hours, working day and night, to get it done in time—and we still just barely made the deadline (although the outcome was a very solid brand—one of my favorites of all the brands we've built). I don't think taking less than three months for a successful brand is realistic, and quite often it could be far longer.

■ **Money:** If a brand is going to be developed by an outside agency, the company can expect to pay a pretty sizable amount to get it done right. Brand-building isn't something just any agency can do—it's a unique and particular skill set that takes a pretty in-depth understanding of how brands work and how markets react. Depending on the size and scope of the brand in question, companies have to budget to get the brand built right.

■ **Reason:** This is especially true in situations where an existing brand is getting rebuilt. Rebranding is no joke—it's a serious undertaking, and doing so means your company will be going through a lot of changes in the way they present themselves and the way they're seen by their market. To do this, there has to be a compelling reason; ultimately, the brand must be built to solve a problem or fill a specific need.

As for the other definition—brand-building as the deliberate and purposeful marketing of the brand to spread its message to the market and increase exposure—time and money continue to be key factors. As with any marketing effort, consumer recognition of the brand will come through prolonged exposure. Whether this exposure happens through pointed marketing efforts or personal interaction with the brand, time is a necessary ingredient for both recognition and trust to be built. And prolonged marketing efforts can be expensive to conceptualize, execute, and sustain, so money becomes an equally important piece of the puzzle.

Reason, however, is not as important in this definition, because the reason is fairly obvious: Brands get built to gain consumer trust and increase market share. Instead, we can replace "reason" with "goals." Goals—numeric goals, whenever possible—need to be set and measured against on an ongoing basis throughout the brand-building process to make sure that the efforts being taken are cost-effective and are producing the desired results. Goals also help ensure that the efforts being taken to market the brand are, in fact, helping to move the brand forward—*not* being seen negatively by the audience and causing the brand to be set back.

GENEVIEVE SMITH
THE BRAND PERSPECTIVE

This is easy. The most important element in building a brand is something else entirely: It is a distinctive (and disruptive) brand promise. The brand promise is the sum total of who the brand is, what it does, and how the world views it. A brand must stand for something. It must be able to connect with consumers. If it doesn't, all the time and money in the world won't make that brand successful.

Let's look at three online companies and what they stand for as examples:

- **YouTube:** YouTube doesn't manufacture any product or content; they rely completely on crowd sourcing, meaning that people who use the site generate both the original content and the comments about the content. So this brand is all about the consumer as the creator—and sometimes the star.

- **Google:** Essentially, the only product Google sells is the integrity of its search results, earning its revenue from advertising related to those results. If the integrity of the results were in question, the ad revenue would disappear—and so would Google. The Google brand, then, stands for integrity.

- **Woot:** Woot pioneered the "one deal a day" business model on the Internet. It started as an employee-store-slash-market-testing site for an electronics distributor, but it's taken on a life of its own. Their core brand promise is selling cool stuff cheap.

Deep pockets and time definitely have their advantages, but a brand that has deep meaning for consumers will develop its own fan club and loyal community—regardless of the marketing budget.

# Q: Is Building the Brand More a Matter of Corporate Success or Corporate Survival?

Jason Miletsky
The Agency Perspective

A company doesn't need a brand to survive *or* be successful. The corner hardware store in a small town may not spend a dime on brand-building, but that doesn't mean it can't be successful or survive for decades or even generations. But chances are, you're not reading this book because you're looking for ways to keep your corner hardware store in business. You want to learn about branding. So, to answer the question, in my view, building a brand is more a matter of corporate success than corporate survival.

To really understand why, have to consider what the *opposite* is of being a brand is. If you're not a brand, you're a generic, which basically means you'll be competing on price alone. As a generic, you don't need to have a personality, a USP, or even a promise. This is the no-frills, no–value-added avenue for selling products to consumers. Marketing costs are significantly lower, which helps keep retail prices lower, allowing generics to capture the portion of the audience that makes their purchasing decisions based on price.

While there is absolutely a market for products based strictly on price, and generic companies can survive, turn a profit, and be financially successful, they'll be limited in terms of their upward potential because price is not an emotion and loyalty isn't built on cost savings. Brands have a greater ability than generics to interact with their market and stand out with one or more unique qualities that make them more desirable. More importantly, brands have the power to forge an emotional connection and bond with their audience, generating a loyal consumer base that can become brand advocates—something that generics can't achieve. Expectation *is* built into the generics model—consumers don't expect much more than the standard product at a low cost. For brands, however, expectation is developed over time with continued fulfillment of the brand promise, usually based on far more significant issues than price.

The potential for growth is far higher for brands than for generics. While each can survive, and each can generate profit, only by building the brand can a company succeed beyond the ceiling created by price-based sales.

GENEVIEVE SMITH
THE BRAND PERSPECTIVE

 It is both!

We've already discussed that a brand is more than marketing or a tagline or an advertising campaign. It is what the corporation stands for on a fundamental level, how that corporation operates, and, most importantly, how that corporation intends for consumers to interact with it. How do you create demand for the products and services being offered? Through the brand. So building the brand is a matter of corporate success.

But commerce is rarely if ever a walk in the park, so it's also a matter of survival. There are ever present competitive threats, economic variables, fickle consumers, and, in many categories, commoditized products and services. The corporations that survive, let alone thrive, are inevitably the ones focused on defending and promoting their brand. These companies are very focused on doing what they do better than anyone else—and they don't stray from the core reason that consumers buy from them.

My point is, a brand is both a matter of corporate success and corporate survival. There is always going to be the latest and greatest new product or flash-in-the-pan buzz right around the corner to potentially threaten a company's competitive position. But if a brand is strong, it can't really be threatened. Take everyone's favorite example, the iPod. There is a plethora of small devices to which a consumer can download and play music; some might be even *very* similar to an iPod. But who owns the market? Apple does—and it's because of their brand.

# Q: IN BUILDING A BRAND, IS IT IMPORTANT THAT THE AGENCY HAVE EXPERIENCE IN THE BRAND'S INDUSTRY?

**JASON MILETSKY**
THE AGENCY PERSPECTIVE

Over the years, I've argued both sides of this coin many times over—and pretty convincingly, I think. In situations where we haven't had experience in an industry, we make the case that this enables us to bring fresh, new ideas to the table, while agencies *with* experience are locked into a set way of thinking and their ideas are tired and uncreative. On the flip side, when we're pitching an account in an industry where we do have depth of knowledge, we proudly display our experience and explain that our work in their field has given us a unique insight into their market—and with that insight, we'll be able to craft marketing messages that less-experienced agencies could never come up with.

But what do I actually believe? Well, at the risk of killing my chances with 50 percent of my future prospects, here's my answer: I do not believe that prior experience in an industry will make an agency more successful. What's more important is whether the agency has had experience with a specific *market*. With any market demographic, there will be subtleties in messaging, approach, design, and strategy that can make a campaign more or less successful, and prior experience with a market will give an agency insight into those nuances. The more experience an agency has with a particular market, the better they'll be able to drill into the minds of the audience, hitting touch points that the audience will likely respond to.

For example, suppose a national home goods retailer, like Pier 1, is looking to reach married females between the ages of 30 and 45 with a household income over $100,000. (I'm just making these numbers up—I've never done any work for Pier 1, but I can't imagine my demo assumptions are far off.) In their search for an agency, it will be less important for them to find a shop that has worked their specific vertical than to find a shop that really understands the affluent female market.

That doesn't mean an agency without experience in a particular market can't learn it on the fly—they can. But if a client decides to work with an agency that has no experience in the even most broad definition of the intended demographic, they must be willing to accept a potentially steep learning curve on the agency's part, that the agency may be slower to respond to necessary changes, and that the creative may not be on target in the early rounds of campaign development.

The other area of expertise that's more important than industry experience is the specific type of service required. This may seem pretty obvious, but agencies can sometimes sell a bill of goods that isn't always legit. Internet marketing, for example, is a complex and constantly changing field that requires specific skill sets. Left to an inexperienced agency, Internet campaigns can easily get botched, wasting time and money and potentially doing long-term damage to a brand. Similarly, a client wouldn't want to hire an agency to produce a national TV spot if the agency has no prior film or video experience. On-the-job training can work in some areas—and there are definitely areas in marketing where services can overlap, with the lines between them becoming blurry—but understanding how to execute and deliver is going to be a far bigger agency asset to a client than simply knowing their industry.

GENEVIEVE SMITH
THE BRAND PERSPECTIVE

⌐ It is the responsibility of the marketing group to select an agency that will partner to produce impactful, creative, and effective media strategies. It is certainly more convenient, but ultimately not critical, that the agencies you employ have experience in the industry. You can quickly ascertain in an RFP or during the agency-selection process whether an agency has the smarts to learn the business or is willing to hire industry expertise. More important, however, is the chemistry between the agency and the brand, and that the client and agencies are willing to put the brand in the center and develop all work with that philosophy in mind. Besides, agencies are often bound by industry exclusivity agreements—meaning that agencies cannot have two clients in the same industry on their roster. (Exclusivity is not as big an issue with brand, digital, and direct marketing agencies; these are frequently smaller and willing to erect a firm line between clients—although one would always prefer exclusivity.)

> Ultimately, I believe it is the responsibility of the internal staff to have experience in the brand's industry. They can then guide creative relevant to the audience within the category by educating the agency about the industry.

Look at the work the agency has produced for others; this will give you a good indication of their versatility. If they are hitting it out of the ballpark for an auto manufacturer, a pet-food company, an electronics firm, a packaged-goods company, and other non-related industries, you can be fairly certain they will apply these same skills to your category. Creative is not about an industry—it must be relevant to the category, certainly, but the real test is: Does it make your employees proud and motivate consumers to choose your brand?

Frequently, the same issue—whether it's important that candidates have experience in the industry—comes up when recruiting talent into a marketing organization. In my industry, however, the question is: Do you want a career in banking, or do you want a career in marketing where you happen to work in a bank?

# Q: HOW IMPORTANT IS IT FOR THE AGENCY AND CLIENT TO HAVE THE SAME PHILOSOPHY OF BRAND-BUILDING?

**JASON MILETSKY**
**THE AGENCY PERSPECTIVE**

Of course it's important—but I'm not sure this is ever really an issue. That is, I've never had a client come out and ask me about my philosophy on brand-building. Typically, this will come out in more subtle ways as the client goes through the vetting process during the initial agency review. If the client determines that the agency's philosophy is different from theirs, that agency will almost certainly be removed from the short list of contenders.

**GENEVIEVE SMITH**
**THE BRAND PERSPECTIVE**

I would state that the agency and client absolutely must share the same philosophy of brand-building. Otherwise, the creative work and the brand will suffer—as will the agency, because they will never be able to please their client.

I was recently involved in a move from one significant agency relationship to another for this reason. We had set very high standards for the brand in terms of communications from signage to collateral to advertising that would really showcase who the brand is, and that it was not just different but better. For two years, we delivered some solid advertising, had good results, and made good progress. In fact, it would have been easier to just keep doing what we had been doing, perhaps making our ads a little better or changing the campaign. But when we assessed the progress in advancing our brand, we decided our advertising wasn't reflecting it enough. We just weren't feeling good about our direction. I spent six months with the agency, working very hands-on to see if we could get the advertising to the next level, but in the end we realized that in order to take our advertising where we wanted it to go, we were going to need to change our ad agency. Now that's a risky move—and not something you do on a whim. But for us, it was a calculated risk we felt we needed to take to move from good to great.

In selecting the new agency, we made a decision to go with a firm who proved to us they were the right partner—that they understood our brand and our passion to make our ads project Simpler Banking and More Smiles. And we were 100 percent aligned on the notion that the brand sits at the middle and the various agencies integrate around that brand to deliver an aligned communications platform to the consumer.

The upshot? Both agencies were well-known, significant advertising firms. Both produce great work for a variety of clients and have long-standing relationships. And both were very sincere in their desire to work with us and with the brand. But at the end of the day, we made the move because we simply didn't share the same philosophy of how to build the brand and the role the brand would play in advertising. I think highly of our team from the first agency—in fact, we stay in touch. I'd even argue that if they were writing the answer to this question, they would say something similar: It came down to a matter of what role we wanted the brand to play in producing creative.

# Q: SHOULD THE AGENCY BUILD THE BRAND FOR THE MARKET, OR FOR THE COMPANY THAT'S PAYING THEM? WHOSE APPROVAL IS MOST IMPORTANT?

JASON MILETSKY

THE AGENCY PERSPECTIVE

Before this question can be answered, one point has to be clear: Even though it is the agency's job to provide our expert opinion, consultation, and feedback, at the end of the day, it's the client that makes the final decisions and gives their approval on all strategies and creative concepts. There may be committees on both sides making their voices heard, but it's usually one individual on the client side who ultimately gives the go-ahead. That being said, this is, unfortunately, a question that comes up all too often. In an ideal world, we'd always do work that we believe the market will respond to. But it's not an ideal world, and the truth is there's a lot more behind every decision than what might be right for the market. For one, there are individual tastes to consider. If the client doesn't like the color yellow, then no amount of marketing data proving it's the right color is going to change their mind. Internal politics and self-preservation also play an important role in decision-making. Chances are, the person we're working with on the client side—and the person to whom that person reports —have families and car payments and mortgages to consider. They're not likely to take risks that could put their end-of-year bonus—or potentially their job— at risk. I once had a meeting with an automotive company where we pitched a viral campaign that would have been…let's just say "risqué" at best, "borderline inappropriate" at worst, but considering their target market of 18–24-year-old males, undoubtedly eye-catching. Sitting in a small, private room at a trade show in Vegas, the director of marketing and one of his associates sat in stunned silence after I finished presenting the campaign. Finally, the director of marketing drew a long breath and said, "This could be huge—we'd get a lot of attention with this." His associate gave a nervous laugh and said, "If we do this, we either end up on the cover of *AdWeek* or we get fired. There's no in-between." With a new baby on the way, the director of marketing ultimately decided that regardless of how the market might react, the conservative nature of his boss created too much of a personal risk. Self-preservation won out, and the campaign has since been shelved, locked away on some remote server, unlikely to ever get a chance to shine.

Agencies need to take all of this into consideration when making their recommendations to the client. In my experience, the best way to deal with this is to always give three options for every creative concept or marketing tool:

- One option that you think is perfect for the market you're trying to reach. If the stars are aligned, your client may go with it; they're not always at odds with what the market wants.

- Another option that you know the client will like. Find a way to do this so that if they choose this route, the market will still react positively.

- A third option that is deliberately okay, but not as good as the first two. This will make the first two options look better by comparison.

This method shows that the agency is being sensitive to all of the client's needs and concerns, and puts responsibility on the client for making the right decision.

GENEVIEVE SMITH
THE BRAND PERSPECTIVE

I'm going to be controversial here and say that an agency shouldn't build the brand for the market *or* the company. Why? Because the agency shouldn't build the brand at all! I believe a company should build its brand—with agency support. Great agencies can give a lot of expert advice and guidance and will bring the brand to life in unbelievable ways, but they cannot judge what a company is capable of executing on. Mutual success requires that the client be surefooted in understanding their market and articulating their objectives.

That aside, let's cover who needs to give their approval. As I've mentioned, employee and executive support and belief in the brand are key. Without these constituents, the brand will go nowhere. What, exactly, is belief in this context? Belief is:

- We can be successful operating this brand.

- We can execute on this brand promise.

- This brand appeals to our audiences.

So the company's feelings about the brand are important. But consumers vote with their feet, so how they as "the market" perceive and purchase from the brand is, at the end of the day, what matters. The brand must resonate with its market in order to be successful, so you build the brand to attract the market.

Many times, I've heard executives or groups of employees make statements like, "I'm not the target market, so I'm not a good judge of what will appeal." This attitude makes for good branding decisions because it ensures that those decisions will be consumer directed and data driven. There are, however, those who feel that because they manage a brand, they are a focus group of one—that their opinion or taste is what matters, regardless of all evidence to the contrary. This is ego. What you end up with then is an agency stuck in a situation where the work is done for the executive who's paying the bills, even if it's known to be off mark, not for the market.

# Q: SHOULD YOU GET EMPLOYEES' INPUT WHILE THE BRAND IS BEING BUILT? OR IS THAT JUST A NIGHTMARE WAITING TO HAPPEN?

**JASON MILETSKY**
**THE AGENCY PERSPECTIVE**

If the legal department of a large company offered employees of that company an opportunity to give their thoughts and feedback on some obscure legal issue, they'd be met with some blank stares and a whole lotta people trying to figure out the best way to politely turn them down. Legal is boring, and not particularly memorable, and like accounting, most people who aren't trained in it are more than happy to admit they don't really get it.

Unfortunately, the same isn't true for fields like advertising, marketing, and branding. When it comes to anything creative, most people think they totally understand it and just ended up working in customer service because they missed their calling in life. (I'm perversely amused when I tell people I'm writing a book and their response is, "You know, I was thinking of writing a book, too...." Because of course, writing a book is just that easy! I mean, *anyone* can do it! Jerks.) Because most people like to think they're creative, and because the brand is going to be so visible in the public eye, anybody who's asked to give their feedback will eagerly do so—and almost always suggest some kind of pointless change if only to get their fingerprints on it somehow.

Clearly, my suggestion is to *not* get employees' input into the brand while it's being built. You'll just be asking for trouble. If you need an insider's opinion, find a couple of people inside the company who you know understand marketing and brand-building, who understand your audience, and who are likely to give you useful feedback.

That said, although I am hard-lined *against* getting employee input into the brand as it gets developed, I am very much *for* letting employees know what's going on. Developing a brand the right way is usually a pretty involved process, and getting it done right is going to take at least three months—and that's if everyone is on top of their game and nails everything the very first time.

It's going to be next to impossible to keep the effort quiet; sooner or later, word's going to get out, and employees will know that something big is going on, even if they won't totally understand what it's about. And change—especially mysterious change—is *never* good for the mental health of a corporate workforce. Change scares employees. It breeds anxiety, reduces productivity, and eggs on the gossipers. Brand-builders need to make sure that although they are not exposing the brand to their employees, and are *definitely* not asking for feedback during the development process, they *are* implementing an internal communications strategy that lets employees know that yes, there is a change in the works, and that the change is positive, and that it is being undertaken as part of a natural evolution spurred on by recent growth, blah, blah, blah—all the typical spin that we marketing types are so good at spewing. Unveil the brand to the employees little by little, teasing it out over time, culminating with an internal launch where all employees are simultaneously presented the new brand and can celebrate its introduction into the marketplace.

GENEVIEVE SMITH
THE BRAND PERSPECTIVE

Input or feedback can always be a nightmare, but if you don't engage the hearts and minds of the employees while the brand is being built, then you can be sure the brand idea will never truly come to life—and could in fact meet with much resistance (if not downright rebellion) when launched. When we evolved the WaMu brand promise, we did it in lockstep with employees, our approach ranging from one-to-one interviews with the most senior executives to focus groups with the newest hires working as tellers, mid-level management, and support staff in the back office. (Interestingly, when we conducted the one-to-one executive interviews, we discovered that there was no unified viewpoint of the brand platform, what it meant or could mean, or how it affected and guided business operations. In fact, several of the most senior executives could not articulate the brand statement, as they did not know one existed!)

When we began our brand-development journey, we asked ourselves the following questions:

- Do customers like or love us?

- Is our current brand platform working hard enough for us today?

- Will it work hard enough for us five years from now?

- Is our brand still unique to us? Or do we have competitors encroaching on our space?

- Customers' needs are changing. Is this brand still what the customer needs?

- Is the platform something that everyone across the company can focus on?

- Is the platform actionable?

- Can we all execute against it?

When we looked at everything—how we did things, how our competitors did things, what the customer loved us for, what the customer didn't love us for, and fundamentally what we were capable of delivering—we saw that the former platform provided a great foundation, but that there were some issues in terms of how we, inside the business, interpreted our platform "Great Value With Friendly Service for Everyone." We found, too, that there was somewhat of a disconnect between how *we* interpreted "Great Value" and how the customer interprets "Great Value." Very simply, internally, "Great Value" was something living in the product group, limited primarily to rate and features, which of course in banking equates to product price. Our customer, on the other hand, told us there were a whole host of other factors that influenced their decision-making processes—among them price of course, but also ease of choice, competence, service quality, respect, clarity, brand, and more. And how about "Friendly Service?" Our employee and consumer research showed that "Friendly Service" is a real differentiator, but that it might not always be enough. For example, if we make a mistake but apologize in a friendly way, that isn't really good enough. The real competitive advantage, inherent friendliness, was being undersold by its being limited to service—suggesting that "friendly" existed only in the front-line customer service–delivery positions.

Ultimately, we concluded from our research that we didn't want to lose a great heritage, but we did want to deliver on a brand position that is clear, actionable, and differentiated. These two critical constituents—our employees and our customers—had told us we needed to expand the notion of "value" so that we could concentrate on things the customer really cares about, and that we needed to liberate "friendly" to apply it across the whole business, not just to our front-line customer-service staff.

Once the brand position was developed, we tested it with employees to determine their thoughts about the re-articulation from both the employee and customer perspectives. Specifically, employees were asked to give their thoughts and opinions about the following:

- How will "Simpler Banking and More Smiles" be received by employees?

- Will it create a competitive advantage?

- How can the promise best be communicated and executed?

Here's what they told us: This brand position exactly mirrors how we see our brand, our customers, what people love us for, and why we love working here.

Perhaps a few brand types and smart creatives from an agency could have worked in isolation to develop a re-articulation of the brand promise—but I don't think the results would have been as unique or as inspiring. Fundamentally, the brand promise needs to be something that connects emotionally with consumers and employees—and the only way to get to that is by listening and including employees in its development. Otherwise, you are likely to end up with a few words on a piece of paper and *maybe* a marketing campaign.

# Q: WHAT IS THE DIFFERENCE BETWEEN BRANDING AND MARKETING?

JASON MILETSKY
THE AGENCY PERSPECTIVE

↳ This is *such* an interesting question! It's just not one of those distinctions you have to make very often, and to be honest, it's almost humbling to try and answer it. I sat down to my laptop ready to crank out what I was sure would be an easy couple of pages, but suddenly found myself at a loss for words. I know the answer, but I don't know the answer. Suppose someone asked you to define the word "cow." Obviously, you know what a cow is; you could draw one, point one out, and moo 'til the...well, 'til they come home. But can you really *define* it? In a weird way, this question is kind of like that, which makes it really interesting —espccially because although branding and marketing are each distinct, there is also significant overlap. So let me start by breaking each of them down and looking over the deconstructed pieces to see where the differences (and similarities) are.

Let's look at branding first. As I've already said (and will undoubtedly repeat), a brand is the sum total of all experiences that consumers have with a company, product, or service. It's a reputation. It's what people base their expectations on when considering future purchases or uses. Branding, therefore, can be viewed as two distinct action items:

- The consistent fulfillment of the brand promise and raising of expectations

- The development and assignment of distinct visual and personality-driven characteristics and the ongoing effort to reflect the brand positively through all marketing and communication vehicles

This may sound fairly easy, but it's actually quite complex. As with an ocean, there is constant churn. Sometimes there are small ripples, other times there are larger, foreboding waves, and every now and then a tsunami hits. But one thing is for sure: It's never perfectly calm. And thanks to the Internet—specifically, social-media tools and instant access to information—markets can shift faster and more radically than ever before. Complicating things is the fact that brands require both ongoing (though usually subtle) evolution *and* consistency—yes, two opposing concepts that make the branding process even more challenging.

Marketing, on the other hand, is the act of bringing a product, service, company, or brand to market. Notice I listed "brand" as one entry in a longer list. That's because marketing is in fact a huge umbrella that can encompass anything being sold to any audience. The high-school track team raising money with a weekend car wash is marketing when they put up signs around the neighborhood letting drivers know about their service, just like Coors is marketing when they air TV commercials and plaster their name everywhere they can fit it on stadium walls. But the track team's car wish is hardly a brand.

Brands can't rely on unprompted word of mouth among consumers to pass along positive messages. Marketing is required to spread the word to larger audiences, help increase recognition, and embed expectations in consumers' minds even before they have the chance to interact with the brand personally. Marketing communicates the brand by effectively pinpointing who the right audience is and where they are, by developing the best message to encourage audience use of the brand, by packaging the message (creative), and by delivering it (media). And of course, that marketing must properly reflect the brand in order to increase its recognition and maintain its integrity.

Now I want to make one thing clear, because it's an important point in terms of the delineation of responsibilities: Agencies may assume responsibility for building the brand identity and communicating the brand message, but the company/client alone is responsible for fulfilling their brand promise and maintaining their reputation. If you promise great-tasting food and people spit it out after the first bite, there's not a lot an agency's going to be able to do for you. We can try to spin information more positively ("Our brand can help you lose weight!") and we may be able to slow down the spread of bad reviews, but eventually it's going to catch up with you. Branding and marketing are not about smoke and mirrors—they're about setting realistic expectations.

GENEVIEVE SMITH
THE BRAND PERSPECTIVE

It is commonly thought that branding is marketing, and that marketing is branding. In fact, branding—or, more specifically, the brand promise—sits in the middle of business operations. Think of it as being like quadrants, with brand at the middle informing products/services, people, distribution, and communications. And marketing—the planning and execution of a concept, pricing, promotion, and distribution of goods and services that create sales—is a part of that communications quadrant. Good marketing creates consumer awareness and converts that awareness into purchasing. Put another way, marketing is what's used to make the cash register ring! When it comes to marketing, the brand informs all the visual elements we've been discussing, including their usage. Additionally, the brand is the lens through which marketing decisions are made.

Let me give you a real-life example of how the brand informs the marketing strategy. As I mentioned in my answer to Question #23, "Should You Get Employees' Input While the Brand Is Being Built? Or Is That Just a Nightmare Waiting to Happen?" the WaMu brand had a heritage of providing value. But when we rearticulated the brand, we found that consumers and employees defined "value" much more broadly than to mean "rate and features." Yes, price was important, but many other factors such as ease of choice, competence, service quality, respect, clarity, etc. also influenced their decision to choose our brand over another. In essence, what we discovered was that screaming price was unnecessary. In fact, being known as a "discounter" was bad positioning for the brand because of how broadly consumers interpreted "value." (This is particularly true in the financial-services sector, as consumers are suspicious of banks and their hidden fees and "tricks.")

Interestingly, this position flew in the face of the experience of a colleague of mine, who was responsible for a major business unit. His belief was that the best way to market was to conduct continual rate and price promotions, including "red tag" or "blue light" special type marketing campaigns. And as it happened, he was responsible for a significant portion of the company's profits. Naturally, whether his approach was the one we should adopt was hotly debated at the executive table. But ultimately, we determined that in this case, the approach related to specific marketing campaigns and changing our position would not be advantageous to the brand and what it stands for. We decided to be true to the brand—and we found that by doing so, sales increased, as did our brand consideration.

# Q: WHAT ARE THE CORE REASONS A CONSUMER WOULD STAY LOYAL TO A BRAND?

**JASON MILETSKY**

**THE AGENCY PERSPECTIVE**

 One of my favorite jokes has to do with the power of loyalty:

*Q. How do you know that a dog is man's best friend?*

*A. Lock your wife and your dog in the trunk of your car. Let them out an hour later and see which of them is still happy to see you.*

Loyalty is one of the most powerful forces in the universe. It's also the brass ring in branding: There's nothing more valuable, but it's extremely hard to grab. Why? Because a brand-loyal customer is revenue in the bank—and a disciple on the street.

Loyalty is derived from a mix of many different ingredients, each of which must be fully present for the magical formula to become—and remain—potent:

- The brand needs to exist in a category the user cares about. For example, even if every other item on this list were present for a particular brand of trash bags, I'll never be loyal to a particular brand of trash bags because I simply don't care about them.

- The brand needs to promise something that the market desires or requires.

- The brand has to consistently fulfill its promise.

- The brand's personality needs to somehow reflect the personality of its market.

- The brand needs to be true to its personality and not waver.

Notice that "price" and "accessibility" are not on the list. Consumers who are brand-loyal are largely indifferent to higher prices or accessibility issues.

Apple is perhaps one of the best examples of a company that commands tremendous brand loyalty. Even in the '90s, before their ultra-hip ad campaigns and retail stores, Macs had reached an almost cult-like status. Back then, Macs were two, three, four, or more times more expensive than their PC competitors (they still are); more difficult to find; way more difficult to fix (good luck finding an Apple repair shop in the mid '90s); and extremely limited when it came to compatible software (in your average 1995 computer store, past the gleaming white shelves jam-packed with PC programs, games, and applications, stood a single dusty, cobweb-covered shelf housing a few Mac programs—each a version or two behind). But Mac users knew a secret that their PC counterparts didn't know: Their Macs were better. They were cooler, easier, more intuitive, and they were the anti-Microsoft—and *nothing* was going to get them to change their minds. Not price, not accessibility—nothing. That's brand loyalty at its finest.

GENEVIEVE SMITH

THE BRAND PERSPECTIVE

↳ The answer to this is everything you would expect—they like the product, the experience, the service, the value, the access, and the ease of purchase. In short they trust the brand. It is reliable, and so they are loyal.

Let's talk about a real-life example of consumer loyalty, how much it can withstand—and when enough is enough. At WaMu, we continually monitored our brand attributes, measuring those dimensions we knew are important to loyalty, consideration, and purchase, such as convenience, security, professionalism, simplicity, advocacy, and value. But when the financial markets melted down in 2008, WaMu was front and center in the media as a "troubled" financial institution.

A survey conducted in April of that same year revealed that our brand was strong. It beat the competition in almost all attributes, even though we'd had our fair share of negative publicity at that point. We were surprised by this; we thought consumers would be reacting as we were internally. Our survey in August of 2008, however, told another story. This survey was conducted after the government seizure of Indymac and daily news predictions that WaMu would be the next to go under. The brand monitor showed considerable weakening in key areas such as trustworthiness, expertise, and simplicity. Then the FDIC seized the company. Not surprisingly, our post-seizure brand survey data showed the brand had contracted on all attributes in a statistically significant way—and as you would expect, sales and retention followed suit.

One of the best measures of loyalty is willingness to refer a friend to the brand. As part of our ongoing brand-monitor studies we also measured this statistic monthly with consumers. We asked, "How likely would you be to recommend your primary bank to a friend?" At our peak, 57 percent of consumers said they would recommend WaMu to a friend; in the August timeframe, 53 percent said they would; and post-seizure, 33 percent said they would. This aligns with brand consideration where, at our peak, 47 percent of consumers said they would consider WaMu for their next financial product/service; in August, 39 percent said they would; and post-seizure, 23 percent said they would. As you can see, as the perceived reliability of our brand decreased, so did our customer loyalty.

We'll talk about repairing a damaged brand and the role of PR in managing a brand crisis later in the book.

# Q: • What Are Some of the Steps That All • Successful Brand Managers Take?

Jason Miletsky
The Agency Perspective

I have to say that I am *crazy* excited to be sharing the pages of this book with Genevieve Smith, who is truly a rock star when it comes to building a brand. Even *I'm* looking forward to reading how she answers this question! She has many of the qualities I have seen in a number of great brand managers who have made their brands a success:

- **They look beyond what they like and consider what the market will react to:** While I think it's important for brand managers to share some of the personality traits of the brand itself, they shouldn't allow their personal tastes to interfere with the right decision. The brand manager may not like the color blue, but a good manager will use it anyway if it's what the brand needs.

- **They understand the value of marketing the brand internally:** Revenue might be made outside the office where the consumers meet the register, but a good brand manager knows that company employees can be the best brand advocates anyone could ask for. Everyone directly associated with the brand must believe in it if it's really going to fulfill its external promise, and successful brand managers will invest the time and expense needed to get employees on board.

- **They consider all available information and research, and they gather the opinions of trusted advisors, but they can ultimately make firm decisions:** The mark of a true leader is the ability to make decisions. A lot of people want to give their opinions, and it's understandable that any individual who manages something as important as a brand will want to consult with many others before making hard decisions, but ultimately, those decisions have to be made. This sometimes means going against the grain—and against the advice of the people around them—and making tough decisions based on raw instinct alone. In the end, though, a good brand manager will be able to make those hard decisions and stand behind them.

- **They treat their agency as a partner, not a bunch of yes-men and doers:** No, I didn't just add this to the list to be self-serving. The truth is, many brand managers can't get beyond their own egos to allow their hand-picked agencies to give them the proper advice and insight they were hired to provide. The benefit of the agency is that they can provide an outside point of view that the people managing the brand just don't have. Successful brand managers strongly consider the counsel of their agencies in determining the direction of their brand.

- **They keep an constant eye on the market and evolve the brand as needed:** Complacency is not an option for brands. Markets change and audiences must be monitored to ensure that the brand message is still reaching them effectively. These changes may be slow and subtle, but strong brand managers keep an eye on them and adjust the brand accordingly.

- **They don't take unnecessary risks, but they're not afraid of taking calculated ones:** There's no reason to be reckless in brand-building, but brands can't reach their full potential without taking some calculated risks. Successful brand managers won't shy away from risks out of fear for their own career, their hopes for an end-of-year bonus, or their position within their company.

- **They don't sacrifice quality for speed:** It's understood that the faster branding and marketing efforts are launched, the happier everyone at the brand is. But speed can sometimes be the poison that ultimately kills quality. This is especially true in the early development of the brand and the establishment of the brand guide, which is derived from a complex mix of many components. It takes time to put it together. Successful brand managers keep things moving at a strong and steady pace, but with an understanding that stepping too hard on the gas pedal can lead to a major crash.

GENEVIEVE SMITH
THE BRAND PERSPECTIVE

The steps successful brand managers take are related but inherently different, depending on the maturity and health of the brand being managed—and the brand manager's charter. For example, if a brand manager is hired to help build a brand literally from scratch, he or she will be much more development- and launch-focused than a brand manager who is hired to expand a successful brand or repair a damaged one. Nonetheless, the fundamental skills and deliverables are very similar regardless of where a brand is in its evolution, so I'll discuss them from a generic "brand manager" perspective.

They are as follows:

- **Knowledge:** A successful brand manager deals with information including past, present, and potential future trends. This information stems from a broad and deep base of consumer research relevant to the category and encompasses such topics as why people buy the product/service the brand represents, how they buy, what creates loyalty, what is critical to the consumer, what the brand's advantages are, and what threats the brand faces. It also includes general consumer research by segment, ethnicity, and demographic, as most brands will be affected by overall consumer trends. A successful brand manager will also have knowledge of the products and services sold by the brand—which means this individual needs to be very familiar with the business fundamentals and financial drivers. Competitive intelligence and insights are also required. To be successful, the brand manager will use this knowledge to help influence and guide product, price, and distribution. Finally, the brand manager's knowledge base must be broadly accepted and generally used throughout the company, meaning communication of knowledge is key.

- **Charter:** The successful brand manager will work to establish or maintain a charter for his or her function that goes far beyond marketing and advertising. Without a clear and comprehensive charter, the branding function simply doesn't exist; instead, it becomes a marketing or product-manager role. Successful brand managers also articulate the charter for the brands they manage. It is important that everyone working with the brand or who can influence the brand's success understands the goals and charter. This ensures that actions, asks, changes, and investments are contextual for folks, as the brand manager doesn't call all the shots.

- **Influence:** I cannot emphasize how important it is for a brand manager to develop and nurture relationships with all the various constituents who can affect the success or failure of the brand. Unless the president of the company is also the brand manager—the way Steve Jobs is with Apple—a brand manager will always be vying for resources and mindshare, which makes their ability to influence others highly valuable.

Beyond these three, there are a few other fundamental steps that successful brand managers take:

- They build and develop the right marketing assets and brand expressions.

- They ensure that the integrity of the brand's visual guidelines are maintained.

- They broadly influence marketing, product, distribution, and agencies that work with the brand.

- They communicate the brand's status in terms of awareness, consideration, and consumer opinion.
- They influence shelf space and prominence for the products and services sold.
- They constantly challenge the status quo and push the edges for the brand's evolution.
- They show the love. They're passionate and committed to the brand, and they fight for what's right for it.

# Q: • WHAT ARE SOME OF THE COMMON
# • MISTAKES BRAND MANAGERS MAKE?

What's your perspective on this question?
Let us know at PerspectivesOnBranding.com.

JASON MILETSKY

THE AGENCY PERSPECTIVE

During the years I've worked with various brands and brand managers, and have studied other brands to see how they've been developed, and I've spotted some mistakes that brand managers make on a regular basis:

- **Relying too much on data and research:** Let me make this clear: I'm a big believer in research, statistics, data, focus groups, etc. I think research can give you insight into the minds and movement of any audience, and brand managers and marketers should use this information as they make their decisions. But good brand managers should also have a sixth sense when it comes to their brand and what's best for it, and be able to make certain decisions even in the face of conflicting statistical data—not based on common sense, but based on raw, gut instinct. Brand management isn't accounting—it's not always just about looking at the numbers. It's creativity. It's sociology. It's psychology. There may not be only one right answer, and brand managers need to know when to go against the grain.

- **Being reactive instead of proactive:** Being reactive is really just playing it safe. Too often, brand managers wait it out to see what their competition does before taking any action of their own. Or they'll balk at trying something new because nobody else in their industry has done it yet. One brand manager told me that he doesn't like to be the first to do something because, as he explained, "the first pioneers through the canyons were the ones who ended up with arrows in their back. The next ones through knew which roads to avoid." I guess that's true...but it's also true that first one to find the treasure chest gets all the gold. The next ones just find an empty box.

- **Going for the quick buck rather than the long-term gain:** Brand-building is as much a time investment as it is a financial investment—but brand managers are often under the gun at the office, with mandates coming from higher-ups to make things happen faster. It's understandable that this will prompt the brand manager to attempt to accelerate results. But if there is one fight the brand manager must take on, this is it. Going for the quick buck and marketing for short-term results might in fact yield short-term results, but those results will be a far cry from the much greater results that can be achieved with a longer-term brand-building strategy.

- **Not setting firm goals:** No, this does not contradict the preceding bullet. Goals are absolutely necessary; they just can't be too short-term or unrealistic. The importance of firm goals can't be stressed strongly enough, since numeric goals are the only way to determine whether the best, most cost-effective strategies are being used.

- **Not taking their own branding guide seriously enough:** Don't get me wrong: I believe people in branding and marketing—on the client and agency side—can ignore certain mandates established by the guide as long as they maintain consistency in key areas and stay within the spirit of the brand. That being said, though, it drives me nuts when a brand manager makes some flippant comment like, "It doesn't matter if the color is off by a shade or two. Nobody will notice." Yes they will! And if they don't right away, they *certainly* will when a full year and five print runs later the color is five or six shades off. Don't screw with consistency—it's a brand's best friend.

Every brand manager is bound to make mistakes and will need to retrace their steps at some point to get back on track. To be honest, I give any brand manager a lot of credit—there's a lot of weight on their shoulders, and very often they're flying in a fog as they try to move the brand forward. But avoiding the pitfalls outlined here will go a long way toward keeping everyone moving in the right direction.

GENEVIEVE SMITH
THE BRAND PERSPECTIVE

As you saw in the preceding question, someone with the right education, capabilities, and experience can follow a fairly standard roadmap to be a successful brand manager because there is a lot of science to the discipline. The mistakes, or derailers, are not so easily categorized, and they're much more subtle than a capability to use research, develop visuals, or perform analytical assessments. So let's talk about some mistakes that go beyond managing the fundamentals, which, quite frankly are simply the "price of entry" for being a brand manager.

I've said a brand manager has to "show the love" for the brand, which means they must be passionate about the brand and nurture it along the development journey. There is a fine line, however, between doing what is right for the brand and awarding oneself the title of Ultimate Brand Arbiter and Grand Poobah of All Things Brand, because unless you own the company, you do not have that discretion. Specifically I have seen brand managers go to battle on business fundamentals, arguing along the vein of "This brand would never do/sell/act that way"—to the point that business ownership began to reject the brand tenets as not being flexible enough to support their growth objectives.

This is exactly the opposite outcome you want in the role of brand manager; it shows the brand manager is either myopic, unable or unwilling to collaborate with those accountable for profit to provide the brand with enough flex to support changing business objectives, or rigid and holding on too tightly to the brand promise by not allowing a dialogue about how a given business need can be accommodated.

I've also had experience with brand managers who literally terrorized others with the threat of reporting non-compliance with the brand. Instead of listening, reasoning, and influencing, they would simply push the "brand button" anytime someone issued an opinion that diverged from the one they had formed about implementation. At first, when that happened, I couldn't understand why the brand-management group seemed increasingly at odds not only with the operating units, but also with marketing and our creative agencies; once I was able to see that the brand manager was using the brand as a weapon, it was possible to repair those relationships. The lesson: You can be the dogmatic and heavy-handed brand police if you want to, but sooner or later it will come back to bite you in the ass.

There are a few other areas where a brand manager can fail, these being:

- Too heavy on creative (focused purely on how things look)
- Too analytical (buried in the data)
- Locked into how things are today (can't lead the brand evolution)
- Lacks implementation skills (roadmap looks good on paper, but nothing is ever accomplished)

To close this discussion, my opinion is that brand manager is a key leadership role, and the ideal manager will know how to deliver in both the art and the science of brand-building.

# Q: • CAN A BRAND BE BUILT
### • WITHOUT A LARGE BUDGET?

**JASON MILETSKY**
**THE AGENCY PERSPECTIVE**

A brand should always fulfill its promise, regardless of budget. That's a given. Whether a brand can communicate effectively enough to broaden its consumer base without a large budget, however, is a different story. What we're really talking about, though, is marketing—can a brand be *marketed* without a large budget? Clearly, higher budgets allow greater opportunities for mass marketing a brand. TV and print can be expensive, as can sports sponsorships, roadside billboards, and other marketing efforts. Not every brand will have the deep pockets required for these types of strategies. But it's naïve to think that without large budgets, brands can't exist, thrive, and grow. They can.

That being said, it needs to be understood that there are challenges involved— the biggest of them being reach. Lower budgets reduce the potential reach of a marketing effort, limiting it either by geography or by the number of people a message can touch. Google AdWords, for example, can be shown around the world, but at $50 dollars per day, there will be a limit on how many people will see them. Similarly, TV commercials can be produced and aired on a shoe-string budget, but on a local or regional level rather than a national broadcast.

So the basic reality is that limited budgets will result in limited audience exposure, limited geographic coverage, or both. Larger budgets, on the other hand, will result in the potential for increased audience and wider geographic coverage (I say "the potential for" because big budgets don't guarantee anything— sound and savvy minds still need to spend the money properly).

There is, however, a potential exception: word of mouth. Word of mouth is the best form of advertising you can get, as people will believe their peers before believing a marketing campaign. The problem is, word of mouth that passes from one person to another during random conversation just won't reach critical mass (which is why, in my answer to Question #24, "What Is the Difference Between Branding and Marketing?" I noted that marketing is required because a brand can't expect to be built on word of mouth alone). That is, unless a clever marketing campaign eggs them on.

Enter viral campaigns. Viral campaigns are marketing communications that encourage consumers to do the marketing for them by passing the message on to other people, most typically through e-mail. The basic concept is that an individual receives a viral message and, because he or she thinks it's funny or informative, forwards the message on to a number of his or her friends, who in turn forward it to a number of *their* friends, and so on. Before you know it, thousands or even millions of people have received the message and been exposed to the brand it's promoting. Usually these messages contain videos that are over-the-top outrageous, shocking, or just really funny, like CareerBuilder's Monk-e-Mail, which was reportedly seen by more than 25 million people. (If you haven't seen that one, you should Google it and check it out.)

The benefit of viral campaigns is that they can be far less expensive than more traditional, mass-media types of marketing. In fact, one amateur video that hits the right buttons may be all it takes to spark a viral explosion. The problem with them, though, is that there's really no control over the campaign. It can be hard to determine what people will like so much that they'll be willing to pass it on, and even harder to establish who receives it. And even if the viral campaign is a certified hit, it's still just a one-time effort. While a single successful viral campaign can help gain quick, short-term notoriety, it takes long-term, ongoing communications to truly build a brand.

GENEVIEVE SMITH
THE BRAND PERSPECTIVE

Building a brand isn't really about money. If you have the internal talent and the desire, you can build many elements of the brand without making a large investment. I would estimate that the conceptual work associated with building the Simpler Banking and More Smiles brand for WaMu comprised approximately 5 percent or less of the annual core marketing budget—and if I include the line of business marketing budgets, it was less than 2 percent of the total annual investment made in marketing.

The largest investments are made not in the conceptual work involved in building a brand; rather, they are made in the brand's highest-exposure communications opportunities. These are advertising, merchandising, point of sale, packaging, direct marketing, digital marketing, and Web presence. If you work at a company where investments in these media are already part of the annual operating budget, then the assignment is to implement any updated or new brand expressions across all of these. If this is a well-managed exercise, most companies will find efficiencies during implementation simply by taking the time to evaluate all the media and the materials used.

If you are a start up with no brand awareness and no baseline marketing investment or existing work to leverage, then the expense will be relatively more—both because of the effort in creating materials and design systems as well as the investment levels required for brand recognition as the brand will build with exposure.

To net this out, conceptualizing and operationalizing the brand can be done with a modest budget; marketing the brand is where the money will be invested.

# Q: • CAN BUILDING A BRAND
     • REALLY GENERATE INCOME?

JASON MILETSKY
THE AGENCY PERSPECTIVE

I would dismiss this question as being too silly to answer if not for the unusually high number of times it gets brought up as a point of discussion within marketing circles. Here's the deal: Last time I checked, businesses exist to turn a profit—at least, that's their goal. Brand-building isn't just a fun hobby that marketing execs dabble in while the rest of the company is busy bringing in the bucks. Building the brand—marketing the brand—plays a large role in establishing an audience, which in turn generates revenue.

The reason people even think to debate it is that the revenue it generates isn't direct, which makes it harder to make a correlation between investments in brand-building and consumer purchasing. Run a series of print ads announcing a sale the upcoming weekend, and by Monday morning you'll know whether or not the ad efforts paid off. But the math's not as easy to do when you're trying to see the up-tick from signage inside a sports stadium or a radio spot that broadcasts your brand in some clever way but with no real call to action.

Does watching those truly annoying Hillshire Farms "Go Meat" commercials make anybody want to break out the barbecue? (Check them out on YouTube if you've never seen them; just search for "Hillshire Farms Go Meat.") Probably not. Do consumers think about those ads when they hit the grocery store? Again, probably not. But consumers who are not driven primarily by price are more likely to purchase products they've heard of. It's just human nature. It's like this: You need directions, and there are two people standing on a street corner. Person A you're sure you've never seen before; Person B you recognize. You're not sure from where, but you know you've seen or talked to that person before. So Person B is a little easier to approach because of that recognition. Even a small amount of recognition is enough to instill a modicum of trust.

It's no different with branding. The consumer is thinking of barbecuing, so when they go to the meat section, the Hillshire Farms name is somehow recognizable.

They're not sure why—maybe they've had it before, maybe someone recommended it, maybe it's just been around a long time, or maybe they've always thought their TV spots were really funny (I guess someone must)—but they're not going to spend too much time figuring it out. They're just going to make their selection and keep on shopping. But for that brief period of time when the consumer was trying to choose from among a large selection, Hillshire Farms' branding initiatives have helped tilt the odds in their favor.

**GENEVIEVE SMITH**
**THE BRAND PERSPECTIVE**

You build the brand to create awareness and consideration for the products and services it sells. A strong brand allows the company to charge a price premium that equals profits because it creates the following benefits versus the competition:

- **Higher awareness:** More consumers know about the product/brand.

- **Higher consideration:** More consumers, when in the market, will choose this brand's products.

- **More loyalists:** A community of consumers who refer friends and family to the brand will emerge.

- **More "unpaid" marketing:** Media and online forums can be leveraged.

Firms like Millward Brown, which provide brand-valuation services, create models that estimate the value of a brand to a franchise. I'll discuss this type of financial modeling later in the book, but for now I'll note that basically, the models calculate brand value, generally expressed as a percent of the franchise value, by analyzing business value based on a firm's financial projections, economic capital, and franchise value (in addition to awareness, consideration, loyalty, and other benchmarking indicators versus the competition). This is one way to look at the brand as a financial asset to determine how much shareholder value it contributes.

# Q: Is Brand-Building Just as Important to B2B Companies as It Is to B2C Companies?

**Jason Miletsky**
**The Agency Perspective**

Clearly, if the average person is asked to name a brand off the top of their head, they're going to name a consumer brand—Nike, Coke, McDonald's, or something along those lines. Those are the brands that are in our faces all the time—the brands we buy on a regular basis, and the ones we see on TV when we come home at night. But—and I have been beating this drum for a lot of years now and will continue to do so—brand-building is not strictly limited to B2C companies. It's every bit as important for B2B companies to build their brands. In fact, in some respects it's even *more* important due to certain limitations on marketing and there being more at stake with each decision (more on that in a minute).

First, let me lay down two fundamental truths that form the basis for my beliefs about B2B brand-building:

- Brands help to build trust, and the importance of trust is directly proportional to the cost of purchase. That is, the higher the price, the more trust is required.

- B2B means "business to business," not "bricks to bricks." Behind every business decision is a real, live person with their own unique personality and a life outside of their office. We market to people, not to buildings.

Brand managers and marketing directors often forget that even in a sales environment of negotiated prices, personal relationships, and potentially longer sales cycles, the brand still plays a heightened role in purchasing decisions. The people behind those decisions are real people—and like any market, those people often share very similar characteristics. But they shouldn't be confused with their jobs. For example, if you're looking to reach HR directors, chances are you'll be reaching a largely female audience over the age of 45. But just because they run HR departments doesn't mean they're boring or that they love HR as a rule. They are people with real feelings who have families, go out with friends, and want to be entertained like anybody else. These are the very same people that Dove soap tries to reach by strengthening their brand, so why should a payroll company put in any less effort when trying to get them to choose their company as a vendor?

Because of the expense and potential for waste (waste being people the marketer isn't interested in reaching), B2B brands don't usually have the luxury of using mass-media tools such as television for marketing purposes. Once in awhile you may see some B2B company advertising on a Sunday morning political talk show, but these are few and far between; and more than likely, they're trying to pique the interest of potential investors, not potential customers. With marketing avenues usually limited to online and offline trade-publication advertising, direct mail, and trade shows, the brand becomes that much more important and provides that much more of an advantage to the salespeople who actively try to close various accounts. Most industries are pretty small, and word about vendors and even individual players gets around quickly, so how the brand is perceived and how easily it's recognized may be the deciding factor in getting a contract or being passed over for someone seen as more reliable.

Once again, the trust issue becomes a greater factor when more money is stake, and the brand is what tells the decision-makers whether their money will be well-spent. Plus—and this is an important distinction—decision-makers are not spending their own money. They're spending their *company's* money—and will be responsible for explaining how they've spent it. That means they won't necessarily be looking for the lowest price around; they'll be looking for the smartest buy. The wrong decision could mean the difference between getting a promotion—or remaining employed—and not.

In my agency's marketing of JVC Professional—the B2B arm of the electronics giant, which sells professional-grade cameras and display equipment to other companies and studios—the toughest hurdle we've had to overcome is the overarching belief by the market that "Nobody ever got fired for buying Sony." The Sony brand has become synonymous with quality and innovation, and the feeling is that purchasing Sony products is not only beneficial, it's safe. Buying anything else—JVC, Panasonic, Sharp, anything—would be taking a chance with your budget and your job. You don't fight that just with lower prices; you fight it by building a better brand.

**Genevieve Smith**
**The Brand Perspective**

↳ In a word: Yes! If you buy the notion that people choose one company's product over another because of brand even when the product and price are essentially the same, then the brand of a B2B product will likewise be important, potentially influencing a company or buyer to select one supplier over another. While the investment levels and focus on brand in B2B can be less than in B2C companies, savvy management will focus on how their B2B brand is perceived in order to influence choice and loyalty. (Besides, no company—B2C or B2B—can escape the fact that they have a brand regardless of whether they choose to manage beyond the name; a company's brand is what the company is.)

In the mid 1990s, I worked for a company that wanted to grow market share by creating a B2B channel dedicated to mortgage brokers. The challenge was how to build a trusted brand with mortgage brokers as the brand also wanted to continue to originate mortgages through our dedicated sales force—which was in direct competition with the broker. So this was challenging for two reasons: One, the new channel was a threat to our existing direct sales force, because they would be in competition with brokers, and two, our sales force would now be distributing the same product to consumers on a direct basis in the same marketplace as brokers, potentially fostering mistrust among the brokers. The solution was to provide 100-percent parity to both groups in terms of price, program parameters, and service, putting in safeguards so that consumers would get exactly the same deal whether they had a relationship with a broker or with our employee. We then had to extend the brand so that the broker community would know we were fair, equitable, honest, and transparent in our business dealings with that segment of the marketplace. We needed to ensure that they could trust we wouldn't market to their customers and that we wouldn't undercut them.

We dedicated resources, marketing, direct advertising, and brand management to the channel and were able to grow it from nothing to the number-one home-lender market share with brokers in the USA in just a few years. We had the right products, operations, philosophy, and marketing, which all aligned to create trust, confidence, and loyalty, making our product the most frequently chosen. At the same time, those same brand values of full transparency and parity that attracted brokers also created confidence with our employees that our B2B relationships were not skewed to benefit brokers or create disadvantages for the dedicated sales force. The way we managed this enabled us to go to market directly under the brand name and use the same brand to market to our B2B customers, which was a win/win from a brand-management perspective. And we managed the brand in the B2B space as diligently as our B2C efforts.

# Q: Do Brand Extensions Further Heighten Awareness, or Just Dilute the Core Brand?

**JASON MILETSKY**
**THE AGENCY PERSPECTIVE**

Both. The more your brand name appears on shelves, the more recognizable it will be. That's just simple math. But that doesn't necessarily mean you're opening yourself up to new audiences. It's possible, of course, that brand extensions will attract new markets that you may not have reached otherwise, but they need to be extended into the right areas—areas where a close association can be made between the new product category and the brand promise. Otherwise, the brand can quickly become diluted and lose its meaning.

First, let's just make sure we're all on the same page with what a brand extension is—or at least how I define it—because it's not necessarily as obvious as one may think. Products often come in different flavors, sizes, and varieties; these are *not* line extensions. Hefty, for example, may sell trash bags in a 10 pack or a 24 pack, tall or regular size, with handles or without. These are product or line extensions, not brand extensions. But if you were to walk into the kitchenware aisle and see a line of Hefty baking trays, *that* would be a brand extension. It's applying a recognizable brand name—its reputation and what it stands for—to an entirely differently line and type of products. In this case, Hefty would be leveraging its brand image as strong and durable to create an impression in consumers' minds that the baking trays are similarly strong and durable.

But the more that a brand name is used on different lines of products, the more it's possible to dilute its value. Spread anything over a larger surface and it's going to get thinner and lose its substance. As more extensions are added, the brand will come to represent more promises and personalities and will need be meaningful to new markets. That's a lot to ask. Eventually, the brand will need to represent so much it'll end up not representing anything at all.

In order for it to work, the brand has to be firmly established and the extensions need to be well thought out. The Hefty example before was fictional and for illustrative purposes only (to my knowledge, Hefty does not have a line of baking trays). But there are plenty of examples of companies that have extended their brand thoughtfully and successfully. Arm & Hammer, long known for making the orange box of baking soda in everyone's refrigerator, successfully extended its brand into oral healthcare. In fact, in a true testament to power of branding, Arm & Hammer's toothpaste (which I use myself) tastes simply awful the first dozen or so times you use it. But taste doesn't matter because the brand is so closely associated with cleanliness that consumers automatically believe in the effectiveness of the product. Virgin, whose brand has been associated with innovation and, to a certain extent, irreverence, has successfully lent its name to music, air travel, and cell-phone service.

A few years back, I watched an interview with Donald Trump on some talk show. Trump has done an amazing job of creating a highly visible brand from his name. The Trump brand is synonymous with entrepreneurship, 1980s-style big-business deals, real estate, and the art of making money. So it makes sense that the Trump name isn't only on top of high-rise apartment buildings, casinos, and hotels, but on the Trump University online school (which has further extended into a book series), a luxury magazine, and more. Anyway, during the interview, Trump was talking about his new line of—wait for it—steaks. Steaks? Really? I don't know if they're doing well—maybe they are. I mean, Trump has about a gazillion more dollars than I've got, so obviously he's done a few things right. But this was one brand extension that just seemed like a stretch (unless, of course, we're talking about steak and cheese...).

GENEVIEVE SMITH
THE BRAND PERSPECTIVE

 Let's start this conversation by defining brand extension:

Brand extension is applying the brand to products or services beyond its current range or into a new category. Some common examples of this are Arm & Hammer baking soda extending into deodorant and dental care; Ralph Lauren extending from clothing into lifestyle products such as home wares; and most notably, Harley Davidson extending into almost everything!

The idea is that a brand extension will capitalize on a brand's recognition and reputation, riding on the equity of the parent brand. In theory, this equity will have already been invested in or paid for, making it much more cost-efficient to apply the parent brand to a new product.

A well-done brand extension reinforces the perception of the parent brand, creating synergies in terms of advertising. A well-done brand extension also generates "news" about the parent brand; awareness is heightened because there is something new to talk about in advertising and marketing.

Obviously, brand extensions that might foster negative perceptions about the parent brand are a bad idea. As an extreme example, if a bank extended into gaming, it would be damaging to the bank's core business, as part of what a bank sells is safety. That is to say, a brand extension that contradicts the promise of a parent brand is a bad idea because it can foster negative perceptions about the parent brand.

Given the emergence of numerous brand extensions over the past several years, there are naturally many examples of a great brand launching a dud extension or two—jeans and vodka from Virgin come to mind (although Virgin Airlines was a hit). Generally, however, limited test marketing will kill a dud before it can create a negative halo for the parent brand.

I think there is a lot of upside to brand extensions—*if* they make sense with respect to the brand's core idea. One upside is the halo effect—that is, a brand extension creates a new opportunity to talk about benefits the brand. Another is the cost efficiencies associated with advertising and marketing. I think it becomes dilutive only if the extension is foreign to the core beliefs of the master brand or somehow fosters negativity about it.

# Q: HOW CLOSELY DO SUB-BRANDS NEED TO RELATE TO THE PARENT BRAND?

**JASON MILETSKY**
**THE AGENCY PERSPECTIVE**

↳ Sub-brands often are closely related to the parent brand, but they don't have to be. Depending on the sub-brand in question—and its reason for being—sub-brands can have a wide range of flexibility.

Take Disney, for example. They have an amazing array of brands in their arsenal. Many of the properties are brands themselves—and because they fall within the umbrella of the core Disney brand, they need to take on the same core values as the main brand. The movie *Toy Story* is its own brand, but because it's a direct Disney property, it appropriately remains lighthearted, fun, and family-friendly. These sub-brands also have an enormous responsibility, however. If they veer from the Disney brand promise or personality, they can damage the core brand. Nagging rumors of subliminal sexual messages hidden in the cartoon movie *Aladdin* threatened to tarnish Disney's squeaky-clean brand image, as did racy photos taken in 2008 of Miley Cyrus—the 15-year-old star of *Hannah Montana*, a multi-billion dollar Disney property and successful brand in her own right.

But sub-brands can live within a brand family and not reflect the parent brand at all. Along with family-oriented sub-brands, Disney also owns Miramax Films, which produces R-rated feature films, as well as ESPN and other entities. It is hard to conceive how these sub-brands could injure the family-friendly reputation of the parent brand because their audiences are different enough, and therefore don't necessarily make the direct connection back to Disney.

GENEVIEVE SMITH

THE BRAND PERSPECTIVE

↳ Let's start by being clear about what is meant by sub-brands, as they can be executed quite differently depending on the definition. There are three classic or generally accepted brand architecture relationships between a master brand and a sub-brand:

- Single name—for example, Virgin Group

- Endorsed—for example, Sony PlayStation

- Product or line of business—for example, anything Procter & Gamble

How closely a company chooses to align a sub-brand to their master brand, or which method they use based on the preceding definitions, depends on business rationale and the company's brand architecture. For example Sony chose to brand its game system "PlayStation," but it is endorsed by adding the name Sony to the sub-brand. In this case, research may have shown that this endorsement would ensure success for PlayStation, or perhaps their brand architecture conventions require the endorsement model for all sub-brands.

This question points to the importance of having solid brand architecture that guides major decisions like alignment for sub-brands. Absent a master brand strategy, the proliferation of sub-brands can cause the brand's architecture to become a tangled web—which is of no benefit to the master brand or its sub-brands because of diluted messaging and investment dollars.

Managing a brand's architecture can be difficult, however, in situations where a company seeks to extend their business through either acquisition or organic launch of new business units/products, as sometimes the brand isn't considered in these types of business decisions. But if you've got solid brand architecture that influences product development, business strategy, and M&A activity, then you can create alignment by either linking or distancing the sub-brand, depending on how additive it is to the master brand.

I spent three years cleaning up WaMu's brand architecture and can tell you that as soon as we aligned one sub-brand to the master, another 10 popped up for consideration. Fortunately, I was mostly successful in negotiating a minimal number of sub-brands and tight linkage to the master where those needed to exist for regulatory reasons.

Sometimes a business feels a sub-brand is the way to go when it really isn't necessary. For example, at WaMu, our CEO and some of our board members wanted to create a new sub-branded Web site to compete head to head with pure Internet plays on deposit gathering—essentially an unknown bank offering high rates to attract depositors, "powered by" WaMu technology. This suggestion was in part a response to a concern that we would disintermediate our branch business by offering easy account opening and higher rates online—a notion reinforced by a cacophony from the branch network, which insisted that the online division was taking their customers.

We did two things: We priced out the investment needed to establish a new brand (about $100 million in 2007) and we looked at the data about our online customer. What we found was that the online customer represented a *new* market; about 79 percent of these customers were new to the bank, and about 70 percent of the deposits were new money. These consumers chose to do business online with a bank they knew because we had a well-established brand regardless of channel; they simply preferred to open their account and bank online. The business was accretive. Any development of a sub-branded Web presence would have been a waste of investment dollars—and in fact was not necessary. So, based on the facts, we didn't pursue the sub-brand.

There is no right or wrong answer on alignment; it really depends on the business objectives and the brand architecture conventions.

# Q: IS A GOOD BRAND ENOUGH TO KEEP A BRAND ALIVE? IS THERE ANYTHING THE BRAND MANAGER CAN DO TO FIX A FAILING COMPANY?

**JASON MILETSKY**
THE AGENCY PERSPECTIVE

↳ If I had written this book prior to 2008, I'm pretty sure my answer would have been the same as it is now—just maybe a little less emphatic. But we're living through some pretty extraordinary times in terms of politics and commerce. The historic movements within our economy and the shakeout of our financial institutions make this question more important than ever before—and make me think about it a little harder before answering.

Perhaps more than anyone else on Earth right now, my co-author, Genevieve Smith, is in a unique position to answer this question based on facts, not opinions. As Genevieve's employer, Washington Mutual, grew in size thanks to numerous acquisitions, enormous investments in the once-booming subprime housing markets, and innovative approaches to retail banking, Genevieve was the genius behind building and marketing the brand—skyrocketing a once-obscure bank to national prominence. She helped forge new paths to consumers that had never before been tried, creating a brand that was approachable, fun, and funny, while at the same time heavily focused on customer service and providing new opportunities to banking and home-loan customers. Their once-mighty "Power of Yes" tagline summed up their brand—Washington Mutual was the place for acceptance. Later rebranded as the more friendly, less geographically specific WaMu, the bank, whose reputation was never in question, continued to build its brand under Genevieve's leadership. I have no doubt that Gen's marketing and strategies for increasing brand exposure will be studied by communications students for years to come.

But no brand is powerful enough to counteract mistakes made by a CEO or a board of directors, and *certainly* isn't powerful enough to buoy a company when the bottom falls out of a market. When the subprime market collapsed and WaMu found itself overexposed from too much bad debt, the bank fell downward from the top of the mountain in a dizzying spiral until, like so many other banks had in the weeks surrounding it, it failed.

Although historians and economists and CNBC pundits may debate WaMu's failure for years to come, there's one thing that is absolutely certain: There wasn't a damned thing Genevieve Smith or any other brand expert could have done to prevent it. This wasn't a brand issue; the brand made a promise and fulfilled it. It developed a personality and found a market accordingly. It gained exposure and loyalty. No, WaMu's problems started in the boardroom and ended on Wall Street, just like Merrill Lynch's, Lehman Brothers', Citibank's, AIG's, and others that have had troubles. Those who survived the 2008 financial meltdown relatively unscathed, such as Bank of America, Wells Fargo, and JP Morgan Chase, did so because of their limited exposure to bad debt and other smart decisions, *not* because of their brand.

Branding can only take you so far. It can build an audience and capture a market, but it can't make up for poor corporate decision-making. Outside of the finance industry, once has only to look at Enron as proof positive: No brand team alive would have been able to save the energy giant from the mess created by the illegal activities of its own executive staff. Brand-building is a powerful exercise, but it's not magic. It has its limitations. What CEOs and boards of directors screw up, brand managers and agencies can't always fix.

GENEVIEVE SMITH
THE BRAND PERSPECTIVE

↳   I am here to tell you there is absolutely nothing that a brand can do to fix a company if it is failing due to fundamental weaknesses in the operating model. Take WaMu for example. Many people helped to build the WaMu brand. These highly qualified and talented people—not simply in marketing, but from various disciplines throughout the company—dedicated literally years of their lives to creating a winning bank brand. But WaMu's financial model was not strong enough to survive the credit and financial markets' meltdown of 2008. And the brand didn't matter a hoot when the bank was seized and sold by regulators.

The demise of WaMu was a long and drawn-out event, accompanied by a tsunami of media speculation, over a period of almost six months. During that time, the brand group worked with internal management and our external agencies to see what we could do to help position the company with consumers so as to maintain their confidence in the brand. We also developed tools for branches so employees could speak with customers in a confident manner. But as I discussed in my answer Question #25, "What Are the Core Reasons a Consumer Would Stay Loyal to a Brand?" although data shows that consumer loyalty to WaMu remained surprisingly high for a long period of time, the media's speculation that the bank would fail became the tipping point for consumer confidence.

This period of time was surreal to say the least; as the CMO, I felt virtually help-less to improve the situation. While we did manage to connect emotionally with the consumer, at the end of the day, this emotional connection was not enough to save the bank.

# Q: DO CONSUMERS REALLY FEEL EMOTIONAL ABOUT BRANDS? OR IS THAT JUST SOMETHING MARKETING TYPES LIKE TO SAY?

JASON MILETSKY

THE AGENCY PERSPECTIVE

↳ I like this question. It calls us out. For some reason, I just like that.

Marketing types, especially on the agency side, can be so full of crap we could be repackaged and sold as fertilizer. Advertising body copy is filled with useless words and phrases that mean absolutely nothing to anybody, including classic gems like "Our company stands for quality," or "We work to serve you," and don't forget the age-long favorite, "We always put our customers first." Please. This sort of fluffy filler copy has never helped sell a single unit of any product, but marketers continue to litter their advertising and collateral with it.

Consumers aren't the only ones who are subject to rhetorical bullshit. Agencies feed lines to clients like they're hot chicks at a party. "We have over 120 years of experience..." (yeah, 10 years of experience for each of a dozen employees) or "We're a results-oriented agency, focused on providing you with a positive ROI," and my personal favorite, "From concept to completion, we have the resources you need to get the job done right, on time and under budget!" Can someone just shoot me if they ever hear me say anything like that to a prospective client? And then there are the less sales-y, more pressure-driven lines, like "We've got a pretty big project getting started next month...I'm worried that if you don't sign now, we may not be able to fit your project on the schedule and meet your deadlines." Yeah, right.

So there it is—I've 'fessed up. I admit that yes, there are instances where agencies speak just for the sake of hearing ourselves talk or because we think this stuff may actually work on people with an above-moron IQ. But when it comes to branding, the emotional connection forged between consumers and a brand is absolutely, positively *not* a load of BS that we spew in an effort to try to sell more. It's real, it's clear, and even if the new trend among marketing authors is to try to dig an early grave for brand-building as a practice (a growing number of marketing malcontents seem to suggest that branding is no longer useful given our Web-enabled access to greater information, replaced in part by targeting consumer behavior), there is no denying that brands wield a distinct emotional power over people. In fact, according to the Grocery Manufacturers of America, which studies consumer trends in grocery stores, half of all consumers consider the brand to be either the first or the second most important element when deciding which product to buy (other factors include nutritional information, cost, or nostalgia—i.e., they buy products they remember using during childhood). In addition, 13 percent first try a brand because it was recommended to them by someone they trust—further establishing the importance of brands in building a loyal following of customers willing to pass the word on to others.

It's possible that some of the hesitancy relates to the word "emotion." The emotional connection between consumers and brands isn't the same kind of emotional connection between, say, two lovers. A guy's not about to look at an Exxon station and suddenly sport wood. And women aren't going to blush and become coy when they approach the Swiffer section on aisle six. That's not the kind of emotion we're talking about. The emotional connection between consumers and brands is more subliminal, more subtle. It's the difference between longing for something and wanting something. Having an emotional connection to a brand is the consumer's subconscious acknowledgment that the brand will somehow prove beneficial to them and that they want to—and will—seek it out.

For those who refuse to see the emotional connection between brand and consumer, and disregard the connection between brand and sales, I ask you to close your eyes and imagine every product packaged in a neutral gray box, each the same size and texture; every name changed to a single letter; every advertisement simply stating what the product is, what it does, how much it costs, and where it can be purchased. Boring, huh? And for those who believe that branding should be set aside in favor of targeting consumer behavior in a more connected world, I ask that you acknowledge a difference between branding and advertising, and that multiple efforts can be undertaken simultaneously and, in fact, combined. Whether and how advertising models can be improved for greater ROI is a debate all its own—but the answer to that question will never negate the emotional sway that brands hold over their audiences.

**GENEVIEVE SMITH**

**THE BRAND PERSPECTIVE**

⮡ Oh yes. Consumers feel emotional about brands. Just like we do about almost everything in life, people emote about brands. Why do people choose a Mac over a PC? Why do they pay $5 for a cup of coffee? Why do they buy only one brand of car? When consumers feel an emotional connection with a brand, their motivation lives beyond rational decisions like price, which many competitors could match, into an almost unshakable brand belief—which is why successfully attaching a strong positive emotion to a brand is thought to be the nirvana of marketing.

It's important to note that brands can also evoke strong negative reactions. For example, some people absolutely *hate* discount airlines. But since those consumers aren't the target audience, it doesn't matter—as long as people who connect with the category also emotionally connect with the brand that's in the category.

Banking is a funny one—it is a disliked category, kind of like the government or the IRS. But almost everyone needs a bank account, so it's a necessity. One way we created an emotional connection between the consumer and WaMu was to position the brand as the "anti-bank." We studied the consumer pain points associated with banking and worked hard to solve for those through product, operations, branch design, service, and brand expressions, to name a few. What we found was that consumers *could* love their bank and connect with it emotionally—and that the connection was fueled primarily by the experiences they had in the store or on the phone with our employees, and by our consumer-driven Web interface. Marketers can say almost anything through advertising, but great customer experiences are the most direct emotional connection with the brand—indeed, they're the ultimate embodiment of the brand. At WaMu, we had created a legion of brand advocates in our employees who served customers directly and through the way we managed our Web interface. The employees lived the brand and wanted to deliver the WaMu experience to the consumer, and the Web site mirrored that experience.

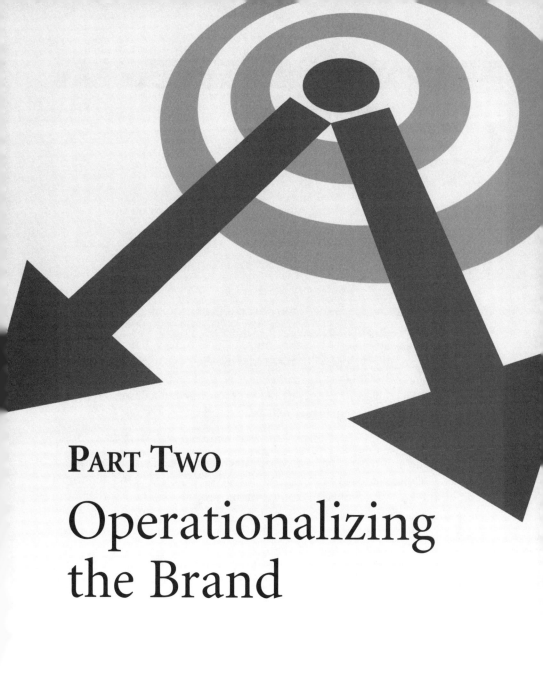

# PART TWO
# Operationalizing the Brand

# Q: WHAT ARE FIVE ACTION POINTS FOR EARLY OPERATIONALIZATION OF THE BRAND?

**GENEVIEVE SMITH**
**THE BRAND PERSPECTIVE**

"Operationalizing the brand" means examining everything a business does, every single nook and cranny, to be sure they are brand aligned. This includes all functional areas and every discipline and business unit. Where they are not aligned, the brand must be operationalized into the practices to create alignment. This is why branding is far beyond a marketing exercise. I cannot emphasize enough the extent to which operationalizing a brand is a journey, not a destination—and the company must have the patience and appetite to see it through.

Here are five areas, in no particular order, that will help kick-start the effort:

- **Develop a road map:** The best way to start operationalizing is to evaluate all areas of the company and develop initiatives to create brand alignment where there is a disconnect. Potential brand projects for the road map can be evaluated across the dimensions of brand impact (i.e., how impactful will they be to the betterment of the brand) and ease of execution (i.e., how hard are they to do). Some things are going to be relatively easy to do, but they'll have a low impact; others will be similarly easy but with a high impact— meaning you'd select those first from the "easy" dimension. This analysis will assist in developing the road map.

- **Get everyone on board:** You must get everyone across the company on board with operationalizing the brand, which means you must take the time to get buy-in and commitment from key influencers and management so that brand projects will be funded and prioritized in the inevitable project queues found in most businesses.

- **Get the brand zealots lined up:** You need a core team of leaders (these are sometimes called "tiger teams") to lead and manage the initiatives on the road map. It should be considered an honor to lead one of these teams.

- **Commission the research you need to make informed choices:** Your "true north" needs to be lead by consumer research. Consumers will tell you what matters to them, which will inform the road map.

■ **Are the basics in place?** Evaluate the brand positioning, architecture, expressions, and guidelines to be sure they are 100-percent tight and strategically sound.

Of course, some of this is dictated by where a company is in the evolution of operationalizing the brand. If much of the operations, product development, and marketing are brand-aligned, then work efforts will be much more in the areas of innovation and continuous improvement. If a company's basic operations are *not* brand-aligned, then you're looking at a much bigger effort, with these as your top-five priorities.

JASON MILETSKY
THE AGENCY PERSPECTIVE

Okay, so we're looking for real answers here, not generalities. Fine. Then let's skip the preamble and get right to it.

1. **Introduce it:** The brand is built; now you have to introduce it to everyone. Celebrate this event; use it as an opportunity to generate some excitement both internally and externally. Be aware, however, that launching a new brand can cause confusion and concern within different parties, so it's important that you get the word out quickly, making sure that everyone sees the brand's benefits. Announcements should be made to people in the following order:

   • Employees, with a special, extended brand introduction and meetings for managers who will likely be asked numerous questions by the employees they supervise.

   • Clients, who need to be shown that the new brand will have a positive effect on their relationship with your company. It's also important to keep them from becoming confused when invoices suddenly arrive with a different name and logo on them.

   • Vendors—again, so there's no confusion on their part, and so that nervous companies and agencies don't freak out when your company suddenly goes through a major change in the middle of a project or contract they're working on.

   • The general public, alerted through press releases, media events, and/or marketing.

2. **Create the necessary physical and visual items:** An inventory should be made early in the brand-development process of each and every visual item that will need to be changed when the new brand is rolled out. This will include signage outside office buildings, truck sides, Web sites (this switch should be flipped the very same day the new site is introduced), brochures, letterhead, business cards, and so on.

3. **Begin internal brand-awareness campaigns:** Introducing the brand might be step one, but just because employees know about it doesn't mean they've bought into it. In order for employees to adjust their behavior to reflect the brand values in their actions and their work, internal campaigns must be constantly implemented. For more information on this, check out the answer to Question #46, "If You Want Employees to 'Live the Brand,' How Do You Train Them?"

4. **Re-examine departmental processes, especially those that deal directly with customers:** There's more to branding than how it looks and how it's marketed. The real value of the brand is in how it treats its audience— whether it's true to its promise and whether the consumer believes that using the brand will positively affect him or her. That means every department from customer service to bizdev must be part of that experience. In many cases, it might mean analyzing workflow and system processes in each department, completely upending everything and rebuilding it to fit the new brand.

5. **Work the brand into compensation models:** These should incentivize employees at all levels to improve workflow and demonstrate the inclusion of brand values in their work. More on this in the answer to Question #47, "Should There Be a Brand Component in Employee Compensation Models?"

# Q: Is the Brand Guide a Firm Law? Or Is There Sometimes Room to Break the Rules?

**GENEVIEVE SMITH**
**THE BRAND PERSPECTIVE**

You cannot break the rules—period, end of subject. Look, the brand guide contains everything about the brand. It's what it stands for, how it operates, how it looks and feels, the values, how it markets, who it hires to represent itself, and how it manages. In short, the brand guide represents who the company is. There simply isn't room to break the rules put forth in the guide.

I don't think you can talk about branding and not talk about Steve Jobs. Here's a CEO who understands exactly why strict adherence to the brand and its guidelines is the key to success. When he returned to the CEO position at Apple in 1997, he stated that the brand is "not about bytes and boxes, it is about values." The values Apple stands for are innovation, individuality, and creativity. So in this example, the brand guide would in its essence state that Apple doesn't make machines, it enables creative people. The stated rules and conventions, which you have to publish and enforce as the brand guidelines, exist so that the brand stays true to its values through all the business funnels that operate at any company. These guidelines serve to chart a true course. There is no room for infraction.

**JASON MILETSKY**
**THE AGENCY PERSPECTIVE**

Brand guides are the bible upon which every strong brand is built. Within their pages lie all the details that marketing agencies, printers, publishers, Web developers, and everyone else remotely associated with promoting the brand would need to know. *What's the RGB breakdown of the logo?* Look in the brand guide. *Do we hyphenate the word "e-mail" in our corporate language?* Check the guide.

Whether it's 10 pages or 100—and I've seen both—it'd be unheard of for a brand of any real significance to embark on a marketing program without having a brand guide at the very center of its efforts. As a believer in and developer of brands, I have beaten the brand drum for many years, always emphasizing the importance of maintaining brand integrity and enforcing consistency. Consistency, after all, is one of the strongest weapons in the marketing arsenal for building immediate recognition over time—and one of the biggest benefits that comes with the development of a comprehensive brand guide.

But for all their value—not to mention the time, thought, and effort that goes into their creation—brand guides are often treated with contempt by marketing professionals on both the client and the agency side. That's because marketers are a creative species. Our imaginations seek out open canvases. The brand guide limits that canvas by providing strict procedures and rules for us to follow—and limits are like Kryptonite to creativity.

This creates a chasm between the "brand police," whose job it is to ensure that the brand guide is followed, and creative marketers, who want to break free from their constraints. The important thing for everyone to remember is that the brand guide is exactly that—a guide. It provides information and direction, details when needed, and answers when questions arise. Brand managers must remember that the agency can't function in a police state. And while people on the production end of the food chain—printers, for example—may need to follow the guide by the letter, creative directors and key strategists should be given certain leeway when it comes to look, feel, and voice. The guide spells out what the brand should be conceptually, but in certain media—like print advertising, for example—going outside the lines to promote a stronger message can benefit a brand.

At the same time, creatives on the agency side need to work within the general umbrella of the brand and absorb the guide on a conceptual level. The guide does more than break down colors and fonts; it defines the personality and promise of a brand. Creatives must work within those boundaries and remember that everything they do is a reflection of the brand to the public—not an isolated canvas for them to paint on.

# Q: WITH EVERYTHING THAT NEEDS TO REFLECT THE BRAND—FROM LETTERHEAD TO BUILDING SIGNS TO INTERNAL AND EXTERNAL MARKETING—BRANDING CAN BE EXPENSIVE. WILL A PHASED ROLLOUT WORK?

**GENEVIEVE SMITH**
**THE BRAND PERSPECTIVE**

This question is about investment, but when addressing it, it's important to remember that rolling out a brand is a journey, not a destination. Even if you had unlimited funding and no budget concerns, there is only so much that can be done over a given period of time. Therefore, a phased rollout is the name of the game, no matter how impatient you are or how much you have to invest.

Let's take signage as an example, as it is a long-term effort. We are currently undertaking this challenge for more than 2,000 bank branches, and it's estimated that the changes will take approximately one year to be fully implemented. No amount of money can change this timeline because it physically cannot be done more quickly. Re-branding the internal store environments involves the same type of long-term effort. As with signage, the interior refresh must be implemented over the course of about a year for the same number of branches. Of course, you can temporarily bag signs and install interim merchandising, decals, etc. while the permanent work is done. This will look like what it is—temporary—but customers are generally forgiving of "pardon our dust" changes and upgrades.

So the short answer to "will a phased rollout work?" is that there really is no other way to conduct the rollout. You just have to live with brand confusion in some areas for a period of time. But if you focus on the most highly visible touch points like advertising, marketing, and merchandising, which can be "easily" refreshed, the brand will begin to look cohesive fairly quickly.

We spoke about the process of re-branding in our answers to Question #14, "The Brand Guide Is Built. Now What?" Once you've got a complete inventory of communications materials, the road map will be coordinated around the highest-impact touch points. Ideally, as inventory is depleted, it will be replaced with the new look and feel. This is a better approach than conducting a whole-sale find-and-replace exercise, which is considerably more costly.

JASON MILETSKY

THE AGENCY PERSPECTIVE

Depending on the size of the brand in question, a phased roll-out is far more the norm than the exception. With larger brands, there's a mountain of work that needs to get done—and even if budgets don't slow you down, time most likely will. Logistics are also a concern, especially in the case of a re-brand, which brand managers will most likely want to keep tightly under wraps until they can launch it with a bit of fanfare. It'd be hard to keep the new brand a secret if everyone comes to work one morning and sees a new company name or logo on the sign outside the office building....

During the initial development process, the agency and the brand need to put together a checklist of all of the items that need to be produced and a timeline for each of these items. In my experience, these timelines have extended out six months, a year, or longer, depending on the size and scope of the brand. But no matter how long it takes, there need to be benchmarks in place—and these benchmarks will need to be communicated to salespeople and others in the field who either use the brand image regularly or interface directly with consumers.

Here's my list of priorities and the order that items should roll out:

1. First and foremost has got to be the brand guide. I discussed this earlier in the book in more detail than would keep most people awake, so I'm not going to ramble on about it again here.

2. Along with the brand guide comes the Web site, which needs to be up and running the day the new brand is announced (although the Web site can also have a phased rollout, with the core structure and content reflecting the new brand and new additions implemented over time).

3. Basic essentials need to be completed quickly, including business cards (again, at least for sales and people out in the field), letterhead, and other stationery items.

4. An early round of sales materials, including an overview brochure and an introductory PowerPoint presentation, should be developed and distributed to salespeople.

5. If an ad campaign was previously being run, there need to be transitional ads developed and submitted.

6. Truck sides and outdoor building signage need to be updated.

7. Any additional brochures or sales materials required beyond the essentials (refer to step 4) need to be created.

8. Corporate overview videos should be produced.

9. Internal signage and wall art should be updated, as should promotional materials such as shirts, pens, calendars, etc.

---

One item missing from this list is trade-show booths, which don't apply to every brand. For companies that do present at trade shows, it's often smart to develop the schedule of what items to develop and when based on needs for upcoming show appearances.

---

However you go about setting your agenda, there's no question that if your brand is large enough, you'll be forced to roll it out and market it with parallel efforts.

# Q: • WHO'S BEST TO BE THE BRAND POLICE?
# • THE COMPANY OR ITS AGENCY?

**GENEVIEVE SMITH**
**THE BRAND PERSPECTIVE**

↳ The employees of the company must act as the brand police. Given that companies constantly generate new product, operations, decisions, competitive reactions, and goals, it's unlikely that any agency would be embedded enough to see how each one of these will affect the brand, making it impossible for the agency to effectively serve as the brand police. This question leads us back to a fundamental point: If we agree that the brand is far more than marketing, then delegating the policing to an agency makes absolutely no sense as it's not a marketing issue.

That said, if you look at policing as simply managing the look and feel—e.g., the brand expressions—then although I still say this should be managed internally, I concede that it will require agency work and support. If brand oversight is under the auspices of the marketing department, then this group will undoubtedly lever their agency relationships for opinions and guidance on any issues that are important enough to hit the radar—for example, items cooked up by product development or M&A activities, as discussed in the answer to Question #32, "How Closely Do Sub-Brands Need to Relate to the Parent Brand?" Even so, how you govern the brand guide is up to the employees of the firm and should not be delegated under any circumstances. Anyway, who would want to pay agency fees to police creative?

Internal employees and business requirements drive this creative development, and it's important to hire internal talent who can both guide communications and police creative execution. Ideally you'd like *every* employee to be a member of the brand police—that would be powerful. (Can you imagine having articulated what the brand stands for so clearly that even the newest hire would know if an action isn't brand-aligned?) So those of you readers who work on the client side, get out your badges and have at it. You probably have permission to police far more than colors and fonts, so don't limit yourselves to creative.

JASON MILETSKY
THE AGENCY PERSPECTIVE

I know I'm going to regret putting this in print, because honestly, "brand police" is not a job that *anybody* wants. But if I were to be really honest, I'd have to say the agency is best candidate.

First of all, let's define what we mean by "brand police." As you know, the brand guide will have a lot of rules and regulations that must be followed to keep the brand consistent over time. And, as you also know, as soon as people are faced with rules, the first thing they want to do is break them. Large brands will have an especially tough time keeping track of all the people, departments, and vendors working with logos, color palettes, images, fonts, and messages—but somebody, somewhere needs to do just that to make sure nothing that could injure the brand gets put before the public.

Salespeople will likely be the worst offenders. In my experience, few salespeople give a flying crap about the brand. They'll happily sacrifice it if it means getting a PowerPoint deck finished a little more quickly. It doesn't matter how many months you've spent putting together the brand guide—which will ultimately *help* sales—salespeople will overlook it completely as they jam every last word onto each slide, mixing and matching font styles and sizes like their cooking up some sort of wacky Chinese stew. They must be stopped! Okay, maybe that's a little dramatic, but seriously, someone needs to smack these guys around once in awhile and remind them that the brand guide exists for a reason—and that reason is to help them sell. They can't just make up their own rules as they go along.

So why should the agency police the brand? Because we're more impartial. We don't know these people—whether they're in sales or some other part of the organization—so we don't have a personal interest. Our interest is in maintaining brand consistency, and our loyalty is to our clients in the marketing and branding department. Plus, as the people who designed the brand, we know all the rules, their subtleties, which rules can be bent and which must be completely adhered to in each and every case. Putting the agency in charge also relieves the marketing and/or branding department of having to be the bad guy—an unenviable position when you're sitting down the hall or a cubicle away from the very people you have to scold. With the agency calling the shots, the marketing department can play innocent and pass the buck, keeping themselves out of the line of fire.

# Q: HOW DO YOU REIN IN ROGUE OFFENDERS OF THE BRAND, SUCH AS SALESPEOPLE?

**GENEVIEVE SMITH**
**THE BRAND PERSPECTIVE**

Well, you can beat them, hang them, or fire them—or you can attempt to create processes and operating principles that make it impossible for rogue offenders to offend. I've worked in distributed environments with literally thousands of salespeople, many of whom believed they could sell only if they had license to create their own marketing materials. But I've found that if you provide clear brand guidelines, communicate a lot about these guidelines and their importance, but also maintain a two-way street with the field (i.e., you have a mechanism for capturing and acting on their feedback so as to be responsive in expanding the universe of available sales tools and marketing materials), that you can assume the reins.

I've also found, however, that absent a full-time police force in every market to root out offenders, you will never completely shut down rogue activities—unless there are management guidelines in place that mandate a hit to compensation or even a loss of employment for managers who allow rogue activity. If you can get these strict guidelines in place, you'll get pretty close to shutting down rogue activity; most managers won't risk their own employment or compensation to defend a field-generated flier. Of course, if you decide to implement these types of rules, you'll have to invest in auditors, approvers, and probably also creatives (you'll need someone to make the flier in lieu of those rogue offenders).

One caveat: It is those in the field who deal with real customers every day, and those field personnel are a rich source of input and feedback to the brand expressions. A brand manager who simply lays down the law from corporate without providing some channel for feedback from the field is missing a tremendous opportunity to expand the brand's visual guidelines beyond what are deemed effective at corporate headquarters. I urge brand managers and agencies to listen to those in the field—even if they drive you crazy—because this feedback represents the results of the real test of how your brand resonates with consumers.

JASON MILETSKY

THE AGENCY PERSPECTIVE

Setting policies for dealing with rogue offenders of the brand clearly isn't the agency's place—but that doesn't mean I don't have some opinions on how it should be done.

Obviously, maintaining the integrity of the brand and ensuring consistency based on the rules established in the brand guide are important and must be enforced. It needs to be said, however, that no entity—marketing department, brand manager, brand police, or whatever—will be able to head off every instance of rule-breaking. If a salesperson is going to put together his or her own PowerPoint deck and show it to a client without getting a approval first, well…there's just nothing anybody can do about that. In this situation, the best offense is a good defense. Ongoing internal campaigns and communications must be executed that drive home the importance of everyone upholding the tenets of the brand—especially salespeople, who will represent the brand to their prospects and clients.

Aside from that, I tend to want to take a pretty dictatorial approach to brand enforcement. As far as I'm concerned, the only way to snap people into line is by affecting their budgets. Even though most companies have a central marketing department, various divisions within the company, such as sales, will have opportunities to do their own marketing or somehow use the brand on their own. My solution: Take some amount of their budget—say, 15 percent—and put it under central marketing's control. Then reinforce the rule that anything new that's created for or with the brand must be passed through central marketing before it gets published and sent to an outside source. If the brand police, under the supervision of central marketing, give the okay, then you're good to go. If not, changes must be made and the materials resubmitted until approval is received. At the end of some set period of time, like the end of each quarter, central marketing will do a review of each department. If everything has been done correctly, then a portion of the retained budget for that department will be released back to them. If not, then that portion would be kept by central marketing and used to pay for internal campaigns to promote better brand use.

It's basic, it's rudimentary—and it can't *possibly* work for every company as easily as that. But you get the concept. Simple wrist slaps will be universally ignored; there need to be repercussions tied to budgets in order for rule-breaking punishments to have any real and lasting impact.

# Q: BEYOND STYLE GUIDES AND ADVERTISING, HOW DOES THE BRAND INFLUENCE PRODUCT DEVELOPMENT, DISTRIBUTION, CHANNEL STRATEGY, AND PRICING?

GENEVIEVE SMITH
THE BRAND PERSPECTIVE

The brand represents a consistent value system. It's seen as the company's "way of doing things." So the starting point for brand strategy is to work out what the company stands for. Once that is done, the brand will influence all phases of business operations. For example, I mentioned WaMu's brand promise of Simpler Banking and More Smiles. Given this brand promise, we had to define *how* we would be known for making people's lives simpler and easier—through our products, fees, policies, and distribution channels. It wouldn't be believable if we said we were easier to do business with if we didn't show it in our operations.

First, we knew consumers wouldn't let value slip out the door. Our research showed that people think value is very important in banking—and while they may not pay a premium for simplicity, it is a great tiebreaker when it comes to consumer choice. We then looked at simplicity among various products and services across industries and found that people's lives are made simpler when firms excel in the following ways:

- **They're empowering:** They offer consumers self-service and other tools to help make informed decisions.

- **They offer a time savings:** They're far quicker, they offer easy 24-hour access, and they can take care of multiple tasks at once.

- **They're helpful:** Help is available when consumers want it and representatives talk in the consumers' language (not industry speak) and have solid expertise.

- **They're straightforward:** Things are intuitive, clear, and no help is required.

- **They're consistent and reliable:** They're predictable with respect to good quality, price, or service; they're worry free, solidly accurate, efficient, and things come when expected.

Our challenge was to deliver across as many of these dimensions as possible in order to demonstrate simplicity. Here are a few of the things we did:

- We created the easiest online application process in the industry; our Web interface was consistently in the top three in the "Ease of Use" category as measured by Keynote Systems.

- We developed and used straightforward, clear, every-day language rather than bank-speak.

- Our WaMu free checking account offered unprecedented features.

- We redesigned the in-store customer welcome experience so customers would spend only 15 minutes opening an account and could walk out with one that was up and running.

- We eliminated 18 "nuisance fees."

- We offered clear communications, including account alerts, on how to avoid overdraft fees.

- We streamlined and simplified the home-loans–origination process.

- We changed the name of the company to WaMu.

You can see the brand influence in all these implementation items—all of which are core business operations rather than marketing-related.

JASON MILETSKY
THE AGENCY PERSPECTIVE

So far, there's been a lot of emphasis on brand guides—their purpose and importance. But with this question, I think we'll get to move away from that and see how the brand really winds its way into operational aspects of a company.

With some areas, how the brand influences operational aspects of a company is fairly clear. Let's take product development as an example. Scientists, inventors, chefs, and other product-development people aren't very concerned about how closely the external packaging reflects the brand, nor will they have much to say about the ways their products are being advertised. But understanding the essence of their brand and the spirit of their brand's personality will absolutely affect how they go about coming up with new products.

Take Budweiser, for example. Budweiser is beer for the everyday guy—the factory worker, the truck driver, the sports fan.

Forget the packaging and the advertising for a second—their reputation is for delivering low cost, good tasting beer to the working class guys that make up the backbone of America (reflected in their brand personality). They're not high-brow, like Guinness, nor are they laid back and tropical, like Corona. Knowing that, it'd be surprising if their product-development team spent a lot of time cooking up a new product along the lines of Chimay, which blends high-quality beer with champagne. It'd be a complete departure from what their brand is about. I'm guessing they'll stick with recipes and formulas that won't leave audiences confused as to what their brand is really about.

The brand has a similar impact on pricing. Sticking with the Bud example for a moment, their pricing is in line with their brand, which is reflective of their audience. They're not the cheapest beer on the market; anyone who's gone to college will remember Gold Label, or Red, White, and Blue—the low-cost, low-taste brands for people on a strictly beer-and–Big Mac budget. Bud's won't drop their price to those levels because that's not in keeping with their brand. *Their* brand is reflective of working-class guys, not the "I'll take whatever I can afford" crowd. At the same time, they'd diminish their brand if they started pushing their prices higher, like many micro-brews. Bud's audience is made up of beer drinkers, not beer connoisseurs. We all remember the basic algebra lesson that says *if $x=y$ and $y=z$, then $x=z$.* It's no different here: The price reflects the brand; the brand reflects its market; therefore, the price reflects the market. It's all interrelated, and it all works together.

Other areas of business work much the same way. What the brand is about, its promise, its personality—it all goes well beyond the brand guide, which simply serves as a repository for this information. But the true use of the brand goes far beyond look, feel, and advertising; it permeates employees' actions, their behaviors, and the thoughts, ideas, and strategies they develop and push forward into the marketplace.

All that being said, there are situations in which a company may have one brand reputation for consumers and another for operations. I've never worked for Disney (and I apologize for using them too often in my examples) or any Disney-owned entity, but the general consensus is that although Disney's brand to their audience is that of fun, family-oriented, wholesome entertainment—parks, movies, shows, songs, stories, and more that both children and their families can enjoy—Disney's brand is anything but fun to vendors, competitors, and anyone else not on the consumer side of the equation. They're known to be among the toughest negotiators in any business, adamant about getting their way, and often difficult to work with. Children love them, vendors often fear them. When it comes to doing business, it seems that the mouse is anything but. The people behind the curtain manage the external brand, and new shows, products, characters, and ticket prices continue to be reflections of that brand, but the business itself does not necessarily have to exhibit the same traits.

# Q: WHOSE BUDGET SHOULD BANKROLL BRANDING EFFORTS? OPERATIONS? MARKETING? SHOULD EACH DEPARTMENT CONTRIBUTE EQUALLY? OR SOMETHING ELSE ENTIRELY?

**GENEVIEVE SMITH**

**THE BRAND PERSPECTIVE**

If I were you, I would circle this question with a red pen, highlight it, and add a bunch of exclamation marks—that's how important it is.

In my answer to Question #35, "What Are Five Action Points for Early Operationalization of the Brand?" I recommended developing a road map early on. Once you've established the road map, then the budget to support the efforts should be planned. Undoubtedly, many of the efforts that are the most difficult and take the most time are also those that have the biggest payback in terms of brand effect; to truly change the way a company operates so that it is brand-aligned requires all groups around the company to prioritize work to support the effort—meaning they must allocate budget.

This is very important. People support what they pay for. Operationalizing a brand, when done right, is a significant effort; and significant projects will require IT resources, vendor resources, and investment. That means the business unit or support group who will implement the effort needs to prioritize it above others and fund the work. Truly operationalizing requires that everyone agree this is of the highest priority and that management is willing to put their money where their mouth is. Once you get going and are on the road map, the hope is that the brand will be considered in all new work and efforts, enabling you to capture the "fixes" and fund them over time, prioritizing based on the return on investment.

I suppose a company could create a big pot of investment dollars to be centrally administered and decked against the brand efforts. I would caution against this, however, as I think it would create a "corporately mandated" perspective about the work efforts, which could equate to a hands-off attitude and a lack of commitment (i.e., a shortcut for eye rolling about what corporate is demanding).

JASON MILETSKY

THE AGENCY PERSPECTIVE

Honestly, as long as we get paid, we're happy. As an agency, it really doesn't matter *where* the money comes from—although, as a company interested in making a profit, we'd always prefer other non-marketing departments to contribute to the mix so that marketing has more budget to work with and can spend more throughout the year. We'll even look for opportunities to make these suggestions. For example, I can easily make a case that an initial Web site should be paid for from marketing's budget, but the ongoing monthly retainer for its upkeep should come from IT's budget. We'll do our best as an agency to have other departments contribute to expenses, but beyond that it's really not our call.

# Q: WHAT ROLE DOES THE BRAND HAVE IN ENFORCING SERVICE STANDARDS AND CUSTOMER INTERACTION MODELS?

GENEVIEVE SMITH

THE BRAND PERSPECTIVE

The brand is inextricably joined with service standards and customer-interaction models. Think about it: You can say *anything* in marketing materials and advertising, but the experience a consumer actually has when interacting with the brand and its employees is where the rubber meets the road.

The brand will say, "We stand for this"—and part of its promise will relate to how it treats and serves customers. This aspect of the brand promise will have been checked against what is critical to the customer, and will be used to develop uniform service standards company-wide. This standardization and subsequent training of employees ensures that when a customer interacts with the brand, the brand always feels the same. It's genuine, regardless of channel or division or product.

I work in the banking industry. We don't manufacture specific physical products; we sell financial products and services. So once you get past the product features such as terms, fees, and benefits, how the brand is experienced by consumers is mostly affected by:

- Interaction with employees in-store, on the phone, and through e-mail

- Account information, such as statements, notices, and direct offers

- The Web interface

All these touch points equal service in the customer's mind. So if the brand says our interactions will be simple but not simplistic, the challenge is to define what that means across each touch point and to create standards. You can then train employees to act, speak, and write to the standards; ensure that account communications align; and ensure that the Web interfaces feel the same way.

> Service excellence (or failure) is not limited to, for example, a single phone interaction. Consumers form their opinions about a company's level of service based on their total experience with the brand.

From my perspective, the area of service and customer interaction leads directly to the heart of brand reputation; it's not limited by the boundaries of how well or quickly an e-mail or phone call is answered. We've talked about the brand police; this area requires a veritable brand army because poorly implemented service standards can truly harm a brand's reputation with consumers.

JASON MILETSKY
THE AGENCY PERSPECTIVE

The brand has a powerful voice in how a company relates to and interacts with its customers. Each and every employee within a company who interacts with customers must embody and exude the standards set by the brand for the brand to really come to life.

Clearly, this may be more important for some brands than others. Case in point: In all my years as a Diet Pepsi loyalist, I've never once had to talk to anybody at their corporate office—and I doubt I ever will. If I go into a convenience store and there are no Diet Pepsi bottles available (and no, I won't drink from cans—what are we, heathens?), I tend to blame the convenience store, and not the Pepsi brand.

Other situations are completely different. I've been a loyal BMW driver since 2000—not because I really love their cars (I mean, the cars are good, but I'm personally not much of a car guy) but because of the service BMW provides. BMW's marketing told me I could expect a high level of customer service from their brand, and that the happiness of their customers and quality of their vehicles was important to them—and based on their longevity and on other people's experiences, I took them at their word. Well, it's one thing to boast about great customer service in a marketing campaign; it's another thing altogether actually provide it—and I have to say that as a brand, BMW is true to their word. One of my favorite supporting examples—and I tell this story often—is that a few years ago, when I was leasing a BMW X3 SUV, my headlight blew out at 49,970 miles—30 miles before my warranty expired. So I went straight to the dealership to get it fixed while the car was still under warranty (by the time I got it there, there were only 15 miles left) so I wouldn't have to pay for the new headlight. When I picked up the car the next day, the service rep told me that since I only had 15 miles left before my warranty expired, they went ahead and replaced my brakes and shocks and a bunch of other things along with my headlight so I wouldn't be in danger of having to repair those items soon after the warranty expired. They didn't have to do that—but it's consistent with what they advertise and with what I've come to expect from them over the years. That's their brand. Nobody should think that I just got lucky, that my dealership happened to be staffed by a couple of nice guys; this type of service is planned. They're trained this way. This behavior is the result of a central corporate entity deciding that the BMW brand will go over and above for their customers, an ideal they then pass on to their employees. They teach them how to make it happen. Those employees literally become living embodiments of the brand.

# Q: • How Can Business Processes • Support the Brand Promise?

**Genevieve Smith**
**The Brand Perspective**

↳ Business processes have a huge impact on how the brand promise is actualized. At the enterprise level, it's important that the desired end state for the brand is clearly articulated and that knowledge sharing, alignment, and integration are aggressively encouraged. This leads to an examination of processes within the business units that can affect the brand promise. Following are a few examples of how one might think about business processes as they relate to the brand:

- **End state:** Will the current initiatives get us there? If not, what else must we put in place?

- **Experiences:** What are the most important customer experiences for each business unit? How can we redesign these in a breakthrough way?

- **Problem resolution:** Do we have a common platform, agnostic to LOB?

- **Alignment:** Are there opportunities for alignment in areas with multiple initiatives?

Particularly in large companies, business units tend to function independently of one another, with financial reporting, legal, human resources, and regulatory requirements being the main areas of commonality. This can lead to consumer interactions and communications that are very different from one another, depending on the business unit's protocols. But of course, consumers don't view a brand like an org chart; they view it as one entity. So it's important that the processes that touch a consumer are as aligned and integrated as possible; otherwise, the brand experience will be fragmented for the consumer.

I've observed that there is a constant tug of war at most companies between what is driven by the business units and what is driven from the center. Although I've lived long enough in corporate America to see the pendulum swing back and forth, in my experience, a "federalist" approach works best to balance business unit ownership with centralized leadership support. (By "federalist," I mean the authority is divided between the corporate center and the business units; these share the power of decision-making.)

Take WaMu, for example. At WaMu, it was fairly easy to get everyone rallied around the notion of Simpler Banking and More Smiles. Once we had agreement—at least on paper—about the end state, it was time to pull the business units together to get aligned and prioritized at the enterprise level. That, however, was not so easy to do. In fact, we ended up bringing in a third party to help us create the road map for operationalizing the brand in each business unit. We simply weren't able to move this forward without some outside help. Lesson learned: Business process is critical to the brand promise—but not so easy to change or influence.

JASON MILETSKY
THE AGENCY PERSPECTIVE

As I've said throughout this book—and will continue to say each time it comes up—the brand is far more than a look, a feel, and a logo. It's how the market perceives your company, product, or service based on its reputation, its ability to fulfill its promise, and the emotional connection made through its attitude and personality.

There's no way a brand can be successful through advertising and marketing alone. Just *saying* it'll deliver doesn't mean much; to really become a successful brand, it has to *actually* deliver. That means the people behind the scenes must follow through to ensure a positive consumer experience on a consistent basis. This applies to both B2C brands and B2B brands, and requires significant communication from the branding department to all areas of the company. So basically, it's a cycle. Business processes can (and must) support the brand promise, but the first step is for the branding and marketing people to let the rest of the company know what the promise actually is.

For example, suppose a credit-card brand promises that they have the absolute best security against identity theft. That's a great promise—timely, hard-hitting. There's no doubt they'll be able to build a market. But if all they do is make the promise and then hope for the best, they're destined to collapse, as word will inevitably get around that the company is pretty much full of it. (When Einstein posited that nothing can travel faster than the speed of light, he didn't take into consideration the rapid rate of bad news.)

To fulfill this promise, the company needs to take measures internally:

- The IT department has to be at the top of its game to make sure that all systems are working properly and that fraud can be detected quickly and accurately.

- A security department needs to be put in place that can assess any situation that comes up in which a customer's identity may have been tampered with.

- Customer-service representatives must be trained to deal with cardholders who may have been affected by fraud, working with them to get them new cards and wipe away bogus charges.

- Outside reps need to be trained to work with retailers where false charges may have been made.

All these systems—and more—are needed to fulfill the brand promise in terms of both technical and customer service. If any of them falter, it could negatively affect the brand far beyond the point where branding and marketing can rescue it.

# Q:

CERTAIN DEPARTMENTS MAY HAVE
TO TAKE ON THE "BAD GUY" ROLE,
SUCH AS LEGAL OR ACCOUNTING.
DO THEY ALSO NEED TO REFLECT
BRAND VALUES? OR ARE THEY IMMUNE?

GENEVIEVE SMITH
THE BRAND PERSPECTIVE

By now I've probably proven that I am a dyed-in-the-wool brand zealot with very little tolerance for immunity—for *anyone*. Let's face it: Even the "bad guy" roles—and, more specifically, their work product—can ultimately affect the way the brand interacts with its consumers.

Here's a perfect example: At WaMu, we developed a "brand manifesto," which we planned to send to all employees when we launched the brand rollout. In it, we talked about tipping cows—meaning we weren't afraid to break convention. When legal reviewed the creative, which included an upside-down cow in the "Cow Tipping" section, they wanted us to put in a serious legal disclaimer that no cows had been harmed or killed in the creation of the manifesto. Naturally, this suggestion was like a match around kerosene—the creative groups went wild at the notion we would take ourselves so seriously as to request this type of formal legal disclaimer on an internal communication. So I suggested to the team that instead of grousing about how stupid legal was, they should come up with a disclaimer that was "in-brand"—in other words, they show some leadership! Here's what they came up with:

> "In case you were wondering, we quite like cows. No actual cows, sacred or otherwise, were harmed in the production of this manifesto. The cow hanging upside down is simply the result of modern computer trickery."

Everyone—including legal—loved the solution. In fact, this incident marked the beginning of a long and storied passage for marketing communications and the legal department. One of our basic brand tenets was to speak in plain English; no bank-speak allowed. You know what I'm talking about: the language used in communications and disclaimers from most banks. The reason this language exists is twofold: regulatory requirements and the bank's desire to protect itself from lawsuits. So the question was, how can you communicate in such a way that honors regulatory requirements and ensures immunity, but actually *says* something to the consumer? How do you make sure the language you use is not obscure to the point that it's simply protectionist?

Thanks to the cow-tipping episode, the marketing and legal departments agreed to kill bank-speak (to the degree it was possible) and write in a way consumers could relate to. The legal group hired a lawyer who specialized in teaching legal groups to communicate in plain English and retrained the entire department to do just that. They also rewrote the endless communications generated by a bank to the brand standards. On the other side, we challenged our communicators to truly understand the role of legal opinion and language and to work with our legal group across all media, including advertising, to find solutions that were true to the brand voice *and* addressed legal concerns.

I know—I'm making this sound like we all sat in a circle singing "Kumbaya." It wasn't actually that easy. But once we had an agreement on and commitment to the brand fundamental, which was communicate in plain English, the logjam cleared and we were able to move forward.

That said, I *never* mess with accounting. Maybe accounting has immunity....

JASON MILETSKY

THE AGENCY PERSPECTIVE

Totally immune. In fact, they'll become a brand all their own. They won't have their own logo or tagline, but legal departments, accounting departments, and others will develop their own reputation among the people and companies that deal with them. Nintendo might be all about games and fun, but that doesn't mean their legal department won't come after you like a Sumo wrestler if you piss them off. (That's just an example—I've never worked with Nintendo, and for all I know, everyone in their legal department is super swell.)

Legal and accounting get the shit end of the stick—no question. The people in those departments work thankless jobs, dealing with unpleasant issues and people bitching all day long. They never get to jump in on strategy or creative meetings, and trust me, few people go into their offices just to say "Hey, great job." But their job isn't brand-oriented. Their job is to collect payments, make payments, protect the company's intellectual property, safeguard their company from potential lawsuits, and other issues not related to consumers. Sometimes they need to be pig-headed and aggressive in ways that the brand might not typically call for. But business is business, and they need the room to do their thing regardless of the brand.

# Q: SHOULD YOU DEFINE WHAT "LIVING THE BRAND" IS AND HIRE PEOPLE WITH THOSE IMPLIED TRAITS?

GENEVIEVE SMITH

THE BRAND PERSPECTIVE

Yes, you absolutely have to hire for the brand. If you work at a large company, odds are your recruiting teams—and human resources in general—will be eager to collaborate. They'll want to have influence on the people side of the brand equation, both for hiring and for how the company treats its employees. Indeed, this will likely be standard operations, with HR professionals translating the brand values into hiring standards and creating screens for the traits you've jointly agreed to as fundamental to "living the brand."

Even if you work in a small company, the brand will likely define recruiting—at a minimum because the culture, which is just another way of saying "internal brand," will so dictate. A small firm may not have the luxury of creating complex screening mechanisms, but it will at the very least ask potential hires a series of questions beyond technical competencies, the answers to which will show whether a potential hire is a good fit with the brand.

Some firms take this one step farther, viewing the employees themselves as the brand. Abercrombie and Fitch is a good example. Their employee manual starts with a section called "You Are the Brand" and continues by outlining how employees should look, dress, groom, interact with shoppers, and so forth. In other words, the employee would look and feel like the brand. I was interested in this because A&F has built a pretty good brand with very little advertising; they rely more on their employees and the store experience to generate word of mouth for the brand. And, I don't mean the employees will look like the models in the A&F catalog; that's advertising. But there are very strict standards governing what brand alignment looks, feels, and acts like for store employees.

To be frank, I think hiring for the brand and managing employees relative to the brand is a discipline that warrants much more depth than we've allotted for here. I could wax poetic about how brand practices, processes, and products must align with the customer experience delivered by front line employees, but unfortunately we don't have time. If by managing and monitoring employee-to-customer interactions you can ensure that these are brand-aligned, then you are more than halfway to building a successful brand. Suffice it to say that the way your employees represent the brand is key to success, and I encourage you to focus on this area in conjunction with human resources and line management.

JASON MILETSKY
THE AGENCY PERSPECTIVE

I think I should define what "living the brand" means for readers before I talk about whether or not we need to define it to new hires. "Living the brand" (I'm going to stop putting it quotes now because I'll probably throw out that term often and I don't want to turn this answer into an Austin Powers spoof) is the participation and display of brand values by employees. It's when the workforce—as individuals and as a whole—inject all aspects of the brand, its promise, and its personality into their everyday work, thereby transforming the brand from a philosophical concept into a living, breathing entity.

Years ago, we helped conduct some basic market research for one of our clients, Ceridian Corp., which managed HR and payroll services. One of the bits of information we found was that HR directors, accountants, and other people in their target market saw Ceridian as "stodgy, corporate, too large, unfriendly, and difficult to work with." Believe it or not, that exact quote—which basically summed up the results of our research—came from a focus group of people who had *never used Ceridian before*. Nonetheless, this had become the Ceridian brand—the reputation they had earned themselves. And unfortunately, it's a small world. People talk.

The weird thing was, all the people we knew at Ceridian in the higher executive levels were great people—they were fun, funny, and easy to talk to. They were innovative. They displayed the qualities that *should* have been reflected in their brand. So we went through the basic branding routine: Who are you guys? What do you really want to be? What does the market want and what can you reasonably give them? A new look and feel was developed, new messaging written, new strategies developed, and a new tagline rolled out. Just as importantly, employees who dealt with clients either directly or indirectly were retrained, with internal marketing campaigns reinforcing the new brand principles of being more customer-friendly, light-hearted, and accessible. Office parties were held, letting people know it was okay to have fun at work while still getting business accomplished. Years later (yes, years—while exposure and notoriety can come quickly, reputation takes awhile), new research confirmed that a turn-around had, in fact, taken place. People who had never worked with Ceridian before now described the company as "friendly, approachable, and easy to work with." Yes, some of this was the result of advertising, no doubt about it. But even the best ad campaign in the world couldn't have turned the ship around like that. The transformation came from within, by adjusting employees' attitudes.

There's no question in my mind that marketing is *not* the key to bringing the brand to life—the brand's employees are. I don't, though, think there's a hard and fast rule about hiring people. We can't expect consumers to be loyal to a brand just because we put it in front of them, nor can we expect new hires to live the brand just because they are suddenly getting a paycheck. The brand must give each worker something to believe in, and the employer must help instill brand values in each employee through training, care, and internal mar-keting programs. Employees need to see that the brand really is what it says it is—that it's not just smoke and mirrors in an effort to turn a quick buck. At the same time, though, the hiring process can weed out people who seem to display the exact opposite traits of the brand, who will resist taking part in it, and who could potentially disrupt other employees from living the brand. Some people simply aren't trainable.

# Q: IF YOU WANT EMPLOYEES TO "LIVE THE BRAND," HOW DO YOU TRAIN THEM?

GENEVIEVE SMITH
THE BRAND PERSPECTIVE

I'll answer this question from the perspective of managing front-line or customer-facing employees, but must emphasize that the way in which support groups relate to and are managed to brand standards has a big impact on how well front-line employees can deliver to consumers.

Obviously, it's important to cover the basics, giving employees guardrails that make sense in the industry and are fundamental to how you would treat any given customer. This is simple check the box logic. You can define key aspects of brand training as pragmatically as this:

- Always resolve customer issues on the first call.

- Answer the phone in three rings.

- Stand, smile, and introduce yourself to a new customer with a handshake.

- And so forth and so on.

Most of this will be common sense tempered by what a brand can afford to invest in with regard to customer service—and of course, you have to have standards to measure and pay employees for achieving (right?). But then there are the nuances. Human beings don't fit into a square box, so customer experience—at least those experiences that become legend, going viral to encourage customer referrals (or perhaps generate anti-referrals)—is mostly about the exceptions, not the rules. The magic comes when a company can determine the latitude an employee has to "do the right thing" for a customer, decide how much support there is for this type of interaction (which needs to be brand-aligned), and train for these exceptions. Thinking about the gray areas from a consumer and employee perspective and training employees to handle these is the challenge—and it's an investment that can be quantified only through customer-satisfaction measures and brand-reputation scores.

All this is to say that I think you can be pretty black and white in training, but that you should also take a leap of faith and empower employees—although this is not the most easily manageable, measureable, or controllable philosophy.

Jason Miletsky
The Agency Perspective

 This basically comes down to internal marketing, with specific training as one part of that effort. What's important is to keep the brand values in front of employees at all times, to let them know what the brand is about, and to help to bring them into the internal brand community.

There are a number of ways that companies can market to their employees and get them to live the brand:

- **Give new hires a "brand overview" book:** This book should discuss the brand, its promise, its personality, the market, and how each employee plays a role in the creating a positive consumer experience. This should be required reading so that all new employees start with a full understanding of what the brand is about and how their own actions can affect consumers.

> For more information on this, check out *Perspectives on Managing Employees*, which discusses in detail how to get all employees to be a bigger part of the consumer experience.

- **Set up specific training sessions:** These sessions should teach employees about the brand—what it is, how it works, and why it's important. This is especially true for employees who will directly interact with customers, to make them aware of how the brand is perceived on the outside. They should be trained in the type of language and attitude that should be used during customer interactions, what their specific role is in fulfilling the brand promise, and how their behavior can add to or detract from the brand personality.

- **Make proper use of office wall space:** Floral prints or paintings of landscapes are nice, but your office isn't a New Jersey diner. Use your wall space for internal promotional purposes. Using the brand look and feel, create prints that display the products or services your company sells, announce the brand values, or promote an internal campaign (discussed in a moment).

If your company does any print advertising, have the agency make poster-sized reprints of each ad and hang them around the office so that employees who may never see these ads in their published form can see how the brand is being marketed on the outside. Maybe make a montage of positive consumer feedback received either through regular mail or e-mail. The point is, every company has wall space available that should be used to somehow promote the brand. But whatever you do with it—please, for the sake of all that is good in the world, no more of those horrible Successories posters. Seriously, enough with those. If you have some in your office, put this book away and go take them down. You'll thank me later.

■ **Circulate an internal newsletter:** Sending this out weekly is probably too aggressive, but monthly or quarterly newsletters should be doable. Let employees know what's happening around the company, any good news, new initiatives that are taking place, etc. As always, keep the design, tone, and look and feel reflective of the brand, and make sure to include sections that celebrate the brand itself—how individuals within the company are living the brand and examples of how each employee is helping to improve the consumer experience. Printed versions of newsletters are always good, but HTML e-mail blasts also work if you're looking to reduce internal marketing costs.

■ **Hold town hall meetings:** While these can be extravagant, they don't need to be. A town hall meeting can be held in your company's cafeteria, a local theater, or the ballroom of a nearby hotel. It's a chance for all the employees from a single office or region to get together and intermingle for a day. Seeing that there's a lot more to their company than what happens in their own office or cubicle will help them feel as though they are part of something bigger. More importantly, it gives key executives a chance to talk to everyone at once, fill people in on important news, and promote the brand first hand to everyone in attendance. The more people feel like they are truly a part of the company, the more likely they'll be to really live the brand. Town hall meetings might reduce the work day by one, but you'll get it all back in increased productivity in the long run by having a more engaged workforce.

■ **Promote the brand through the corporate intranet:** If you don't have an intranet, get one. Give employees the chance to go online and get updates and information—anything that will make them feel more connected to the brand and your company. Again, design the site to reflect the brand. Use language that promotes it in a positive way and provide articles and stories that prove that living the brand results in a better experience for everybody, both in and out of the company. Blogs written by the brand or marketing manager are a great way to get messages about the brand across; these people might blog in a conversational way about core brand values and provide tips on how employees can live the brand in his or her position within the company.

- **Create computer wallpapers and screen savers:** This might be a simple idea, but repetition is one of the key ingredients to successful advertising. So keep the brand in front of company employees by making it the first thing they see when they turn on their monitors in the morning, and the first thing they come back to when they return to their computers after being away for a short while.

- **Communicate to employees through department managers:** The single most important effort a brand or marketing manager can make is to get department managers on board with the brand. Larger companies in particular can make appropriate use of these managers, each of whom will have the ability to influence a large number of employees under their supervision. If the brand is about being buttoned up, focused, and dedicated to taking a proactive approach, for example, then these traits need to be demonstrated in the behavior of each manager. It would be counter-productive for a manager in this type of company to consistently come in late, dress in jeans and golf shirts, and take a "que sera, sera" kind of approach to meeting deadlines. Executives should take extra care to properly explain the brand promise and personality to each manager and provide insight as to how each manager can further promote the brand to the employees in their supervision.

- **Wrap all internal brand communications under a finite campaign theme:** Consumer marketing efforts are more effective when they are organized and delivered according to a specific timeline, with pre-established goals. The same goes for internal marketing strategies. While the goals may not be directly related to revenue, they can be pegged to track specific employee behavior or involvement in internal activities, or even in increased production. Create a specific creative campaign theme for all communications. (I'm not a fan of cheesy marketing in general, but internal campaign themes may be the one exception. Themes like "We Are One" or "Yes We Can" are actually appropriate for internal communication efforts, even if they are the marketing equivalent to Velveeta.) Roll out efforts over time, communicate the campaign through wall art and newsletters, and make sure there is a call to action, such as taking part in a contest or internal promotion (discussed in the next bullet point).

- **Engage employees with contests and promotions:** You're not going to be trying to get your employees to purchase a product, but it's still important to get them engaged in your brand. Use internal marketing to get employees to participate in contests with small prizes awarded to winners, with winners being highlighted on the intranet and newsletter. These contests don't need to be complex—they can be anything from collecting names and selecting random winners to asking employees to submit their new ideas for products or external marketing messages. Whatever you do, do it with the idea in mind to get employees involved.

# Q: • SHOULD THERE BE A BRAND COMPONENT • IN EMPLOYEE COMPENSATION MODELS?

GENEVIEVE SMITH
THE BRAND PERSPECTIVE

↳ Yep. You've got to pay for what matters. This is fundamental. The challenge is this: How do you set brand goals and measure them in order to pay employees appropriately? For example, if a brand value is "friendly," how do you quantify "friendly" and pay employees for being so? How would you measure "friendly" on a scale of 1 to 5?

Strong compensation models are generally pretty simple, focusing on the core elements that create profitability for the firm that an employee can be paid to affect. For example a company may have four or five key goal areas—like profit, risk, growth, service, and innovation—for corporate groups, and monthly sales goals for sales groups. So how does the brand factor into these core pay-for-performance measurements? You have to be able to set goals that are measurable to have a pay plan that yields results.

Generally the area you can most easily measure and pay for as it relates to the brand is service, which underscores the importance of setting service standards, measuring these standards, and paying employees for either individual or group achievements against targets. I don't pretend to be an expert in this area; I acknowledge that it is highly complex and requires both time and science to get it so that you're firing on all cylinders.

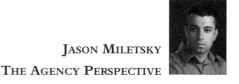

JASON MILETSKY
THE AGENCY PERSPECTIVE

Employees can be incentivized to achieve certain goals through the compensation model. But that alone isn't enough to motivate people to participate—and it's certainly not enough to further strengthen the brand values within each employee. These compensation models still need the creative marketing edge to fully bring the brand to life.

Case in point: Starting in or around the spring of 2001, my agency, overseen by managers under my co-author for this book, Genevieve, ran two three-month internal campaigns per year each year until the end of 2004. The programs we ran were for employees only, and had two distinct purposes:

- To incentivize the national sales force to reach targeted goals based on their geography and the products they were selling.

- To motivate operations staff behind the scenes—the people who facilitate the transactions that ultimately make the salespeople's job faster and easier —to be more productive and efficient.

As an agency, our job was *not* to come up with the specific goals. We couldn't have done that even if we tried. There were numerous goals and prize levels for all sorts of products, places, and situations, and only they could have put it all together. Our job was to package it all up in a creative campaign, communicating the goals to the employees and getting them pumped up to try to reach them.

Now, most companies that run these sorts of incentive programs do little more than announce them, give them a fairly generic name, and send a few e-mail reminders to everyone to inform them that the campaign is in progress. But that wasn't WaMu's M.O. Their brand, under Genevieve's leadership, was big, fun, exciting—they were the best of the best, they did things differently, and they were all about moving forward in an upbeat, positive way. These were their ideals, and the internal campaign, while selling the program, had to also promote the brand. There was nothing generic about this bank, and there could be nothing generic about our campaigns.

In total, I think we did nine of these campaigns with Washington Mutual, and while I liked them all, in my opinion the first one was clearly the best. We had a virtually clean canvas to work with—the only directive we had was that the campaign had to reflect the general concept of "communication," which was part of a larger overall internal message they were promoting at the time. The idea for our first campaign came to me while I was watching a video of their last sales meeting. There must have been about 15,000 salespeople sitting in a massive convention hall with a 15-person band, a stage show, and lighting worthy of the MTV Music Awards. For the salespeople, it looked like an amazing outing where they not only got a lot of great information, but had a great time getting it. It was like watching the brand literally come to life. But what struck me was that while the salespeople got to enjoy all the excitement of the show and the brand, the operations staff remained in their cubicles in offices all over the country, working to support the salespeople. I thought that it'd be great if we could somehow create a campaign that motivated everybody, promoted the "communication" message, and somehow brought the excitement of the sales show to every office.

What we came up with was a campaign centered around a fictional radio station called "W.A.M.U. Radio Yes!" using the letters in WaMu as the station call letters and playing off their "Power of Yes" tagline. The communication message was clear (radio itself being a powerful medium for news and information), it was motivational (everybody likes some kind of music, and will often turn to music as a source of inspiration), and there's no question that radio can be fun! For three months, everything related to the incentive program was run through the Radio Yes! campaign. There was a radio station style intranet site (complete with our own DJ, who gave weekly campaign updates), online contests, rock-themed wall posters for each office, and small radio-style giveaways, such as bumper stickers and t-shirts. But the best part—and this was where we really brought the brand to life—was the van trips. Radio stations are known for having prize vans visit local retailers, so we had a traveling W.A.M.U. Radio Yes! prize van visit 40 different Washington Mutual offices so that anywhere between 50 and 1,000 employees in operations departments per office could come out to the parking lot and experience a little piece of the excitement that the salespeople got from the sales show. With each prize van stop we had a live DJ playing loud music and got the employees dancing, playing games, and just having a great time. We let them live the brand! In fact, we may have been too convincing—at one stop in Seattle, a group of Japanese tourists thought the van was from a real radio station, and came by to join the fun and get the DJ's autograph!

One quick note: While some of what I described here could seem excessive in light of the recent financial meltdown and WaMu's subsequent collapse and takeover by JP Morgan Chase, it was not considered to be excessive at all at the time, when the housing market was exploding and Washington Mutual was in fierce competition to get and keep the best salespeople in the industry. While it's easy to look at any industry and play Monday morning quarterback after the bottom has dropped out, Washington Mutual's strategy at the time led to enormous growth and, I believe, remains a model for how to build a brand and how to incentivize employees. Like many other banks, WaMu was a victim of the collapse of the mortgage industry—and neither their branding efforts nor their compensation/incentive efforts were the cause of it.

# Q: An Influential—and Effective—Department Manager Doesn't Get the Purpose of Branding and Isn't Buying Into It. Now What?

What's your perspective on this question?
Let us know at PerspectivesOnBranding.com.

**GENEVIEVE SMITH**
**THE BRAND PERSPECTIVE**

Welcome to my world. This could be a really complex discussion or a really simple one; I'm going to go with simple. Here's the bottom line: Influential and effective managers generally manage business units or support groups that generate profit or cut expenses in a way that is material to a company's bottom line. They're hired because they have the necessary skills and knowledge to generate results and they can be held accountable for profits.

Managing these relationships is where brand management becomes an art much more than a science. Yes, you could create enterprise metrics and measures that demonstrate the brand effect to the bottom line—and you *should* do this no matter what, as we've discussed. The challenge for brand management in this situation is to demonstrate how the brand creates relevance and value for the influential manager and his or her business unit and bottom line.

The first thing you have to do is work with the manager to define "brand"—meaning brand as a core operation, not graphics, logos, or marketing—so you know you're talking about the same thing. If, even after this discussion, the manager fails to get on board, a somewhat naughty but effective response is to ask that the dissenting manager rebrand his or her business unit and stop doing business under your brand if he or she doesn't want to pay for the privilege (if you allocate brand expense) or doesn't believe in the brand's effectiveness. If this person *really* believes the brand has no value to his or her group, then he or she should be up for the challenge—but chances are he or she will see the light.

JASON MILETSKY

THE AGENCY PERSPECTIVE

The part that makes this question hard is that the department manager is effective. The part that makes it easy is that he's influential. As I've alluded to numerous times in this book, the brand is not a logo, and there's more to it than can fit into a brand guide. There's a spirit of the brand in its personality, and whether a brand resonates with its market will largely depend on how well that personality connects and how consistently the promise is fulfilled. This can't be just a facade—it has to be real, and to be real it has to be accepted and believed in not only by the intended consumer audience, but by the employees of the brand themselves.

Through internal campaigns, brand managers can communicate their message throughout their company—not just the importance of maintaining brand consistency to people who may be in positions to publish marketing or sales material, but the brand values to all employees to really get everyone to truly live the brand. However, most of these campaigns will require acceptance and active participation by various managers, who will be used as conduits to spread the brand to the people under their supervision—not just by word, but by example. They lead, and their employees follow.

That's why it can be a big deal if a department manager just doesn't get the importance of branding and simply refuses to embody it. It can be even worse if that manager goes beyond ignoring the brand and moves right on to bad-mouthing it or otherwise showing contempt. One influential manager can spoil any number of his or her employees, preventing them from understanding the importance of the brand, which in turn can hurt their job performance and weaken the brand overall. When this happens, the company should take whatever means necessary to make sure this individual understands why upholding the brand values is important and how their attitude is negatively reflected on the employees he or she supervises. If, after all honest attempts have been made, this particular manager still refuses to be part of the brand, fire that manager. If there's one thing I've realized over the years, it's that everyone is replaceable. And no matter how good they might be at doing their job, no single person is worth having the attitudes of everyone around him or her poisoned. Living the brand is just too important to allow a couple of bad seeds to deteriorate it from the inside.

# Q: IS THERE AN IDEAL RATIO FOR DIVIDING BUDGET BETWEEN INTERNAL AND EXTERNAL AUDIENCES?

GENEVIEVE SMITH

THE BRAND PERSPECTIVE

There really is no ideal ratio for dividing the budget, although as a rule of thumb, the internal-communications investment will be significantly less than external marketing.

With respect to internal communications, the first thing you should do is figure out how business-as-usual communications could be repurposed to talk about and/or better reflect the brand. For example, at WaMu, we specifically asked management to look and sound like the brand. We requested that every manager in the company do the following:

- Talk about the brand in meetings and regular communications.

- Make sure their materials and communications look and sound like the brand.

To support this, we provided regular updates and suggested discussion points as well as templates so that their communications materials reflected the brand-expression guidelines.

Here are a few other things we did to market internally:

- We launched a blog so that the employees could speak directly with the most senior management of the company and each other regarding the work environment. They could also use the blog to offer suggestions and to ask for help when processes or work conditions didn't match brand standards. This blog was monitored 24/7, and the posted responses came from everyone around the company—including the president, who hosted the blog. We viewed this real-time feedback as critical to the success of the brand.

- We re-branded the intranet and all internal communications so they looked and felt like the brand—again supported by templates and training for internal communicators.

- All of our employee conferences centered on the brand—and these touched literally thousands of employees each year.

These actions didn't cost a bunch of money—and with the exception of the blog, they were not new initiatives. They were, however, extremely high impact in the way they constantly reinforced our brand message.

Your company probably has a budget (built on ROI) to support external communications, including advertising, direct mail, online marketing, merchandising, and all other customer messaging vehicles. Similar to internal communications the challenge is to align these with the brand expressions. We speak quite a bit about external communications in the book, but *vis a vis* this question, there is no "ideal investment ratio" between internal and external communications. The lion's share will be invested externally.

My advice? Be as innovative and clever as possible in using existing communications vehicles to get the word out about the brand, internally and externally. The division between internal and external budgets could prove moot if you can infuse these already funded vehicles with the brand expressions and focus. Done right, by the way, you can end up with highly focused communications that are 100 percent more effective because they are grounded in the brand.

JASON MILETSKY

THE AGENCY PERSPECTIVE

↳ Wow, I really hope Gen doesn't have a great, mathematical answer to this one and make me look foolish, because I'm really not positive what an exact ratio should be—and I don't want to wimp out by giving some generic answer about the importance of internal branding, blah, blah, blah. We've already gone over all that already, and if there's one thing I hate about books like these, it's when nobody gives any specific information. So I'm going to go with this: 92 percent of budgets should be used for marketing to external audiences, with the remaining 8 percent earmarked for internal marketing. (I'm talking about marketing expenses—creative, project management, production, media—I'm not taking into consideration any additions to financial compensation through incentive programs or similar efforts.)

This ratio isn't arbitrary—I put considerable thought into it before answering—nor should the single-digit percentage I've assigned to internal marketing be considered an editorial on my part about the importance of these efforts. Internal marketing is *absolutely* important. If you've read these questions in order, you know that I'm a huge fan of getting employees on board with the brand. I mean, I even suggested firing the rogue manager in my answer to the last question! But here's the way I see it: While internal marketing is important, it should be far less expensive and easier than external marketing.

Consider the following:

- **You know exactly where they are:** Brand or marketing managers will know how many employees there are, how many are in each office, and where each different office is located. There's also no guesswork as to when to reach them, since they'll be at work roughly between 9:00 a.m. and 5:00 p.m., Monday through Friday.

- **You're marketing to a pretty captive audience:** Sure, you still need to get their attention, but aside from traveling salespeople or virtual employees, most employees can be found in the office, factory, or warehouse. Plus, there's no waste—everyone who *will* see the internal marketing program *should* see the internal marketing program. Unlike external marketing, you won't be wasting time or resources reaching people you don't need to reach.

- **There's a clear order of communication:** In this order, each level of manager is available as a conduit to spread messages over larger populations of employees. Do a good job getting managers on your side, and they will save you mega-bucks in marketing to the employee population.

- **There are no mass media expenses:** No TV advertising expenses, no radio, sponsorship, no roadside billboard costs. This doesn't mean there won't be any hard costs—internal marketing programs often include wall signs, newsletters, intranet upkeep, e-mail blasts, even town hall meetings and organized office parties. But while all of these items can add up in terms of cost, it's barely a drop in the proverbial bucket compared to the expense associated with mass media.

- **There is a built-in incentive for the audience to accept the messages being marketed to them:** Unlike general consumer audiences, who need to be convinced of your message and may derive no immediate benefit from accepting your brand, employees spend a good part of their lives at their work—they *want* to like it. They *want* to believe in the brand. So you won't have to try too hard to make a lasting impression.

- **Creative doesn't need to be as clever or integrated:** Internal efforts don't need to be all that out there, so agency fees for creative and even project management shouldn't be nearly as high as agency fees for expansive external efforts.

So, is my 8 percent accurate? I have no idea. I didn't whip out the calculator and do the math, and I didn't ask my bookkeeping department to pull invoices from past work so I could do a compare and contrast between billing for internal versus external campaigns. But based on the preceding points, I would say that while internal marketing is neither cheap nor easy, 8 percent (give or take) of the budget should about cover it.

# Q: Do You Need to Enforce Brand Values to Vendors? As Long as They're Getting Their Invoices Paid, Does It Matter What They Think?

**Genevieve Smith**
**The Brand Perspective**

I view vendors as an extension of the internal employees, and as such I expect them to have the same passion and concern for the brand. Think about it: Vendors are hired for their specialized expertise and are critical to the success of any given program or operation they work on for the company or any product/service they supply. So the values that guide work throughout the enterprise are equally as important for vendors, given that the work provided by a vendor is a component of the whole and won't stand alone.

For example, at WaMu, our brand said we wanted to make interaction between the consumer and the brand "easy" (simple). Any vendor briefed to work with us was told that this attribute was a key input to what they produced for the firm. We wanted them to approach the work we paid them to do with this mindset.

Specific to the values, let's say an internal value is "Treat one another with respect." The successful vendor will understand that this is a core value in terms of how people relate to one another and will adopt the same tonality in dealing with the internal teams. If a core value is "Produce at the lowest cost," then the successful vendor will be very focused on delivery against this dimension as that is what the people who are paying them are focused on.

My belief is that vendors are part of the team, so they must live the within the brand values while working on the business. Especially when selecting marketing and brand vendors, it is important to focus on the chemistry between the agency and the brand. There needs to be very tight linkage and similarity between the vendor and the company in this area, as the work produced is frequently the most visible to the consumer outside of specific product development or outsourced services.

Vendors are people too. They've got money to spend on products—and more importantly, they've got voices that can pass on positive or negative reviews of your brand to others.

First, let's just get one thing on the table—and I say this as a business owner who has both worked with a number vendors and been a vendor to many different clients: Just because you're paying somebody to do something doesn't mean you have to be a dick to them. You may not feel compelled to invite every vendor to the company picnic, but it won't kill you to treat your vendors with at least a bare minimum of respect. It's the best way to get positive results from anybody doing any kind of work for you.

At the same time, it's possible that I've come off as a little contradictory in this book, and I want to use this question to clear some of that up. On the one hand, I've discussed the importance of living the brand. That means training, conducting internal marketing, and promoting compensation models that motivate employees to produce in accordance with your brand's values—put another way, transcending colors, fonts, and images to become a living, breathing brand entity. On the other hand, I've given a free pass to the accounting offices and internal legal teams to work outside the brand values, offering Disney as an example of a company that is notorious for being tough for vendors to work with despite their squeaky-clean consumer-facing brand.

So which is it? Well, it's both. Not every company will have the power, reach, budget, or global familiarity that Disney does—and yes, sometimes different rules exist for richer, larger companies. And I also believe that certain departments of any company are sometimes required to be confrontational—meaning they may need to function outside of the brand values that everyone else in the company abides by. But those departments don't make up the majority of groups that deal with outside vendors. Marketing needs to deal with agencies, printers, media buyers, publications, etc. Manufacturing needs to deal with suppliers of raw materials. Distribution needs to deal with trucking. The list goes on. And in many of these cases, vendors need to be seen more as partners—and the brand needs to be every bit as strong to them as it is to the consumer market. Your reasons for interacting will be different (you're buying from them, while consumers are buying from you), but the brand values, personality, and behavior don't change based on who you're dealing with. If it does, then you may as well admit that your brand is little more than a facade, make as much money as you can before someone figures it out, and then pack it in and move on.

# Q: WHAT IS THE ROLE OF BRAND THROUGH ALL CONSUMER TOUCH POINTS? HOW DO YOU HAVE THE BRAND LIVE AT ALL TOUCH POINTS?

**GENEVIEVE SMITH**
**THE BRAND PERSPECTIVE**

The brand should be reflected at all consumer touch points. That said, it is not that easy, especially at a large firm, to have the brand live at all touch points. A consumer could enter a physical location, speak to someone on the phone, use the Web site, receive statements and direct marketing solicitations, see advertising, and read about the company in the media. It would be nice if all these potential interactions would look and feel the same, but how do you pull that off when there are multiple divisions accountable for operating the different touch points and multiple marketing and communications departments creating advertising?

Let's tackle the operational issues first, as they are the most complex. Different lines of business may adopt their own standards for efficiency of cost and/or of operations. To use a simple example, one division may have a standard that says we answer the phone on the third ring and we solve the consumer's request on the spot without handing it off. Another division might say we put the consumer into the automated phone system and we have three days to resolve any issue or request. If a consumer has multiple products and is serviced by these different divisions, the experience that consumer has with the brand could be very different depending on which product he or she is calling about. Even worse, depending on a firm's infrastructure, consumers may not be able to get help on multiple accounts with a single call—which will be extremely frustrating for them. In their mind they do business with the entire brand, not with its divisions. The way the consumer interacts with the company probably won't reflect the company's internal org chart.

The solution? A road map where the most senior executive in the firm is dedicated to holding management accountable for seamless consumer interactions, regardless of where or how they touch the brand. Sounds easy, but with the pressure of running the business and making money, this type of objective is tremendously hard to implement. Also, the brand must be very well defined from a consumer perspective to act how you want it to across multiple and complex touch points. It cannot be nice marketing words on a piece of paper intended to create aspiration; it has to be defined in very practical and hard-core terms that can be operationalized into the functions that drive and manage the operation of the touch points.

Using the phone as an example, if the brand stands for "easy to use," then you have to do a lot of work to figure out what "easy to use" means to the consumer. Does it mean answer in three rings? Does it mean have all their information available, or is it okay to route through an automated phone system as long as they get a call back within xyz time frame? And then there is cost: What can the brand afford to do in order to be easy to use? This is the hard stuff about operationalizing the brand. But if a company wants a truly world-class brand and believes this asset is key to their growth and sustainability, then these are the type of issues worth addressing.

It is somewhat easier to control the brand expressions through standards and guidelines, as discussed previously. Marketing interactions, including advertising, are touch points, so these absolutely must be brand-aligned, not division-aligned, if you want the brand to look and feel cohesive. But there are nuances here as well. Even if everyone is using the same color palette, fonts, and templates, there remains the issue of the intent of the marketing communications, regardless of how they look. This means things like control over and agreement on how many times a customer or consumer receives direct mail from the brand, how the brand is associated with promotional and price discounts, what companies are acceptable partners for co-branding, sponsorships and events and how they affect the brand, just to name a few.

This is not easy, as again, different divisions have their own business and marketing plans that drive the annual divisional profitability, and frequently it is not in the DNA of a firm to have marketing reviews or cross-divisional plans. Often, you get into a situation where one division's analytics prove they have to mail 15.5 times to get a response, but another believes that is spamming the customer, which they originally sourced. In other words, things can get dicey.

We somewhat solved for this at WaMu by structuring both the centers of excellence (e.g., advertising, research, creative, operations) and various divisional marketing directors as direct reports to me, the CMO. It would have taken a few more years to get the entire marketing community focused around the brand. We were close but we ran out of time.

**JASON MILETSKY**

**THE AGENCY PERSPECTIVE**

Answering this question requires that you first figure out where each touch point exists. They exist in retail outlets and mall kiosks. They live on the other end of every customer-service phone line and tech-support chat box. They exist with every home delivery, every product return, and every response to every suggestion or complaint. Touch points exist at each place the consumer comes in contact with your brand—especially at points that enable or encourage some sort of two-way communication. This includes your Web site, where users gather information about your brand and most closely interact with your products and services on a one-to-one basis.

These are where the brand matters most. Marketing can send the message—it can pique a consumer's interest and even encourage that person to take action. But there is always that point just before the consumer makes a decision—that final second where doubt could still set in and change the game. Brand advertising can compel an audience into a store, but from there it's the salesperson's job to embody the brand—to make it come to life and represent the personality and promise. Similarly, once a potential consumer has become a paying customer, future touch points must continue to reinforce the brand values in order to encourage future purchases, increased interaction, and hopefully loyalty.

There's one thing I need to make clear: These human touch points are not actors, and they're not just putting on airs. These need to be people who genuinely live the brand—who appreciate the company they work for and believe in the brand values. This is where internal marketing and training come in, and hiring the right people can make the difference. Remember: The concept of a brand may be somewhat vague and intangible, but that doesn't mean the brand can just be a smokescreen. There needs to be real substance in it, and that substance needs to come through at each and every touch point in order to make it come to life and really mean something.

# Q:  Is It Possible to Make Customers Advocates of the Brand? If Yes, How?

GENEVIEVE SMITH

THE BRAND PERSPECTIVE

I will be flippant by saying a company cannot "make" customers advocates for the brand. If the company has focused on building a brand people love, then those people will naturally advocate. So the focus is on producing products and doing business with people in a way that is completely consumer centric and designed to make them smile. Then they will show their advocacy, which is really another way to say loyalty, through repeat business and by referring their friends and family to you. Research shows that when considering a purchase, consumers use the Internet quite a bit as well as responding to advertising, but a key step is asking friends and relatives what they know about a product or brand—in other words, asking for a referral.

A way to measure this advocacy is along the dimension of "willingness to refer a friend." It gives a pretty good read about how well a company is doing in creating brand advocates and this metric should be part of the analytics package a company uses to measure the health of their brand.

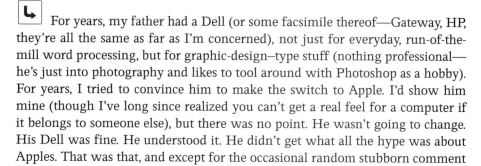

JASON MILETSKY

THE AGENCY PERSPECTIVE

For years, my father had a Dell (or some facsimile thereof—Gateway, HP, they're all the same as far as I'm concerned), not just for everyday, run-of-the-mill word processing, but for graphic-design–type stuff (nothing professional—he's just into photography and likes to tool around with Photoshop as a hobby). For years, I tried to convince him to make the switch to Apple. I'd show him mine (though I've long since realized you can't get a real feel for a computer if it belongs to someone else), but there was no point. He wasn't going to change. His Dell was fine. He understood it. He didn't get what all the hype was about Apples. That was that, and except for the occasional random stubborn comment on my part, there it stayed.

But then, one day, like all computers, his Dell began to die. Before long, you could almost feel the hard drive struggling to complete commands. It was clear: The end was quickly approaching. So my dad said to me, "Okay, convince me to buy a Mac." I replied, "I don't know how to convince you, except to tell you to think of everything you can do with your PC. Now make all of that five times faster and five times easier. That's a Mac." As inspiring as that speech was (so I'm no J.F.K.), it still took a bit of coaxing and more than one trip to the Apple store before the final purchase was made. I'm happy to report that more than a year later, my dad still likes to point out all the things his Apple can do that his Dell couldn't. And on more than one occasion, I've caught him preaching the Apple gospel to others.

Am I an advocate for the Apple brand? Absolutely. And now so is my dad—and so are at least three or four other people I've convinced to make the switch. I didn't become an advocate because Apple asked me to, and I'm not going out of my way to get more people to use Apple because they've enticed me through some sort of "refer a friend" promotion. (Although these types of promotions can work to encourage current users to pass info on, it doesn't make them advocates—it makes them opportunists.) I became an advocate of the brand because:

- It's a brand category I care about, so using the right product is important to me.

- I can relate to the brand, what it stands for, and how they market themselves.

- They have consistently produced high-quality, innovative products that do both what I need them to do and what the brand has promised.

- They live the brand through all touch points, including the products, service, and tech support, ensuring that I'm taken care of as more than just a one-time, see-you-never kind of client.

- They've connected with buyers and created a community. Apple users feel like we know something other people simply don't: Our computers are better than your computers.

- Basically, they've kept me happy.

As an advocate, I wave the banner and talk up a storm. I look forward to telling people about the products I like, and I want to share my experiences by persuading others to get involved.

Want proof that brand advocacy exists and can be effective? Go to the Garden State Plaza in Paramus, New Jersey, on any Saturday afternoon. Check out the Apple Store on the upstairs floor. See how long it takes you to get from the entrance to the cash registers—make sure you have some free time, because the store will be packed. Next, go downstairs and check out the Sony Style outlet—a far roomier store selling far less expensive computers—but try to be quiet. You don't want to wake the salespeople up. Brand advocacy at its best.

## PART THREE

# Marketing the Brand

# Q: • How Do You Determine the Best • Strategic Position for the Brand?

Jason Miletsky

The Agency Perspective

↳ Setting a strategic direction for a brand can be one of the most exciting and nerve-wracking parts of marketing. You've got a pre-determined budget and specific goals to reach, so whatever position you set, it'd better be the right one! Situate the brand ineffectively and you won't just be wasting time and money; you'll potentially be hurting the brand by framing the brand and putting out messaging in ways that may repel your target market. The brand position needs to fall somewhere near the intersection (and there may be more than one) of what the market demands and what your brand can realistically provide.

Suppose your brand provides online-dating services. From research through focus groups, interviews, and surveys, you discover that your target market wants to join sites that have thousands of profiles for them to look through. Great—you know something that audiences will respond to, so it's an easy call to position your brand as being the largest dating site on the Web, where you're guaranteed to never see the same profile twice (unless you want to, of course). The only problem is, it's not true. Your site launched only a few months ago and has so far struggled to get more than a few hundred people signed up. Given this, you can't realistically support your brand position. It won't take long before new members figure out that there really aren't that many singles' profiles to search through, and they'll inevitably abandon your site. Not the best way to build a strong reputation.

But maybe research also revealed that the target demo considers privacy to be really important to them (not as much as having a lot of profiles to search through, but it's up there), so you toss that around the office. Your lead programmers say it wouldn't be too tough to implement a privacy feature that limited users to seeing only a little bit of each profile and required them to request permission to see the full profile or contact someone they want to date. So you now position your brand as a great resource for making a romantic connection while maintaining discretion. With this, you've hit the sweet spot—the intersection between what the market wants and what your brand can realistically provide.

Of course, the position can change over time as the brand and markets change. In this last example, suppose the site grows to be exceedingly popular—to the point where hundreds of thousands of people have posted profiles. The position can reasonably evolve from being a site that provides utmost confidentiality to a site that has an enormous pool of singles to meet. The privacy position will still be there, but will take a secondary and supporting role.

The position you choose for your brand needs to both make sense and be realistic based on your capabilities in the short and long term, while staying targeted to desires held by a significant percentage of your target audience. Research and reality play equally important roles in this determination process; don't slack on either.

GENEVIEVE SMITH
THE BRAND PERSPECTIVE

↳ The first thing you need to be clear about is what is "ownable" by the brand, what is differentiating about it, and what it can actually deliver on that is valuable to the consumer. If you know your business and category well, it's possible to use your own consumer research as well as gut and intuition to come up with a variety of strategic positions that would then be tested for relevance with consumers.

At WaMu we worked with our branding agency, Wolff Olins, to develop the strategic platform Simpler Banking and More Smiles. As I mentioned, we found this was a great direction for the brand, disruptive to the category, and highly believable to consumers and employees. Our challenge was expressing this in advertising and marketing.

To bring Simpler Banking and More Smiles to life, we worked in partnership with TBWA/Chiat Day/Los Angeles, WaMu's advertising agency, who uses a process they've branded as "Disruption." Disruption, in their words, "involves helping a client to unearth and rediscover the essence of their own company and brand, the deep, hidden truths that make it unique. Having done that, we could then articulate this truth in the form of a disruptive idea—one that would run counter to the established way of thinking in such a bold and compelling manner that the world would have no choice but to sit up and take notice." (From *Disruption Stories* by Warren Berger with Jean-Marie Dru and Lee Clow.)

Our disruptive idea was Simpler Banking and More Smiles, which we had developed prior to working with TBWA, but we hadn't found the way to take the brand position to market in a meaningful (disruptive) way. They helped us to put the brand squarely in the center with all the internal and external partners around the table focused there. By working together this way, we were able to develop a highly impactful and integrated creative platform that resonated very positively with employees and consumers.

I am a strong believer in using consumer research to support the thinking that goes into developing a strategic platform. Done right, it gives you a true north and a bead on what people are thinking. But I'm also a strong believer that people who work for or with a brand have the ability to translate what they know about the business, the brand, the category, and the consumer to develop solid strategic positioning that can take a brand from good to great. So when it comes to positioning, I'm one part science and one part intuition (backed by consumer opinion, once developed). Add in a dash of innovative thinking, and you've got soup.

# Q: CAN A BRAND CAMPAIGN INCLUDE A CALL TO ACTION?

**JASON MILETSKY**
**THE AGENCY PERSPECTIVE**

First, let's just make sure that we're all on the same page in terms of what a brand campaign is. A brand campaign is an ongoing marketing effort meant to generate and raise awareness of a brand. It's not a one-time or short-lived promotion advertising an upcoming sale, a 3 a.m. infomercial prompting you to call to order some product, or an ad featuring coupons for discounts on upcoming purchases. Brand campaigns don't advertise events or anticipate immediate action; they work to keep the brand's name in the minds of consumers so that when the time does come for those consumers to make a purchase, the brand's products or services will be more seriously considered. It's the communication of a promise and/or personality and the building of trust through recognition. Two-page spreads in magazines that show a Ford truck sitting magnanimously on top of a mountain in front of a bright blue sky aren't trying to get readers to go purchase a car at that moment; they're working to keep Ford trucks in people's minds in a positive way. The same goes for the big Coors sign next to the scoreboard at the stadium and the TV commercial for Advil.

Now let's look at what we mean by call to action. A call to action is a line of copy that deliberately tries to get the audience to take an immediate or impending action. "Call now!" "This Wednesday only!" "Hurry on over for terrific savings!" "Free piece of crap you don't need to the first 100 buyers!" and other similar lines are typical calls to action (although they're not all quite that cheesy). These aren't branding campaigns because while they may build the brand over time, their main purpose is to encourage immediate action. Therefore, these fall into the category of direct-message marketing.

So let's get back to the question: Can a brand campaign include a call to action? Using my definition for call to action, the answer would have to be no. A brand can run distinct and simultaneous campaigns—one to spur immediate results and one to build the brand—but each will have a different set of campaign guidelines, utilize different media, and work to fulfill different goals accordingly.

This does not mean, however, that there isn't an *implied* call to action in brand campaigns. The implied call to action—and this becomes more true for larger, more expensive brands that are purchased less frequently—is to go to the brand's Web site for more information. This has become the new cycle for shopping: Take interest in a brand, visit their Web site, decide to make a purchase. Somebody thinking about buying a car may see that Ford ad—the one with the truck on the mountain—and then spend a few seconds looking them up online. The ad didn't need to tell them to do that; it's become a natural part of the purchasing cycle. So while brand campaigns don't include an obvious and blatant call to action, it's perfectly reasonable and expected to include a Web URL and/or phone number (usually quite small) somewhere in each ad to aid consumers in any further research they may do.

GENEVIEVE SMITH
THE BRAND PERSPECTIVE

I can think of instances where a purely brand campaign does not need to include an overt call to action. These include the following:

- **Introduction of a new brand:** The purpose of the campaign is to tell the public what the brand does and what it stands for, like introducing a new person at a party. The campaign creates an impression of who the brand is.

- **Introduction of a new product:** The purpose of the campaign is to tease the market with "coming soon" messages with the intention to create purchase consideration and anticipation for when the product launches.

- **Response to external environment (e.g., safety or regulatory):** The purpose of the campaign is to assuage concerns consumers may have about a brand because of the business they are in.

- **Doing good:** The purpose of the campaign is to show community-service or cause-related initiatives intended to provide a positive halo for the brand.

Aside from instances like these, I think a good brand campaign should include a call to action. A brand campaign may say "We are great," but it's not doing the brand much good unless the creative says *why* you should consider the brand and asks for the business, however subtly.

Most brands are highly focused on return on marketing investment (ROMI), measured primarily by sales. Therefore, the most practical way to do some branding work is to develop the creative with the brand at the middle across all mediums, even if it is a product campaign, so that the work reinforces both product sales and brand attributes.

# Q: WHAT'S THE MAIN FOCUS OF A BRAND CAMPAIGN: PERSONALITY, PROMISE, IMAGE, USP, OR SOMETHING ELSE ENTIRELY?

**JASON MILETSKY**
**THE AGENCY PERSPECTIVE**

One of the things I've really tried to avoid doing in this book is give a bull-shit "This is what I'm supposed to say, so I'll say it" kind of answer. There's enough of that in other books. I want to give firm answers that actually take a side, give an opinion, and provide an actual point of view so that even if some-one disagrees with me, I can't be blamed for being safe.

But there are situations where the safest answer is actually the right answer, and this is one of those situations. The answer is "all of the above," depending on the brand in question and the type of advertising vehicle being used. The key thing, of course, is to implant the brand name in the minds of the market. But differ-ent media vehicles give brands different opportunities, so messages may vary based on the method. Can a brand do more with TV than it can with print? Not necessarily—but it can do something *different*. Also, what the brand is, how it will likely be used, how long consumers take to decide whether to make a pur-chase, and what is likely to make the biggest impact on consumers are all factors that will play a role in how the brand is portrayed.

For example, Weight Watchers, Jenny Craig, and other diet companies have their own brand personalities (usually enthusiastic, energetic, young, etc.), but they usually market their brands based on the promise. That is, they show pic-tures of people before they started a weight-loss program and then show how thin those people are now, with them holding up a pair of their old pants as proof, talking about how easy the program was—you get the idea. It's not just a personality play. These brands aren't trying to reach people who may be heavy one day and will need a good diet plan when that happens; they need to get peo-ple who are already heavy to feel like they can accomplish their weight-loss goals, too. Brand personality will play a part, but it's the promise that's going to make the sale.

On the other hand, look at the TV spots for the Canon PowerShot camera with Maria Sharapova, the tennis player. If they say anything at all about the camera itself, I doubt anyone even notices. The information might be there, but the commercials really play up the brand personality. Hot girl, poolside, friends, a cute puppy…clearly they're not going for the geriatric market. They're going for a specific audience and tapping into it primarily through the personality of the brand.

Finally, take a look at air fresheners and the messages they market for themselves (as a single guy living alone, I don't think I've ever actually bought an air freshener, but their TV commercials can help me make my point). One brand promotes itself as the longest lasting, another touts how attractive it will look in your home while making it smell great, another sells itself as being disguised in a candle, while yet another promotes the funky puff of smoke that shows it's still working every few seconds. They understand that you can't smell their products on TV, so they sell themselves based mostly on what makes them unique.

In each of these examples (and keep in mind, I've only touched on TV advertising, not print, radio, or other marketing vehicles), the brands in question led with what works best for them and would be most likely to have an impact with their market. But that doesn't mean that other factors of the brand didn't play a role. The air fresheners may lead with what makes them unique, but they still demonstrate their personality in each spot they produce. Diet plans might promote themselves on the promise, but each finds a way to point out what makes them different from competing brands as well. It's never just a cut-and-dried formula. Brands create their own unique mixture of messaging based on the market, needs, and other factors.

GENEVIEVE SMITH
THE BRAND PERSPECTIVE

Not to be sarcastic, but the focus of a brand campaign is the *brand*. Brands are asked to support a large number of products and to make these products look distinctive and have value. In addition, the brand itself must have depth and substance. It must stand for something. So any campaign needs to tell the story of the brand while at the same time supporting the sale of products and working to continually evolve the brand's image through communications as the world around it changes.

I'm not a fan of purely branding creative work, as with a few notable exceptions—like the ad announcing the launch of Macintosh during the 1984 Super Bowl (which ran only once but is still talked about more than two decades later)—I have not seen this done very well.

This isn't just about creative; it's also about media. How will the campaign reach employees? How will it relate in populist media like wild tags and street postings, on the Internet, in the store, through direct channels, and in mass media? We ask a lot of a campaign in today's marketplace—and here I go harping on the same theme, but if the brand story is strong and the campaign work is distinctive in both creative and media, all this can be done—and very well at that. Who's the best? For my taste it is Apple.

# Q: WHAT ARE THE MOST EFFECTIVE WAYS OF GETTING CONSUMERS INVOLVED WITH THE BRAND?

JASON MILETSKY
THE AGENCY PERSPECTIVE

↳ Getting consumers involved with the brand is often a matter of being creative and taking advantage of the right opportunities. I think one of the best examples I've seen is Charmin's New York City restrooms, which opened in Times Square in late 2008. Charmin saw an opportunity in New York City, which is known to be unfriendly to people when nature calls (there are few—if any—decent public restrooms, and practically no store or restaurant will let non-customers use their facilities), putting up 20 restrooms on Broadway for people to use as needed. They're free, they're clean, and they're comfortable—and of course, everyone who uses one gets a chance to use Charmin toilet paper, be exposed to their marketing messages, and walk away feeling good about the product for giving them what was probably some much-needed relief. For Charmin, it's not only a great PR opportunity, it's a brilliant way of getting consumers directly involved with their brand. They saw an opportunity, approached it creatively, and took the concept of grocery-store sampling to a whole new level.

Clearly, not every brand is going to have the budget or opportunity to pull off something as large and expensive as Charmin's NYC bathrooms. But that does not mean brand managers who keep an open mind to new ideas can't use other creative methods.

With social media, the Web provides another great (and, for many brands, more realistic) forum for getting consumers involved with a brand. (Keep in mind, this is about involvement with the brand—not necessarily direct involvement with the product.) For example, any number of brands have run successful online contests in which they have asked entrants to upload pictures or videos of themselves using their products, with the winner being the individual with the funniest or most creative upload. Blogs are another way of creating interaction by providing commentary on brand-specific topics and letting consumers voice their opinion through comments.

No matter how you do it, one of the keys to gaining market share is getting new consumers interacting with your brand and keeping current customers continuing their interaction. The Web offers tons of opportunities for interaction, and a little creativity can go a long way toward keeping people engaged.

GENEVIEVE SMITH
THE BRAND PERSPECTIVE

My experience leads me to believe it is a combination of three primary elements, working together, that causes consumers to get involved with a brand:

- The first, most basic element is a compelling, consumer-driven brand proposition. Without this, you can market and advertise and create promotions that will cause sales (and sometimes, this is all a company wants to do) but you will not create brand loyalists.

- The second element is employees who are committed to the brand and who live the brand in all their consumer interactions. I spoke about this earlier, but it's worth mentioning again as it is so key to consumer engagement. Really great brands know they are only as good as each and every interaction a consumer has with their employees.

- Third, you need to have products and services that people want to buy and use and that are reasonably priced. If these are no good, then forget it.

So those three key elements—proposition, employees, and value—are the basics. Then there is the way you go to market and interact with consumers. Let's loosely call this "the toolbox." It includes

- Great distribution in terms of location and facility design (assuming the company oversees physical locations)

- Effective Web presence with a site that consumers find easy to use for both finding information and buying goods

- Compelling advertising and relevant marketing

- Community involvement and values

From my perspective, if your company is good in these areas, consumers will involve themselves with your brand.

# Q: HOW DOES BRAND ADVERTISING DIFFER FROM DIRECT ADVERTISING?

JASON MILETSKY

THE AGENCY PERSPECTIVE

Direct advertising is about as straightforward as marketing can get. These are the commercials that shout, "On sale this Saturday only!" and "Call and order within the next 30 minutes, and we'll include a useless piece of crap absolutely free!" They're the one-color, boxed-in ads shouting the names and phone numbers of local accountants, dentists, and attorneys on the placemats of small diners and local pizzerias. Direct advertising is basically any ad effort that disregards the brand personality, doesn't bother trying to make any sort of emotional connect with its audience, and uses its time or space to send a very specific, typically flat message about who they are, what they do, how much they cost, what they sell, and when a special event (such as a big sale) will be taking place. They say what they need to say as directly as possible.

Agencies rarely like to do these kinds of ads because they're usually devoid of anything resembling creativity and have about as much energy as a Steven Wright stand-up routine (although that may be a bad example because that dude is hilarious). They also tend to be pretty cheap to produce, and usually run in smaller, cheaper media outlets (which means there's less money in it for us). But while they may be boring, direct ads do play an important role for many companies—particularly smaller companies or retail chains that cater strictly to a highly targeted and/or local audience, and are more interested in generating short-term revenue than long-term ROI. These marketers need consumers who are ready to spend money immediately.

Brand advertising, on the other hand, usually involves a more long-term strategy. It plays up the personality of the brand and seeks to forge an emotional connection with its market in an effort to increase recognition and trust, which can later turn into sales and possibly even loyalty. Brand advertising very often revolves around a creative concept that sends a message in a more clever way without trying to pressure consumers to make an immediate purchase. Look at the AFLAC duck or the classic "Aaron Burr" spot in the "Got Milk" campaign.

(That's the one where the guy eating a peanut-butter sandwich misses out on his chance to win a radio contest because he doesn't have any milk on hand to wash down the peanut butter and as a result can't answer the question posed by the deejay.) The brand is being built through clever, creative messaging that increases recognition and leverages the brand personality rather than flatly stating benefits.

In many cases, direct advertising and brand advertising can be a tag-team of sorts. A grocery-store chain, such as Shoprite, is likely to run direct advertising to get local audiences into their stores (by promoting upcoming sales price specials, etc.), while the brands they stock will run more brand-centric campaigns designed to build trust and compel the consumer to buy their products once in the store.

The line between direct advertising and brand advertising isn't always totally clear. The definitions I've given are the extremes; there is plenty of gray area in between. For example, Macy's runs TV and print ads for upcoming sales that have very direct messaging but at the same time build up a brand personality and create the emotional connection that they clearly rely on to maintain brand loyalty and reach their market. Automotive manufacturers often do the same, running ads that promote rebates or special pricing while also building the brand personality (and leaving the more hard-core direct advertising duties to the local dealerships).

GENEVIEVE SMITH
THE BRAND PERSPECTIVE

By definition, direct advertising generally has a measurable call to action whereby the advertiser can track the results of an offer and thereby measure the ROI of the campaign. It can be managed to a science using test and control methodology. This method facilitates predictable sales results for the marketing investment. Generally, the media used for direct advertising are direct mail, e-mail, online advertising, print, direct TV (and some radio), and coupons. This advertising will include limited-time offers that prompt the consumer to call, click, or come in to receive the offer. The advertiser measures the response rate against the investment made (including offer, advertising, and fulfillment) to generate the ROI analytics.

In contrast, brand advertising speaks about the company, its products, and its services, but may not include a specific offer or any predictable short-term way to measure the results in terms of direct sales made for the investment. Generally, the media used for brand advertising are TV, out of home, radio, sometimes print, and online advertising. If the brand includes a distribution network, the in-store merchandising can also include brand advertising. Brand advertising also includes experiential marketing that generates buzz for the brand and PR. There are multiple ways to measure the ROI on brand advertising, including tracking the effect the advertising has on brand attributes, awareness, and consideration. When all these are expanding, you know your advertising is supporting the growth of the brand.

At WaMu, we built a very sophisticated analytic model called Marketing Mix Modeling (MMM) to evaluate ROI for non-direct marketing mediums. It took us about three years to complete, as the data collection was quite complex and had to run a few cycles to provide results. What MMM did was differentiate between economic conditions, competitor actions, pricing, advertising, direct advertising, distribution, and many more elements in order to isolate the contribution of media like TV, print, and radio, which are not measurable on a direct basis. You can also build test and control markets wherein everything except mass advertising is static in order to measure the lift received from brand advertising as it works with the other forms of advertising.

Note that while they are different, direct and brand advertising work in concert with each other. Figuring out the optimum mix for a company's products and service in order to guide the investment in brand advertising versus direct advertising, however, takes time.

# Q: Do Brands Need to Be Marketed Differently Depending on Their Stage of Life? For Example, Do New Brands Need to Be Handled Differently from Well-Established Brands?

Jason Miletsky
The Agency Perspective

You wouldn't take a newborn to shop in the men's section—and you shouldn't market a new brand the same way you would an established one. Both the messaging and the theme behind any marketing efforts should be determined by how familiar your audience is with your brand and what their expectations will be if they get involved with your brand.

The message or purpose of a campaign is the idea it is trying to convey. General messages may be used to establish or underscore the brand promise, with the objective of increasing recognition of the brand name. The message behind a marketing campaign could be something like, "We provide the healthiest recipes of any cooking site on the Web" or "Be part of a more elite community of consumers by purchasing our brand." Usually these messages are not articulated as bluntly as that, however; rather, they're communicated more subtly through imagery and copy. Other messages might be less brand-oriented and more direct. These types of message might be intended to highlight one specific idea or promotion, such as "Half-price Wednesdays now through Christmas" or "Refer a friend to our Web site and receive a $50 gift certificate with his or her first purchase."

Thematically, concepts in advertising and marketing support the message, establish the personality of a brand, and make the brand more attractive to one audience versus another. Conceptual approaches particularly rely on a theme, which usually evolves over time and is consistent throughout various media. Popular concepts have included the Geico cavemen, the MasterCard "Priceless" campaign, the Energizer Bunny campaign, and the infamous "Got Milk" campaign—considered by many to be one of the greatest advertising campaigns ever. Direct messages tend to not confuse their messages with brand-oriented concepts, but rather show products, people, buildings, or other appropriate images to support their point.

What the message should be, and whether or not it's presented with a clever campaign or product-driven imagery and copy points, often depends on where the brand is in its life cycle. The younger and less well-known a brand is, the more direct its messaging needs to be. As a brand becomes more universally recognized and trusted, its messaging can be less direct and its approach more conceptual.

The following table provides a general overview for effective messaging at different points within the brand life cycle.

| Stages of the Brand | Appropriate Actions/Messaging |
| --- | --- |
| **Stage 1:** Brand infancy (Little to no brand recognition.) | Campaign should focus on establishing the brand and building name recognition. |
| | Explain the brand promise. |
| | Make the USP obvious. |
| | Concept should be clear so as not to obscure the message. |
| | More marketing dollars should be spent to ensure a Web site is solid, functional, and beneficial to its audience. |
| **Stage 2:** Brand elevation (Base market established, increasing recognition, and expanding growth. Trust in USP taking the brand is growing.) | Message should reinforce the brand, continuing to seek heightened brand recognition. |
| | Benefits of the brand should be highlighted, with the center stage in most efforts. |
| | Concept should be clear, although if research has shown that the company or product already is familiar to the core audience, the concept can begin to show more of the brand personality. |
| **Stage 3:** Brand maturity (Significant brand recognition either in a general market or among its desired market demographic. Trust is well established.) | Message can stray from mere brand recognition to particular aspects of the brand, product, or Web site. |
| | If research indicates that the USP has been understood and accepted by the market, then the message can promote aspects of the brand other than the USP. |
| | Concept can be largely personality driven, with heavy creative elements. |
| | Campaigns should revisit basic brand recognition (as outlined in Stage 1) if direction of the brand changes. |
| | Marketing to current customers should be a primary focus. |

GENEVIEVE SMITH
THE BRAND PERSPECTIVE

↳ Yes, brands need to be marketed differently depending on their stage of life. Generally speaking, you can think of it like this: Established brands *stand* for something in consumer's minds. If the company is happy with its position and reputation in the marketplace, then the job of marketing is to reinforce this position—in other words, reaffirm, defend, keep it fresh, expand its reach, etc. But if an established brand is unhappy with its position, has suffered a PR or other setback, is being overtaken by competition, or is becoming irrelevant to its market, then the job of marketing is to carefully reposition the brand. I say "carefully" because even if a company is facing one or more of the challenges I mentioned, there will still be a pool of consumers who like the brand the way it always was, and they will need to be coaxed along and kept loyal to what was appealing to them. Also, a radical change can look desperate, and can seem very jarring to consumers in general. It's better to keep what's still good and build on those components or attributes than to attempt to become something new overnight, as generally that won't ring true to consumers.

Marketing supports a new brand in different ways. First, it is used to launch the brand in the marketplace. That means introducing the brand, its products, and its value, as it is unknown. It's akin to introducing someone new at an event. No one knows this individual; who are they? Once the new brand is launched, marketing will continue to define the brand as this is not yet established. At the same time, marketing will work very hard to create market share and customers for the company, as growth will be very important to ensuring the business makes it. This is not to say an established brand doesn't need marketing to create growth; it does. But during this phase, with no proven marketing models and start-up financial pressure, there will be a lot of attention and focus on marketing.

As an aside I also think it's marketing's role, regardless of the brand life stage, to continually lead the brand forward and keep it fresh and vibrant. No one can rest on their laurels.

# Q: • HOW DOES THE MARKETING • STRATEGY GET BUILT?

JASON MILETSKY
THE AGENCY PERSPECTIVE

↳  Time, talk, and a lot of coffee. (Well, a lot of Diet Pepsi for me.) Nobody should expect the process to be quick or easy, but it can definitely be fun! This is where each and every brand manager or marketing director gets to be a general for a little while. In fact, I've known plenty of brand managers who have a space they call the war room, where they go to brainstorm on their market strategy. And a war room is exactly what it is—piles of magazines, papers strewn around haphazardly, volumes of ideas scribbled on dry-erase boards, walls covered with oversized Post-It notes, and marketing geniuses wandering in and out, jacked up on a case of Red Bull (having not slept for 48 hours) and mumbling to incoherently to themselves. These are the times when you remember why you got into branding and marketing to begin with!

This might not be the scene in every brand and agency, but it's pretty common. One of the most interesting things about this industry is that it's packed with creative types, all with their own ways of finding inspiration. But no matter how individual people might go about developing their market strategies, there are some baselines I think should be followed to create a workable and effective strategy:

1. I believe that strategies don't work as well when the agency and brand build them together. Quality brainstorming can only happen when everyone in the room feels free to bounce around ideas, no matter how stupid they are—and also feel free to shoot down someone else's ideas when they're no good. That just can't happen when agencies and brands tackle the initial brainstorm together. Instead, the brand should tell the agency the budget they have to work with and let the agency then go about doing their work.

2. Knowing the budget they have to work within and the brand in question, the agency should start eliminating media outlets that don't make sense. For some brands, television may simply be too expensive for their budget or may not be the right vehicle for them even if they could afford it.

3. With the media vehicles that are not possibilities out of the way, the agency then needs to consider what's left and start to peel away methods that seem less viable based on the market, money, and message. These early decisions should be made with a mixture of common sense (based on knowledge of the audience and the brand) and preliminary research on the pricing, reach, and timing of each method.

4. With respect to the outlets remaining on the table, the strategic minds at the agency should talk about what makes the most sense and what will gain the brand the greatest yardage toward its goals. These decisions need to be based on research and cost analyses of each avenue in the mix and should consider the potential results based on how the budget is divided among these marketing outlets.

5. With a first pass at the strategy completed (this doesn't need to be crazy detailed yet), the agency should present their preliminary strategy to the client. It should be clear, show the process the agency went through to arrive at the strategy, and provide a compelling rationale for why this strategy is being recommended.

6. At this point, with a plan to act as the foundation, the brand and the agency can start brainstorming together. The marketing minds on the brand side will like part of the plan and want to change others, and together, the brand and the agency can come up with a new version of the strategy that everyone believes in.

7. With the mutually blessed plan, the agency must do the detail work, get it approved by the brand, and get started on executing everything.

These are obviously broad strokes. In real life, there are smaller steps between each of the steps I've outlined here. But there's enough here to make it clear on what to tackle as you get the strategic planning effort underway. You may even find that steps 2 and 3 blend together and that you already have a pretty clear idea of the general direction you want to take as soon as the need for a strategic plan comes up. However you go about it, this can be one of the most exciting, challenging, exasperating. and fulfilling parts of the brand-building process.

**GENEVIEVE SMITH**
**THE BRAND PERSPECTIVE**

I believe the marketing strategy should be built off of the business strategy. It can't be built in a vacuum. Marketing may have certain strategic objectives particular to the discipline that they will include in the strategy to be more effective, such as upgrades to talent, agencies, support systems, creative designs, and new functionality. But in the main, marketing is not a line of business. It's an investment the business decides to make because of the return relative to other investments that could be made.

Once the business strategy is articulated, it's the role of marketing to use their expertise to create programs that support the business. These can generally be thought of as strategic, as they will be high-level objectives or recommendations not yet translated into the detail of the annual marketing plan.

An example of a strategic marketing direction is the decision to be a direct advertiser versus a mass advertiser. At WaMu, one of our lines of business was the credit-card group, which had built a veritable marketing machine fueled by direct marketing alone. They could control the machine for quality and results across account generation, receivables management, and collections (which is essentially what that business is) through formidable DM expertise. In the Chief Marketing Officer organization, we wanted to expand the brand by mass-advertising our credit cards in order to have brand proof points for the breadth of product we offered beyond free checking. Well, my colleagues in the cards group had zero interest in building the brand or experimenting with media they didn't believe would work for managing their business. They very nicely allowed us to produce a few spots (although they wouldn't pay for running them), but as they saw little to no lift in their business by running TV advertising, they would not change or expand their strategic marketing direction beyond the direct marketing machine. So the card group's strategic marketing direction/platform was direct marketing; underneath that platform were multiple tactical programs that used mail, Internet, e-mail, and statements, all of which were the pillars for the annual marketing plan.

It is helpful when the business has a long-term—at least five-year—plan to key off of in creating the marketing strategy. I realize five years is a long horizon, and many things—even the fundamental profit streams—can change dramatically in a much shorter time frame. But marketing strategy generally operates best when there are relatively long-term core objectives articulated by the business because some marketing programs build over time. (This is particularly true with direct-marketing models.) Others, however, can be operated with fast turnaround, such as quick, in-store campaigns or rate advertising, which are not strategic.

# Q: • Is Television Necessary • for Building a Brand?

Jason Miletsky
The Agency Perspective

Of course not. Television is a great way to get a brand noticed by a lot of people over a large geographic area in a highly targeted way. And there's no denying that not only can TV spots help get the brand name and message ingrained in the minds of the market, but they probably have more power to establish a brand personality than any other marketing medium. With TV, a brand can send a message, raise awareness, create an emotional connection, start a buzz, and drive people to take action—all within a single 30-second spot (well, a really well-done 30-second spot, anyway...).

But to use TV as the single distinguishing factor between what is a brand and what is not a brand, or whether or not a brand can be successful, is to both underestimate the usefulness of other media and misinterpret what a brand actually is. TV advertising is only one element that can be used to determine whether or not a company, product, or service can be considered a brand. The truth is, there are brands all around us, all the time, and only a small percentage have the budget or need to advertise on television.

Consider companies that strictly market their products or services to other companies. B2B brands spend serious amounts of money to reach their audiences— companies such as AmerisourceBergen and Dendrite, which market their distribution services to pharmaceutical companies, and ADP and Ceridian, which market their payroll services to accountants and any company with employees. For most companies like these, television would be a waste of their budget. They're trying to reach a highly targeted audience of specific decision-makers, not the general public, most of whom would have no connection to their brand or ability to sign off on a purchase. For these companies, online and print advertising, direct mail, trade-show marketing, and public relations are more efficient and cost-effective ways of building their brand.

The same goes for B2C brands: While many rely on television advertising to support the national distribution of their products (such as major-label apparel, home goods, or food or beverage brands), television isn't the only way to reach large audiences. Nobody can deny that rock bands like Kiss, Aerosmith, or Metallica are brands in their own right, having built a worldwide market hungry for anything new they produce—and none of these would point to television as the main reason for their growth and popularity. Radio, live public performances, in-store promotions, and great PR were clearly the main factors behind their success. Smaller brands that rely more on a local market might also avoid television as well, as may brands that rely strictly on an online audience. Amazon, MySpace, Wikipedia, and Google have all built amazing brands without having to rely much—if at all—on television.

The trick to building a brand through marketing is not to get caught up in the allure and romance of television advertising and simply run TV spots for the sake of running TV spots (read: for the sake of stroking your ego). The best way to build a brand is to be realistic about who your audience is and where they can be found, and to determine the best media mix to reach them given your available budget.

GENEVIEVE SMITH
THE BRAND PERSPECTIVE

Although in many categories, using television to build a brand is desirable, as well as the fastest and easiest approach, it is not mandatory. Some brands that do not use television but have done great brand work include the following:

- **Altoids:** Altoids used some very creative out-of-home and print vehicles to introduce and promote their "curiously strong mints."

- **Mini Cooper:** Like Altoids, Mini Cooper also used great out-of-home concepts, very clever experiential displays, and attention-getting 3D techniques to promote their brand. Plus, they let it be known that annual production of the car was limited.

- **Google:** Google became the only game in a new town by providing the most reliable search engine on the planet, and thus became more than a product—it became a verb.

- **Starbucks:** Starbucks leveraged their distribution and store experience to build a brand while making the $4 dollar cup of coffee an almost mandatory fixture in consumers' lives.

None of these firms put one dime into television advertising. They built their brands through superiority of product concept, first-to-market position, alternative media, strong creative, and distribution. These are good examples of the product or the concept being so far superior or differentiated as to build the brand in and of itself. This stands in contrast to the more traditional approach of investing heavily in television advertising to foster awareness and recognition.

Television advertising is also infrequently used in the very high end or luxury category. It's simply not targeted enough to the people who can afford the purchase. Likewise, margins on highly commoditized day-to-day products may not allow for the cost of television advertising. Instead these may rely on techniques like price and in-store promotions to generate sales.

# Q: • HOW HAS THE INTERNET CHANGED • THE WAY BRANDS GET MARKETED?

**JASON MILETSKY**
**THE AGENCY PERSPECTIVE**

Recently, I had a B2B client get upset with my agency because the print ad and direct-mail campaign we ran for them didn't make their phone ring. We pointed out that although new potential customers weren't calling them for more info, traffic to their Web site had spiked considerably during the campaign. (We didn't design or develop the site, by the way, but we did have access to the traffic analytics.) They didn't care. Traffic to their site wasn't what they wanted; they wanted their phone to ring.

Well, I would like a date with Heidi Klum, but that ain't gonna happen, either. The new reality is that the purchasing cycle has been forever altered by the Internet. The Web has become such a large part of everyday life that consumers rarely make a purchase directly after receiving a marketing message. The Web is often the intermediate step that consumers take before deciding to make a purchase, for reasons that could include any of the following:

- To make sure that a company is legitimate. If they don't know the brand, consumers will typically want to make sure the company behind it is reputable before making a purchase. Consumers are wary of most marketing efforts and are often skeptical of messages sent directly from brands—especially lesser-known ones—and Web research gives them added comfort.

- To see what other people have to say about their experiences with a brand.

- To get more detailed information about a brand than they might have been able to discern from an advertisement.

The amount of research that consumers conduct on a brand prior to purchase tends to increase in parallel with the price of the product or service being considered. People rarely engage in significant research before buying low-cost items like toothpaste or gum. But larger, less-common, and more-expensive purchases like vacations, furniture, and cars will be researched more heavily. Also, people making a business-to-business purchase are especially likely to do heavy Web research prior to beginning a relationship with and making a purchase from a company.

For some brands, it's a simple matter of providing information, retaining users, and enticing them to come back for future visits. The goal here is to make sure the site represents the brand in a positive manner and accurately reflects the brand's promise and personality (as well as the offline marketing creative). For brands that take advantage of e-commerce functionality, the challenges are a bit more daunting. Why do people shop online? What are the benefits and drawbacks when compared to traditional, in-store shopping? Marketers need to understand the pros and cons from the perspective of the shopper before undertaking an e-commerce effort.

For many, the pros of online shopping include the following:

- **Convenience:** According to Nielson research, 81 percent of all online shoppers cited convenience as their number-one reason for shopping online. Convenience goes beyond being able to shop in one's pajamas; it includes being able to shop at any time of day, not having to wait in lines, and not having to push through crowds. In 2008, as gas prices soared past $4 per gallon in most parts of the U.S., convenience also included driving less and saving on gas.

- **Not being bothered:** One of the more annoying parts of shopping is being interrupted by pushy salespeople. This can be avoided by shopping online.

- **Online reviews:** As more online stores add social-media components, shoppers can read what other consumers think of a product before making a purchase as well as leave their own opinion for others.

- **Easy comparison shopping:** Online shopping enables consumers to compare prices and features between retailers far more quickly than they could by going from store to store. Some sites have been established to provide comparison-shopping services for consumers, saving shoppers even more time.

- **Less expensive:** In most cases, retailers would prefer that consumers purchase online, as it helps to reduce the retailer's overhead (fewer salespeople means less salary expense). To help promote online shopping, many retailers offer reduced prices for online purchases. This has been particularly successful in the travel industry.

- **Personalized selection:** When a consumer makes a purchase in a store, that typically is the end of the transaction. The next time that person comes to the same store, the salespeople are not likely to remember that shopper's purchasing habits. In contrast, online searching and buying habits can be tracked, stored, and used to offer a more personalized selection.

- **Wider selection:** Retail stores have limited shelf space, so they need to limit the selection they offer. Because Web retailers don't have to contend with shelf-space issues, they can offer a wider selection. Plus, if one site doesn't offer what a consumer wants, that consumer can broaden his or her selection by visiting other sites.

- **No sales tax:** Most states do not charge sales tax for online purchases (although this is changing in some states). This makes it less expensive to buy products online.

- **Historical order record:** If shoppers lose their receipts after a purchase from a traditional retailer, they are typically out of luck—especially if they used cash. When purchases are made online, however, a historical record is kept.

Marketers also need to have a solid understanding of the aspects of online shopping that consumers might view as drawbacks to purchasing. These can include the following:

- **Shipping payments:** Online shoppers typically incur a shipping charge, which they would not have to pay if shopping in a store (except for large purchases, such as furniture). Shipping can be fairly pricey—and the quicker the shipping, the more expensive it usually is.

- **Delivery wait time:** Online shoppers usually have to accept a lag time in receipt of material. Depending on how much they are willing to pay, consumers may have to wait anywhere from 24 hours to a month or more before they get their purchases. This is far different from the immediate gratification that shoppers get when they shop in a store and can take their purchases home with them.

- **Lack of a non-cash payment option:** Cash is not an option for online shoppers, who must pay via credit card or through other non-cash methods.

- **Inability to experience:** There is a big difference between touching, feeling, tasting, wearing, and trying products prior to purchase, and simply looking at their picture and reading about them. Online shopping does not give the consumer the ability to try on clothes, smell perfume, or feel the texture of a pair of pants before buying, which heavily reduces the product experience.

- **Lack of trust:** Although online transactions are largely secure, online shoppers need to trust that their private information will not be stolen by hackers or sold by the retailer. In the case of lesser-known sites, customers need to trust that they will receive their purchases in the time guaranteed. (And in some cases, customers have to worry about whether they will receive their purchase at all.)

- **Wider selection:** How can a wider selection be both a pro and a con? While wider selections give shoppers more to choose from, the additional choices can be overwhelming. Traditional retailers, with their limited shelf space, do part of the selection work for consumers by offering only the best products available from manufacturers. This helps reduce consumers' confusion and saves them time.

- **Unsocial:** With social media, online shoppers have the ability to interact with other people by leaving comments on products, writing and responding to blog entries, etc. That is still a far different social experience from shopping with friends and interacting with others in real life.

- **Lack of assistance:** Although salespeople at traditional retailers can be intrusive, they are also available when shoppers have a question. Even e-commerce sites that have online chat (and not all do) would have a hard time providing the same level of service as traditional stores with in-person salespeople.

Brands need to have a full and complete understanding of their consumers—who they are, what they want, and what they'll respond to—if they want to make the best use of the Web. The Internet has changed the way people interact with a brand—how the brand and its consumers communicate with each other—and it's made each brand's Web site the center of the universe for finding deeper and more relevant information when it comes to deciding whether or not to buy.

GENEVIEVE SMITH
THE BRAND PERSPECTIVE

In the most traditional sense, the Internet has become another marketing channel. Most brands use it in the media mix for advertising, to fulfill, or to communicate information. And most everyone has a Web site plus some form of search-engine optimization, link strategy, or display advertising programs that supplement traditional media buys. What money cannot buy is viral marketing, which is highly desirable when it comes to leveraging the Internet—that is, if the opinions are positive!

I think what has changed from the media perspective is the capability of a product or brand to gain almost instant recognition and ubiquity through smart use of display, search, link, and affiliate networks. Another thing that has changed is the respect that the Internet user expects to receive from marketers. There is a fine art to Internet advertising and marketing in terms of relevancy so as to not be intrusive or annoying. And this goes beyond the virtual mute button; it means don't do it. Communities are another big deal. We saw some major U.S. brands join Second Life when it first launched, but because the community simply did not want them there, the results were somewhat disastrous. I think there is still much to be learned in terms of what a commercial brand can do online, how it may be accepted, and what constitutes "good marketing" on the Internet.

# Q: SHOULD BRAND STRATEGIES FOR INTERNET MARKETING AND TRADITIONAL MARKETING BE SEPARATE OR INTEGRATED?

JASON MILETSKY

THE AGENCY PERSPECTIVE

For the life of me, I can't understand why clients continue to keep Internet marketing strategies separate from more traditional, general strategies. I get why this was the case back in the '90s, and the Web was brand new; clients didn't yet see the true value of Internet marketing, and the older, established agencies had no clue how the Web worked. The general fear of the Internet during that period made sense. But even though we're rounding out the first decade of the 2000s, not that much has changed in the way some clients handle their Web marketing. Yes, they all get that they need a site, and that the site has to be a serious reflection of their brand. Most even understand that they need to have an Internet strategy in place, whether that means planning out how to build and evolve their site, adding streaming-video components, blogging, including CPC advertising, implementing e-mail marketing, or something else. But it still seems like most clients insist on separating these efforts from more traditional strategies the way a kid tries to keep the peas on his plate from touching the mashed potatoes.

I'm not saying a single agency needs to be at the helm of each and every effort. Clearly, different agencies have different strengths and these should be leveraged properly. But as hard as it might be, I think agencies must force themselves to play nice and develop strategies together. There's no longer any question about the magnitude of the Internet's importance to marketing; what seems to remain in question by many brands is how many new avenues the Internet opens for finding and capturing new audiences. It's not just about building a great site; it's about driving the right traffic to it, keeping them there, encouraging them to take the desired action, and enticing them to return.

The danger is in the potential for a disconnect. Not everything will just automatically work together. Like trying to retrofit a turntable to play CDs, getting a site or entire Internet strategy to work in sync with a traditional marketing strategy could be inefficient and seemingly forced or, worse, simply not possible.

Setting the general strategy first and then forcing the Internet strategy to comply underscores the naïveté of brands that have yet to grasp the Net's complexities.

In an ideal world, brands would develop a single strategy that simultaneously considers both traditional and Internet efforts in a somewhat layered fashion, sharing concepts in the online and offline space so that there's consistency in creative, design, and messaging. Brands should also consider the potential actions of consumers as they are exposed to various marketing efforts, the likelihood that they will (encouraged or on their own) visit the brand's site for more information, and how that reaction will be managed. By doing this, brands can fully exploit the power of all media outlets rather than concentrating on the strengths of traditional strategies and potentially weakening their Internet strategy.

**GENEVIEVE SMITH**

**THE BRAND PERSPECTIVE**

↳ My bias is that Internet and traditional marketing need to be completely integrated. The consumer is going to interact with one brand, regardless of channel, and it creates a disconnected experience if there isn't linkage between all marketing media and channels of distribution.

A few years back, companies in a wide variety of categories experimented with managing their Internet efforts separately from their offline efforts. Generally, this was done to avoid channel conflict, because many times traditional channels felt the Internet would cannibalize their customers and sales. There was a lot of chatter and the general opinion, if you remember, was that the Internet would be the death of physical distribution. Funny how that didn't happen. What *did* happen was that the Internet empowered the consumer (which I'll talk about a bit later on) in terms of shopping how they want as well as informing themselves prior to shopping.

In the mind of the consumer, they should be able to navigate seamlessly between online and offline channels. For this reason, brand strategy needs to be fully integrated, centered around the brand (which is how consumers see us) in order to be effective.

# Q: • IS BLOGGING GOOD FOR THE BRAND?
# • OR IS IT TOO DANGEROUS?

---

What's your perspective on this question?
Let us know at PerspectivesOnBranding.com.

---

**JASON MILETSKY**
**THE AGENCY PERSPECTIVE**

 Blogging can be great for a brand, but like anything else when it comes to marketing, you have to do it the right way. This means having a full understanding of blogs and the blogosphere. So at the risk of being terribly long-winded, I want to use this question (since it might be my only chance in this book) to talk in detail about the pros and cons of blogging and to offer tips on how to run a successful blog.

While blogs have inspired millions of individuals to tap into their inner writer, blogs offer far more than simply a personal creative outlet. For businesses, blogs offer an opportunity to reach new and larger audiences in a unique way. For all companies, blogging provides opportunities that other online and offline marketing tools do not:

■ **Easy provision of information:** Updating a blog does not require a highly coordinated effort. In fact, the only real time commitment is the time it takes to create the content. Compared to other forms of marketing communication such as print ads or brochures, which need to go through significant quality-control checks, blogging is a relatively uncomplicated form of wide-scale communications.

■ **Establishing a more human voice:** Most companies speak to their audience through a variety of marketing materials such as brochures, Web sites, radio ads, and TV ads. Each of these is designed to deliver a specific message in marketing language that's carefully crafted but hardly conversational.

Corporate blogs, however, give companies an opportunity to break away from traditional marketing language and speak to consumers directly using a more informal tone. This helps to humanize the brand, making it easier to forge an emotional connection with the audience. Corporate blogs still need to maintain some semblance of their brand voice, but blogging provides significantly more room for relaxed communication than almost any other method of marketing.

- **Increased credibility:** Because corporate blogs give marketers the opportunity to support their products in their own words while allowing reader feedback, blogs can increase a brand's credibility with its audience. Product and service claims made in mass-media advertising are traditionally met with a degree of skepticism by the market because they're viewed as having a single purpose: to sell. A blog, however, gives the brand the opportunity to communicate with its market with a different purpose in mind: to inform. This may come through blog posts that establish the author (a representative of the brand) as a thought leader or expert in a given field, in turn engendering market trust and credibility with consumers.

- **Marketing-campaign support:** Large-scale marketing campaigns that use a variety of media outlets are typically centered on a unifying theme and promote a message from the brand to its audience. Often, large campaigns incorporate an online component that includes a campaign-based Web site (separate from the brand's standard corporate site). The addition of a blog lets the brand further promote the campaign, explain the concept behind it, and involve the audience in the campaign by soliciting reader opinions.

- **Improved customer service:** Customer service is central to any company that needs to maintain long-term relationships with customers. But because it is an expensive endeavor that doesn't translate directly into increased revenue, many companies see customer-service programs as a necessary evil and often do what they can to decrease the cost of customer service (potentially resulting in poor quality and unhappy customers). Blogs are an inexpensive and effective way for companies to improve their customer service by enabling businesses to proactively tackle issues they know will be problematic and giving customers a forum to ask questions that brand representatives can discuss in a public setting.

- **Opportunities to draw a new audience:** By promoting a blog through traditional marketing, tags, and listings in blog search engines, corporations can draw audiences they might not otherwise be able to attract. Blogs often include links to other company Web pages to drive traffic to specific areas of the main site for more information or to other pages where products can be purchased.

Clearly, there's a good case to be made for blogging being a benefit to a brand. And while I'm a fan of blogging as part of a marketing strategy, in fairness, I also have to let you in on the potential dangers. As I've mentioned, branding is about building trust. Making mistakes when blogging can be potentially harmful and, if egregious enough, irreversibly damaging to this trust.

■ **Lying:** People see blogs as honest expressions of opinions and experience. They may vehemently disagree with the opinions that a blog editor expresses —and will say so in comments—but at the very least they believe those opinions are honest. Marketers, however, sometimes create fake blogs, or flogs, in support of their campaign efforts. Flogs are established to trick people into believing that the opinions and stories they are reading are true when in fact the posts are purely marketing-driven content written for the sole purpose of promoting a brand and its products. This can backfire dramatically. Blog readers don't like to be fooled and will hold the brand accountable for lying. Very often, if the brand that is perpetrating the deception is big enough, they can be persecuted in the media and the blogosphere will spread the word throughout the Web, potentially harming the brand image. I'm not talking about blogs that are clearly fictional. There's nothing wrong, for example, with Batman having his own blog in support of a campaign to promote an upcoming movie. I'm talking about creating a seemingly independent product-review site and filling it with positive reviews of your brand from made-up users. That kind of thing will never go over well.

■ **Substandard execution:** As with any marketing program, corporate blogs have to be carefully crafted and maintained to build and keep an audience. Brands need to pay close attention to the execution and development of blogs. Companies can do themselves considerable harm by not fully executing their blogging efforts. Some potentially damaging practices include the following:

- **Publishing a blog that is rarely or randomly updated:** When a visitor comes to a blog only to see that the last entry was weeks or months ago, he or she will get the impression that nothing important is going on in the company. Obviously, no company would intentionally create such a negative impression.

- **Poorly policing the blog and failing to delete spam:** Too many spam-generated comments will drive real readers away from the blog and reflect poorly on the brand, which can be seen as sloppy and disorganized.

- **Publishing inconsistent messages:** Posting poorly developed content that runs counter to the beliefs, promises, and personality of the brand will ultimately confuse readers as to what the brand is really about.

As mentioned, corporate blogging is a commitment. Even though it is easy and cost-effective, blogs can be digital lightning rods for audiences, and companies need to pay considerable attention to ensure that these audiences are fed information properly.

- **Longevity:** Although specific entries can be deleted from a blog and blog sites can be shut down entirely, a simple copy-and-paste by a single blog reader can keep a controversial or damaging blog entry alive and in the blogosphere forever after. Like a politician running for office, every brand has its enemies, all looking for an opportunity to tarnish its image. Brands should be sure that each entry they post will position their brand in a positive light in both the short and long term because often, there simply isn't any erasing of old mistakes.

- **Representation:** Whoever does the writing for a corporate brand becomes the voice of that brand, and any opinions expressed by that representative will be seen by readers as the official position of the brand. A single misstep or a poorly worded blog entry can do untold damage to a brand.

So here it is, after all that, my list of what you need to do to get a successful blog up and running. (If you're reading this for free in the café at Barnes and Noble or Borders, you'll want to write these down.)

- **Update content regularly:** Once you decide to maintain and promote a blog, you need to make a commitment to keep the blog updated with new entries. The frequency of new entries is partially determined by the amount of traffic that comes to the site—the more traffic, the more new entries should be posted. At the very least, new content needs to be added on a scheduled basis so that readers know when to expect it. Posting entries on a seemingly random basis or missing scheduled updates is a sure way to lose core visitors who can easily become confused or indifferent, taking their blog-reading elsewhere. (Before you call me a hypocrite, I am well aware that I regularly break this rule on the Perspectives blog, my agency's blog, and my personal blog.)

- **Maintain a friendly but brand-oriented voice:** Blogs offer companies the opportunity to communicate in a friendlier, more conversational tone— but take care to avoid letting this more casual style dilute the image and lifestyle that the brand represents. A tone of voice that is so informal that it runs contrary to the brand image can actually work against the company, detract from other marketing efforts, and drive away customers. Successful marketing is about having control over the message. Blogging, with its conversational style and open forum for responses, can reduce the control a marketer has over the message, so extra attention needs to be paid to ensure that the blog is friendly but still brand-oriented.

- **Keep content relevant:** For the most part, blogs are based on a central theme, as determined by the blog writer. This makes it easier for readers to find the blogs that they are most interested in. Writers should know that readers will come to their blog because they're interested or curious about that particular brand and/or the industry in general. It is important for marketers to remain on topic and not deviate from the stated focus of the blog.

- **Don't (completely) ghost-write blog posts:** While the content of a blog is important, so is the name behind the blog. Like a TV news anchor whom viewers tune into because they have come to trust him or her, the validity of a blog post will often rest on the shoulders of its author—and it's not uncommon for readers to examine the blog author's biography. Blogs by definition are meant to be more personal and intimate. Once readers (or worse, the media) catch on to the fact that a blog is being ghost-written, there could be a severe backlash, causing audiences to question any future statements or claims by that company. At the same time, it's impractical to think that people in high-profile positions will really have the time to write their own blogs. Hell, even politicians have speeches written by someone else. At the very least, if a blog is going to be written on someone's behalf, the person whose name is attached to the blog should review each post and sign off on it prior to it being published.

- **Don't sell, and don't be too quick to delete:** Blogs are meant to provide insight and opinion, personal thoughts, or expert advice that other people can benefit from. They are not meant to be straightforward sales pitches, which are best left for advertisements or the content on a company's primary Web site. Blogging can work in a company's favor as long as the subtle connection between information and trust is maintained and allowed to unfold and the direct-sales route is avoided. Similarly, because blogs are meant to be public forums where readers can comment on each post, it's important that bloggers allow negative comments to appear as readily as they allow positive ones. While it's fine to delete rude or baseless attacks (such as "This company is terrible") and especially fine to delete spam-tinged comments, marketers must be careful to avoid deleting comments simply because they offer a dissenting opinion. Consumers want to judge the quality of the content themselves and will put more trust in a brand that provides all the ideas available—including ones that work counter to the company's goal—than companies that "stack the deck" by providing only the comments they want readers to see.

**GENEVIEVE SMITH**

**THE BRAND PERSPECTIVE**

⤶ I asked a colleague of mine, Rick Starbuck, who has worked with me in e-commerce for many years, to provide his opinion on subject. Rick is now Senior Vice President of Customer Experience with Chase.com, a position he assumed after Chase's acquisition of WaMu.

One note for readers before Rick gets started: I believe that the brand can be most present with consumers through its Web interactions. It's the ultimate 1:1 with the consumer, which, by the way, can be viewed and commented on by all, around the globe. If you think about it that way, considering the Internet as one of your primary consumer touch points, then I'd suggest you staff the team who manages this with talent like Rick Starbuck.

### GUEST PERSPECTIVE: RICK STARBUCK

Much like any online trend, blogging should be thought of in terms of the following:

- What problems it solves for the company or its customers
- What risk it introduces, if any

That is to say that starting a company blog for its own sake is not worth the effort and risk. If, however, there is a genuine need, then a blog can serve as a bridge to communities of customers and the general public.

I think of a blog as primarily a piece of marketing that has as its goal top-of-mind brand recognition and maintenance. The tricky bit is that this particular medium has a few peculiarities in that it demands transparency. It is ultimately a populist, inclusive medium, and it is a two-way, interactive conversation.

Taken in combination, these attributes make a blog more like a live press conference than anything else. The real tension, I think, for a large company in the blogosphere is between transparency and control. I've often remarked that a company can't control its brand because that lives between its customers' ears. It can, however, control its branding—that is, all the messages and prompts it puts out to customers.

The blog is, in some ways, a pure expression of this phenomenon. What is painful is that the company must choose to endure directly the co-mingling of both its branding (the messages it puts out onto the blog) and the expressions fed back by its customers either inside the blog or in reaction to it on the Web.

# Q: WHAT'S THE ROLE OF PR IN ESTABLISHING AND PROMOTING A BRAND?

JASON MILETSKY

THE AGENCY PERSPECTIVE

I've read a lot of books on marketing and branding. Some of them I like quite a bit. They definitely have some interesting things to say. But I notice that many of these books end up being little more than 300+ page advertisements for the author, who's trying to sell creative or consulting services. I really don't want to do that here. You bought this book to learn something, not to give me business. So while I've mentioned my agency now and then, I've really tried to keep it low-key, bringing it up only when it closely related to a story I'm telling.

But I'm going to break my own rule now and be a little self-promotional. My agency, PFS Marketwyse, is a full-service agency. I oversee the branding and advertising departments and my partner, Deirdre Breakenridge, oversees our PR/communications department. One of the main reasons why PFS has grown as quickly as it has is because when it comes to PR, Deirdre is really about the best there is. She has an amazing eye for strategy and she's a leading voice in her industry. (Although it's for a competing publisher, you really should check out her books *PR 2.0: New Media, New Tools, New Audiences* and *Putting the Public Back in Public Relations*. Both are required reading for anybody looking to understand the intricacies and subtleties of today's PR landscape. Also check out her blog at http://www.deirdrebreakenridge.com.) With such a brilliant resource at my disposal, it seemed silly for me to answer this question myself, so I've asked Deirdre to provide a guest perspective on PR's role in establishing and promoting a brand.

## GUEST PERSPECTIVE: DEIRDRE BREAKENRIDGE

PR serves many functions for brands that want to increase awareness, manage their reputation, and build relationships with key stakeholders. Although companies have valued PR for years, they do more so today because PR is one of the most powerful weapons in the interactive-marketing arsenal. Communication professionals have learned that the new PR 2.0 landscape allows a brand to interact one-on-one through social-media tools including RSS, podcasting, streaming video, blogging, and social networking, to name a few. These 2.0 resources enable brands to talk directly with customers, prospects, media, and of course new influencers or bloggers.

PR 2.0 is not a new principle. As a matter of fact, it's been around for over a decade. It's only recently that a tremendous focus on enhanced Web 2.0 collaborative applications allows professionals to fully take advantage of the communications resources available in Web communities. Pre–Web 2.0, brands used PR to go through the media and other important groups as credible third-party endorsers. Today, not only can professionals develop those relationships—for example, using 2.0 sharing tools to help journalists build their stories with social-media releases (SMRs)—they can also interact with new influencers or bloggers in ways that were never possible and with more reach and impact.

However, bloggers, like other influencers, have expectations too. Similar to media relations and a PR person's approach to media outreach, there are rules of engagement with new influencers. Brands can engage with bloggers to increase brand awareness and build relationships that lead to endorsements, but you can't just jump right into their conversations. It's very important to listen first, to hear what your influencers are talking about, and to discover what interests them—and *then* provide meaningful information or communication that they can then share with their followers or members of their communities. In many cases, these very influencers are the people who buy a brand's products/services. Because social media allows sharing in communities, brands are reaching people directly and can listen, learn, interact with, or engage in new ways to build awareness and brand loyalty through a great experience.

New PR provides a direct experience with key stakeholders in addition to the traditional endorsement approach of the past. For instance, brands can use a social media release, which is becoming a popular new social-media communications tool, to reach the media, the blogosphere, customers, prospects, etc. This doesn't necessarily mean you abandon the traditional news release to your media outlets. On the contrary, you can still have a traditional-style release that is distributed via a wire service—but with a PR 2.0 enhancement that allows you to give new influencers/bloggers, customers, prospects, and other groups in communities the ability to take parts of your release and share them. The SMR is a viral PR tool. The body of the release houses links, MP3 downloads, video, and sharing tools, including the ability to pass the release virally to members of different communities through Twitter, Facebook, Redit, Delicious, Digg, Technorati, and Newsvine, to name a few examples.

The PR landscape has changed dramatically, enabling PR professionals to promote and enhance their brands' reputations through social media. Engagement and conversations with the media, bloggers, and people in Web communities provides real-time, direct communication that builds loyalty and trust. Brands, through PR 2.0 and social media, have a voice. They are no longer hiding behind their monikers, but can actively engage and show their human sides to the people that want to hear from them directly. Brands will continue to build awareness and loyal brand followers through PR 2.0.

GENEVIEVE SMITH

THE BRAND PERSPECTIVE

↳ In my answer to Question #60, "Is Television Necessary for Building a Brand?" I highlighted several well-known brands that used no television advertising and very little paid media. They generated a lot of positive attention with PR because they are clever in managing their marketing and branding. It's the role of PR to generate unpaid media impressions, which are positive reinforcement of the brand. People tend to believe news much more than paid advertising, so media generated by PR is a great way to promote the brand. There are many techniques that can be employed—such as sponsorships, events, community commitments, executive speaking opportunities, and cause-related involvement to name a few—where the hope would be the media would pick up the story to generate buzz for the brand.

I view PR as part of the overall communications team that supports the brand and its development. It does require focus, a plan, and constant attention to media-worthy occurrences, either generated by the firm or levered opportunistically by the firm. In other words, this isn't just going to happen on its own. I think it is helpful to have PR at the table with the core brand group so they can be involved and accountable for this part of the brand's development. Plus, because media is their business, frequently they can suggest ways of doing things in order to generate media attention.

Something else to consider here is disaster communications: You never want it to happen, but if a brand has difficulties, it is very important for negative media to be handled in such a way that it doesn't permanently tarnish the brand's image. So another role for PR is to provide caution on any activities that would be damaging to the brand as well as to have stand-by messaging and good media relations in case those are needed.

# Q: • CAN YOU BRAND YOURSELF • OUT OF A PR CRISIS?

JASON MILETSKY

THE AGENCY PERSPECTIVE

I'm sure there's nothing I can write that will be nearly as interesting or insightful as what Genevieve will have to say based on her experience with WaMu during the 2008 financial crisis, but I think that clearly, the answer to this question is a resounding no.

PR crises come in all shapes and sizes. Some may come and go with hardly anyone noticing, while others will be big and serious enough to really do some lasting damage to the company's viability. Severe issues often require a swift and immediate response, which usually involves a PR team springing into action to try to combat whatever bad news is out there. A strong public-relations team may be able to catch the attention of the media and change the stream of public sentiment or, at the very least, get their voices heard. But bad news travels faster and more potently than good news, so in more serious crises, even really good PR efforts may not do the trick.

The same goes for marketing. Running more happy, positive TV commercials about the quality of your food while the news is busy reporting the growing number of people who have been rushed to the hospital due to illnesses stemming from ingesting your products isn't going to make the problem any better. In rare cases, companies have used advertising vehicles to try to combat negative publicity by directly sending a message to the public, usually by taking out full-page newspaper ads that have little production costs and can be inserted quickly. But again, the power of an ad can't possibly match the power of the media, especially when it comes to negative press.

Beyond that, the brand itself needs to continue its main mission: to fulfill its promise. This can be tough because part of being able to function as a brand is creating an atmosphere where the employees actively live the brand, particularly at consumer touch points. During bad PR crises, employee morale will likely be down, opening the door to increased gossiping and making it more difficult for employees to properly reflect the brand values. Employees who work directly with consumers may have to be trained quickly on the best way to answer questions about the issues that are in the news, and throughout each and every department within the company, managers will need to be extra careful to ensure that everything is functioning properly and problem areas are fixed quickly. Continuing to fulfill the brand promise consistently will be even more important during times of crisis, and missteps will only aggravate the issues and make it harder to recover. Even with all this, as we've seen time and again with companies that have fallen after bad news hits (Lehman Brothers, Enron, WorldCom, and more), the hard truth is that when the news is bad enough, there ain't a damned thing the brand manager can do about it.

GENEVIEVE SMITH
THE BRAND PERSPECTIVE

I am here to testify that you *cannot* brand yourself out of a PR crisis if it is of such magnitude that anything a company says is suspect. I am certain you're familiar with the financial crisis of 2008 and with the brands that were once considered solid that went out of business during this time. (Note that in my view, to some degree, the media frenzy during this period contributed to or perhaps hurried on the demise of some of these firms through their non-stop speculation and speculative reporting, but I guess that's neither here nor there.)

That said, there are examples of companies that have leveraged the brand to get through a PR crisis, one of the most famous being Tylenol, which now controls about 35 percent of the pain-killer market in North America despite the "Tylenol scare" that occurred in September, 1982. In case you don't remember it, seven people in metropolitan Chicago died after ingesting Extra Strength Tylenol capsules that had been deliberately contaminated with cyanide—a crime that was never solved. Although Tylenol sales collapsed temporarily, the brand was rebuilt and recovered in a few years, thanks in part to the company's contributions to the invention of the tamper-proof capsule and use of tamper-proof packaging. While the Tylenol scare was one of the most brand-damaging PR events I have witnessed, the company turned it around and became one of the most trusted and used pain relievers. It can be done.

# Q: Can B2B Companies, Which Typically Don't Use Mass Media, Market Their Brand?

Jason Miletsky

The Agency Perspective

Of course. Not only can they, they need to. B2B companies will likely have a much tougher time reaching their market than B2C companies because their audience is so much more finely targeted.

For B2B companies, reaching the masses is rarely the call to order. Instead, they need to pinpoint, reach, and engage key decision-makers and the employers who influence that decision-maker's opinion. Talk about a needle in a haystack! In some cases, companies may get tripped up in the discovery process: Should an IT-management company try to reach and sell to someone with the title of IT manager? That would seem like the obvious choice, since he or she would most likely influence decisions made by a chief technology officer—unless said IT manager considers an outside IT-management resource a threat to his or her job, in which case that person will end up being a roadblock to getting a new account. And what about smaller companies that don't have a CTO—is the company president or owner the person you want to reach directly? Or is there somebody else?

Agencies often help clients determine who they need to reach as well as help put together a demographic and psychographic profile of who these people are. Once pinpointed, highly targeted marketing campaigns need to be run to gain their attention. It's neither easy nor quick—with B2B marketing, the sales cycle can go on for awhile. And even after you've piqued their interest and started a dialog, if the potential contract is high enough or may have a serious impact on their company, they may need to do their due diligence and research competing companies before signing.

But I'm getting ahead of myself. Let's start with the specific type of marketing that B2B companies usually do once they know who they're trying to reach:

- **Trade-show marketing:** The Internet has not killed off trade shows. True, trade shows have slowed down a bit, but they're still a great escape from the office and a powerful way for a brand to reach other businesses. Successful trade-show marketing should include:

  - A really well-designed booth that reflects the overall brand look and feel. You'll be competing with lots of other booths for people's attention, so make sure your booth stands out. Try to include something overhead that people can see when they look up, and don't use a booth layout that keeps people from seeing inside the booth. Light, open, and airy booths tend to work best.

  - A corporate overview brochure, as well as individual sales sheets or brochures on individual products or services you're trying to push.

  - One or two short videos that show off your product or services that can keep booth visitors engaged, entertained, and informed.

  - If it's in the budget, live presentations should be used to demonstrate systems and products. Don't try to do this yourself; get a professional speaker or actor.

  - Have some sort of giveaway—something of some value, like an iTouch. But don't just give it away in a random drawing of business cards. Contestants should at least be required to sit through a presentation before they can walk away with a nice prize.

  - Purchase space and display signage in and around the entrance hall to let people know about your company and booth number.

  - Every show has at least one publication, and longer shows will have daily publications. Make sure you have an ad in one or more of these, and issue press releases to get news about your company written about in these publications.

  - Prior to the show—and possibly during the show—send e-mail blasts to your house list. (With most shows, you can also pay for them to blast an e-mail to their registrants.) These e-mails should announce your booth number and the giveaway, and allow people to sign up in advance for meetings or for live demonstrations. (Nobody will register with you, but it fosters the impression that your booth will be really popular.)

- **Print advertising:** On the B2B side, print advertising can sometimes be surprisingly affordable. There are usually dozens of publications in any industry that will reach the specific audience your brand relies on. Plus, these ads usually suck, so if you're really creative, you can easily grab some attention. (Note to B2B companies: Don't do this yourself. Hire an agency.) And don't be afraid to run brand advertising. Just because you're B2B does not mean you're not trying to build a brand. Other companies need to trust that you're established and can do what you promise if they're going to invest their resources in you. That's not going to happen in a call-to-action print ad (which typically don't work well in B2B).

- **E-mail marketing:** The hardest thing about e-mail marketing is developing the contact list. Beyond that, make sure e-mail blasts aren't too over-the-top promotional. Give recipients something to read—something that will help them in their own work. Set yourself up as an industry expert, not as a used-car salesperson. Make sure there are plenty of links back to your site. Keep close track of every blast that goes out—their open rates and click-through rates—and make special contact with recipients who consistently open each blast you send.

- **Direct-mail marketing:** Skip the postcards. Postcards and letters end up getting thrown out by admins. If you want to get something on someone's desk, make it substantial—and whatever it is, put it in a box (in addition to making it creative and memorable, of course). If there's dimension to it, there's a far greater likelihood it'll get where you want it to go. But don't rely on the recipient to pick up the phone and call or take action; B2B direct mail works best if it is followed up by a sales call. Salespeople can use the direct-mail piece to break the ice on an initial call.

- **Public relations:** PR can be a highly effective tool in building trust—as much for B2B companies as B2C companies. So maybe you won't end up on Fox News or CNBC, but you can definitely get coverage in important trade pubs. And depending on the type of company, there's the potential for heavy-hitting business media like the *Wall Street Journal, BusinessWeek*, etc.

Beyond these efforts (and there are others, like event sponsorships; you just have to be creative), you need to continue being the brand. Continue fulfilling the brand promise and creating a strong reputation in your industry. As I said earlier, the B2B sales cycle can be a long one. Marketing can help bring people to the table, but the brand you build will help seal the deal.

GENEVIEVE SMITH
THE BRAND PERSPECTIVE

There is a fairly standard set of marketing tools B2B companies use (although these may vary a bit by industry):

- Web site for information about products and services and general industry communications

- Informational e-mail or newsletters to clients

- Selected trade publication advertising if appropriate

- Sales calls to key influencers with leave-behind collateral, samples, etc.

- Informational seminars

- Referral programs to select partners if the brand advertises its products to consumers but doesn't sell direct

- Top-notch sales representatives and/or customer-services agents

- Personalized service, as in "know the business of the business" as well remembering personal things about key contacts such as kids' names, birthdays, and so forth

- Processes and access designed to support the business partners so they can be successful (i.e., the marketing is all about helping business partners do more, and better)

- Price consideration, rush orders, courteous and prompt service (i.e., doing all that can be done to help the business partner)

These are some of the marketing activities that reinforce to the business community why they should do business with the brand.

It is my belief that person-to-person relationships are key in the B2B arena; therefore, it is also important that the brand have long-standing and highly reputable and knowledgeable employees, as they *are* the brand. A business wants to know its partner is knowledgeable in the category, reputable, sells good products, and employs people who are going to stick around and serve the account.

# Q: THERE'S A LIMITED BUDGET. NOW WHAT?

JASON MILETSKY

THE AGENCY PERSPECTIVE

Just pack it in and go home, of course. What else is there to do? Kidding. Come on—now's the time to get creative! Have some fun! Be strategic!

I love the large accounts we work with, and it's always great to have a big budget behind a campaign because it gives us a lot more opportunities to reach the market through a wider variety of media vehicles. But some of the most fun I've had has been with smaller clients who didn't have a lot of money to spend. Obviously, those situations are going to be harder, and those clients need to understand that while we can maximize results, they can't realistically expect to achieve with thousands what other companies will achieve with millions. But that doesn't mean we can't develop a campaign to get the brand out into the market and start the building process. You just need to work on a smaller scale and understand that some things will be off the table.

When you're dealing with a limited budget, the first thing that has to go—and I hate to say this—is any kind of formal market research. I'm a big believer in research, but the reality is that research can be expensive. So if you don't have a lot of money to work with, you can pretty much wave goodbye to focus groups, surveys, and heavy-duty analysis. Instead, you'll be looking to good, old-fashioned common sense and what you already know about the market to lead the way. (It's not a bad idea, however, to run things by a small group of people working at either the brand or the agency who know the market to get their honest opinions.)

You'll have to give up other things as well. (Don't worry—I'll get to the creative and more positive parts in a bit.) Things like high-quality TV production and national media buys will obviously be off the table, as will print ads in national consumer publications. I'm not going to go down the full list of all the expensive things that you *won't* be able to afford with a small budget, but you get the idea.

So now what? Well, pretty much all traditional mainstream marketing outlets that we tossed out before are still available on a smaller level for brands that can benefit from marketing locally or in only a few spot markets. Local cable TV advertising can be surprisingly affordable (if you produce the spot on the cheap), as can local radio and print (neighborhood newspapers or region-specific specialty magazines).

But small brands shouldn't just rely on smaller doses of traditional marketing to get word of their brand out to the public. Now's the time to get creative! Think outside the box and be open to taking some chances. Here are just a few things brands with limited funds can do to help themselves grow:

- **Retain a PR agency or independent publicist:** An ongoing public relations effort doesn't have to be expensive: even retainers of $3,500 or $5,000 per month can produce exciting results and get your brand out into the market by harnessing traditional and online media.

- **Turbo-charge your Web site:** Without a huge budget to put into advertising, your brand will need to develop a particularly strong presence on the Web. Make sure the site's design and organization is clear and in line with the brand personality. Use images that are really outstanding and can capture attention, and add content that can bring people back on a regular basis, such as information that may be useful to them even if they aren't buying your product or service, polls and surveys, or online contests.

- **Get others to do the marketing for you:** Viral marketing is a great tool for brands with smaller budgets; if it's done right, consumers will ultimately do your marketing for you. Largely run through e-mail, viral marketing happens when something (often a video, Web site, or image) is so funny, shocking, or otherwise eye-catching that people feel compelled to pass it along to friends, family, and coworkers, usually through e-mail. The benefits of a viral campaign include the relatively low production costs and the possibility of no media expenditures—with the potential for tremendous brand exposure. Drawbacks include the high possibility of the effort having no results at all (it can be hard to predict how people will react and what they will want to pass on to others) and the near impossibility of reaching a targeted market (once a viral campaign takes off, it's out there, and it's impossible to control who will receive it). For a more detailed look at this, check out *Perspectives on Marketing*, where I discuss the power, benefits, and drawbacks of viral marketing in Question #55, "How Powerful Is Viral Marketing? Can Viral Marketing Be a Planned Effort, Given That It Relies So Heavily on Consumer Involvement?"

- **Pay-per-click advertising is a great way to market your brand without blowing your load too quickly:** Google is still king when it comes to PPC advertising, but you can also look into smaller players like AdBrite or specific networks like Facebook. With PPC advertising, you can control when your ads appear, where they are geographically, and what keywords or sites they're associated with. More importantly, you can control your daily budget and track results to measure ROI. Just make sure you don't waste clicks—your Web site really should be well done if you're going to pay to get people there.

- **Keep lists of contacts and send your message through e-mail blasts:** E-mail marketing is cost-effective, easy, and measurable—and a great way to get your brand in front of a lot of people and drive them to your site. There are a lot of subtleties that go along with running an e-mail marketing campaign (way more than I have room to go into here), including list procurement, content, and ways to design your e-mail so it doesn't come off as "cheap Viagra"–type spam. So although you should do your research before getting anything started, for any brands on a small budget, e-mail marketing needs to be a serious consideration.

These are just five ideas that popped into my head while writing. Clearly, there are a lot more. Like I said: Be creative. Look at things differently. Call smaller traditional and online publications, skip over the sales rep and go right to the manager, and tell that person to throw out his or her price list and come up with something really outstanding that makes sense for you and your budget. Don't be afraid to ask for things—salespeople, especially at smaller media outlets, are hungry and will work things out with you. Don't let smaller budgets keep you from building your brand; look at them as a tougher but more interesting challenge that you'll just need to sharpen your creative and strategic approach to overcome.

GENEVIEVE SMITH

## THE BRAND PERSPECTIVE

There is always a limited budget—and we marketers are *always* going to want to spend money! Those are the facts of life. Okay, so I'm being a bit sarcastic, but truly, there will never be enough money to fund all the marketing activities that a great staff and agency can come up with to promote the brand. So we have to ask ourselves, what are the activities that are most important as investments for this particular brand to use to communicate with? Where is the audience? How do we reach them? And how can we do so cost-effectively? I am going to spend a little extra time here and approach things from multiple angles because I know from a very pragmatic perspective that investment in marketing is always going to be a hot topic, regardless of the size of company you work for.

First of all, just to be point-blank honest, it's pretty difficult to secure a budget for purely brand marketing. Normally, marketing investment is part of the P&L of the business and those are mostly managed to ROI targets. So unless you work at one of very few companies where imagination rules over the bottom line, you will be held accountable through results for every dollar invested. So the first objective is to get painfully clear with management as to the goals associated with any proposed investment. That means you have to invest in measurement, either by employees or some other trusted source. I would also advise you to have all measurement managed by an outside party—e.g., your finance department or their designee for third-party endorsement.

Once you have agreement on what the investment needs to achieve and you have measures in place to evaluate the results, it's a matter of once again reaching into the toolbox to find the methods most appropriate to the level of investment. For example, if you have a budget that won't fund both quality TV commercial production and TV media, then you shouldn't use TV. Otherwise, you'll wind up scrimping on production and delivering a sub-par commercial, which might actually *tarnish* the brand due to its lack of quality. So what's a good alternative to TV for your company? Out of home? Internet? In-store?

Most established companies have financial targets for both investment and return that they like to work within unless there is something extraordinary to communicate. So really, it's a matter of evaluating the marketing media for effectiveness against the goal *and* producing the best-quality creative and innovative media in order to leapfrog the competition.

With respect to funding re-branding or a new brand in terms of the expressions and touch points: As mentioned previously, this needs to move along with sufficient momentum but will not be a "big bang"—meaning it can be funded over time. If you use the methodology I talked about in my answer to Question #28 "Can a Brand Be Built Without a Large Budget?" you probably can self-fund and/or even cut expenses by closely evaluating every piece of communication.

My final thought is, budgets grow with success and adoption. While it may seem like you have to make some tough tradeoffs initially, you can change this when the brand is viewed as an investable asset.

# PART FOUR

# Brand Evaluation and Evolution

# Q:
THE CAMPAIGN'S DONE. BRAND RECOGNITION INCREASED, BUT SALES ARE FLAT. WAS THE CAMPAIGN A SUCCESS?

**GENEVIEVE SMITH**
**THE BRAND PERSPECTIVE**

I have some experience with exactly this subject matter, so I will use my recent experience as CMO for WaMu to tell you what I know. We launched a great new campaign across all media. Our tracking showed recognition and consideration moving upward, as well as good expansion on the important-to-consumer brand attributes. Plus, the campaign was an absolute hit internally and in the distribution network. We were feeling pretty darned good—until the head of sales approached me, noting that all brand metrics were up, but sales were not. Why?

I pulled in my research group and gave them the assignment of answering this question. It was a bit of a head scratcher, even for them, because of the number of variables beyond the campaign that needed to be examined in order to provide an answer or at least a solid direction. We approached the assignment by attempting to determine what factors were influencing the recent downturn in sales:

- Were fewer people in movement or opening accounts?

- Was it competitive pressure?

- Was it due to our own policy changes or declining service levels?

- Was our brand suffering/free-checking message stale/campaign underperforming?

- Was it due to macro-economic and environmental conditions?

What we found was there were a variety of factors that, when taken in combination, accounted for these results:

## Were Fewer People in Movement or Opening Accounts?

- The percentage in play and percent choosing WaMu appeared to be stable.

- Gross checking sales were down overall—below prior-year levels

- In-store existing-customer sales were fairly solid and increasing slightly year over year.

- In-store new-customer sales declined about 20 percent year over year.

- Online existing-customer sales appeared flat, but new-customer sales fell by about 25 percent year over year.

## Was It Competitive Pressure?

- Offline was stable.

- We'd seen a sharp increase in competitive checking ads from our leading competitors online.

- Nearly half of the online spots were from Bank of America in 2008, and their spending skyrocketed.

## Was It Due to Our Own Policy Changes or Declining Service Levels?

- Customers appeared less delighted with WaMu in recent months. They reported that changes in service drove changes in their opinions of WaMu, good or bad.

- Executive complaints increased 50 percent over a year ago.

## Was Our Brand Suffering/Free-Checking Message Stale/ Campaign Underperforming?

- The free-checking message diluted after 2006 but not between 2007 and 2008. It could possibly have accounted for lower new-customer sales after 2006.

- The campaign had performed more or less as expected. The goals of mass campaign had been as follows:

  - Move away from attack stance and "foil" to talking about WaMu alone.

  - Showcase customer experience and WaMu's customer-centric approach.

  - Sell free checking and other aspects of the bank (small business, cards, online).

  - The pre-campaign research predictions were as follows:

  - Brand attributes around customer service would increase.

  - Persuasion and consideration numbers would be weaker than in the past because of the softer, passive tone of the ads and the struggle of consumers to fully connect emotionally to some of the spots.

## Was It Due to Macro-Economic and Environmental Conditions?

- We were unable to tell with the current data.

At this point in time, in April 2008, we had seen a slight uptick (which had subsequently leveled off) in the number of consumers who had heard negative news about WaMu, but the general economic news was not good. So, was the campaign a success? I guess as it framed the brand in a new way and fully engaged employees and customers it was, on those dimensions. Softer persuasion and consideration was a choice we made with the creative. As you can see, though, the competition had increased dramatically in our online channel and our sales to *new* customers were down significantly. As well, our service scores had declined quite a bit as a result of new fees and policies. In combination, many choices we made about the business affected our sales; marketing was one component of many.

### JASON MILETSKY
### THE AGENCY PERSPECTIVE

↳ Maybe, maybe not. Ultimately, yes, revenue needs to be generated and brand-building campaigns need to contribute to that. But just because the needle doesn't move and the cash register isn't ringing doesn't mean anyone should suddenly conclude that the campaign crashed and burned. There are a few variables that need to be considered before that determination can be made:

- **What were the pre-established goals of the campaign?** If the goals that everyone agreed on prior to execution were to increase sales, then no, the campaign did not succeed if sales stayed flat. But there are other goals to shoot for that might not be revenue-based. Maybe the goal was to increase brand recognition, or to improve consumers' perception of the brand, or to successfully and smoothly introduce a new brand look and feel. Success for these types of goals would more likely be measured by comparing pre-campaign market research with post-campaign market research, and may receive a stamp of approval without even looking at sales figures.

- **Has the brand been pulling its weight?** The agency can only market the brand. We can't fulfill the promise. Any problems a company faces that might be harming their brand and negatively affecting consumer sentiment could be too powerful a deterrent for even the best marketing to overcome. (But don't pay too much attention to this bullet point; it flies in the face of the "blame the agency" route that brands are famous for taking when things go wrong.)

- **Is there a secondary component that's not doing its job properly?** In my answer to Question #61, "How Has the Internet Changed the Way Brands Get Marketed?" I told a story about a client that was unhappy with us because they got very few new leads from a brand campaign that we developed for them. In response, we pointed out that throughout the campaign, traffic to their Web site had increased significantly—and we had recommended from the beginning that they improve their site (which was developed by another agency before we were retained, and was truly awful). So it's entirely possible that the campaign worked but the Web site failed. If you run a B2B branding campaign through direct mail, but the salespeople who call recipients afterward screw it up on the phone, that's not the campaign's fault; it's the salespeople's. Similarly, a brand campaign could increase traffic to a retail store, but if the cashiers are unfriendly or the selection is weak or the store is dirty? Well, those problems will contribute to poor sales, but be completely unrelated to any campaign effort.

Of course, flat sales could also be the result of a poor campaign. Believe me, I'm not saying the agency can't be at fault or that the campaign may not be effective. I'm just saying you may need to consider other reasons before any final judgment is made.

# Q: CAN BRANDING CAMPAIGNS HAVE SHORT-TERM GOALS, OR IS BRANDING ALWAYS A LONG-TERM EFFORT?

**GENEVIEVE SMITH**
**THE BRAND PERSPECTIVE**

From my perspective, branding is not a campaign. It's a long-term—indeed, forever—effort that involves much more than marketing. A company *could* decide to launch a purely branding campaign, however. So what might this branding campaign entail? Would it be a standard campaign mix of mass media, direct marketing, and online marketing, plus in-store or online merchandising? Should it talk purely about how cool the brand is, or does it include product proof points and offers? These decisions will need to be made prior to establishing goals, either short- or longer-term.

Once you've defined what will comprise the branding campaign, you can apply goals—and these can be short-term goals if you have measures in place for consumer awareness, consideration, and attitude about the brand. When the campaign is launched, these can be measured weekly during the media buy and also measured post media to test for sustainability of message and brand lift. (You can measure more frequently than weekly, but typically the trend won't move enough on a daily basis to provide you with any additional useful data.)

While specific campaigns will be additive to the brand and can be measured in short time frames, the true test is brand health and vigor over the long-term. For this reason there will be longer-term goals for the brand beyond those associated with a campaign.

JASON MILETSKY
THE AGENCY PERSPECTIVE

 I know brand managers don't like to hear this, and it's easy to think that agencies just like to say this because it makes us less accountable for achieving a positive ROI, but branding campaigns really are meant for developing long-term results. The more the brand is marketed, the more it's understood, and the more trust is built. And the more trust is built, the more people will feel compelled to buy. It's a simple equation, but not a very quick one.

Of course, there are exceptions to every rule. Although Monster.com had been around in one incarnation or another beforehand, it launched itself to global prominence with a single (really good) TV spot that played during the Super Bowl in 1999. Direct-mail campaigns, especially B2B campaigns that are meant to introduce and build brand recognition, can also be good for achieving short-term goals. However, these efforts ordinarily require the follow-up of a sales team to get the best results.

And while I'm a believer that brand campaigns should largely be created for the long term, one short-term result that can be watched carefully is evidence of increased traffic to the Web site. Even though it may take some time for trust to be built, curiosity usually gets piqued on a shorter timeline. Increased Web traffic is a good indication that a brand campaign is effectively reaching people.

# Q: WHAT'S THE BEST WAY TO MEASURE THE ROI OF A BRANDING CAMPAIGN? IS IT EVEN POSSIBLE TO MEASURE?

GENEVIEVE SMITH
THE BRAND PERSPECTIVE

If you are going to operate a pure branding campaign, then by its nature, the intent of the campaign is not to generate an immediate profit. Rather the campaign will have some other purpose, such as growing awareness, overcoming negative press, highlighting some upcoming philanthropic endeavor by the company, or other objectives in this vein.

That's not say that a brand campaign cannot be measured, however—it's just that the measurement may not translate directly to ROI like one expects when evaluating direct marketing. For example:

- You can measure the impact of the campaign on brand attributes, consumer opinion, awareness/recognition of the brand, and other non–ROI-specific analytics.

- If your company has invested in models to measure the brand effect, you can track this outcome.

- You can measure the marketing efforts, the market environment, and the cognitive factors like awareness, brand image, loyalty, and customer satisfaction to judge whether a branding campaign has caused a lift or sales through its halo effect.

- You can measure the number of media impressions generated by any PR used in a branding campaign; these can be translated into equivalent media investment.

This very question is why it's critical to have agreed-on goals and objectives for each campaign—and to have agreed on which measures will be used to evaluate the results.

JASON MILETSKY
THE AGENCY PERSPECTIVE

 It's not just possible, it's necessary. A lot of people outside of the industry think that marketing is all about being creative and coming up with new ideas. (I love it when I tell someone about an account I'm working on and they respond by saying "Hey, I have a great slogan for that company," because of course my job is just that easy and all it really takes is a great *slogan*. Ugh.) People don't realize that behind the fun, creative part, there are numbers, statistics, and goals.

As far as I'm concerned, when it comes to building a brand, nothing of any significance should be done without knowing why it's being done and what the specific numeric goals are. Campaigns take time and money, and represent a brand's opportunity to speak to its market. If mistakes are made, then these opportunities might be missed. The market might not be reached, competition could gain market share, or even worse, the wrong campaign could damage the brand. One way or another, every campaign effort needs to be measured.

Brand campaigns aren't necessarily meant to generate sales—at least, not directly. They're meant to penetrate the minds of the market and keep the audience constantly aware of the brand so that its promise and personality are increasingly recognizable and they instantly understand what to expect from the brand (even if they've never had direct contact with it personally). Because the purpose of a brand campaign is to generate awareness, basing goals on increased sales is probably not the best way to measure success. Building exposure and trust in a brand takes time. The more consumers are exposed to a brand, the more they'll start to trust it, which will eventually lead to increased sales—but it's not going to happen overnight. Plus, there are other things that need to be considered when setting goals, such as the role that salespeople, store designers, and other factors play. An aggressive brand campaign may get people through the door, but after that it's up to the brand to make the sale.

Instead, the best way to measure a brand campaign is to base goals on something that is needed and that the campaign can realistically accomplish. Getting more people through the doors of a retail store is a good goal, as is getting more people to visit a Web site. (Each of these, and other goals like them, should have hard numbers attached. I'm just using "Get more people through the door" for illustrative purposes.) An even better goal is to base success on brand exposure and perception among the target market, measured through exacting pre- and post-campaign research.

# Q: IS INCREASED TRAFFIC TO A WEB SITE ENOUGH TO DETERMINE THAT A BRAND HAS BEEN MARKETED SUCCESSFULLY?

**GENEVIEVE SMITH**
**THE BRAND PERSPECTIVE**

The short answer is no. Increased traffic to a Web site is not enough to determine that a brand has been marketed successfully.

First of all, I would hope your marketing efforts would be intended to create sales. The ultimate metric is cost per sale in order to evaluate the effectiveness of online marketing. Of course we measure click-throughs, time on site, and abandonment, all of which go into the constant analysis of what needs to be tweaked in order to hit the cost per account (CPA) targets. But those don't necessarily help us to determine whether or not a brand has been marketed successfully.

Beyond looking solely at visits there are a few other metrics besides Web traffic that could be considered to ascertain whether you have been successful:

- Some metric of "buzz" outside of the Web address itself. This can be a Google search trend (as can be found at http://www.google.com/trends) or number of mentions in the press.

- Some kind of action commitment, however small, on the part of the customer. The customer should show some second-level interest in the brand via a mechanism that can be measured. This could be signing up (and staying on) an e-mail list or engaging with some part of the Web site (such as a widget that delivers some info/value).

At WaMu.com, we built the number-one Web site for bank-account generations (according to Comscore) and we measured our marketing success based on CPA and account growth. In an interesting conversation I had with a competitor, we compared our visits data and our results from this metric were in fact similar. But while we opened 1,000,000 accounts in a year, they opened 70,000. They felt very successful based on Web visits, but we evaluated success much differently.

As in many areas, it all depends on what you are trying to achieve. If it's purely buzz for the brand, then consider these additional metrics to evaluate success.

JASON MILETSKY

THE AGENCY PERSPECTIVE

↳ A campaign might be able to get people through the doors of a particular store, but it can't sell the product on its own. There are other factors at play, including (but not limited to) the following:

- Can the shopper find the product they're looking for easily?

- Is the store design simple to navigate and in keeping with the brand personality?

- Are the prices for the product reasonable—what the consumer expects and would be willing to pay?

- Are the salespeople helpful or pushy jerks?

- Is there a competing product on the shelf right next to your product that has a really eye-catching display and is on sale?

Marketing campaigns can do a lot. They can increase exposure and improve consumer perception of a brand, build trust, and even compel people to take action—all of which is measurable. And the agency creating the campaign should be held accountable for reaching their stated goals. But the goals have to be the right goals, and must take into account other non-marketing elements that may be needed. Otherwise, a perfectly good campaign could be scrapped for the wrong reason or, worse, a poor campaign could be kept longer than it should.

All that being said, I'm a big fan of using increased Web traffic as a primary gauge of whether a brand has been marketed successfully. If a campaign is successfully reaching its audience, there is every reason to believe that traffic to the Web site will increase. (As I've mentioned elsewhere, aside from curiosity being piqued, the new purchasing cycle is for consumers to first check out a brand's Web site and then make the purchase, especially for larger and more expensive items.) And for all the faults that may be found with traffic-analytic programs, Web traffic is relatively simple to measure. With just a couple of clicks, it's easy to tell whether traffic has increased over the last hour, day, week, month, quarter, or year. You can compare the net difference between traffic rates before a campaign and during or after it, and you can set firm, numeric targets as a percentage increase over previous traffic rates.

Even with increased Web traffic as a stated goal, however, there need to be limits. A good marketing campaign should bring new visitors to the site, but it can't make them look through more pages or make them stay longer—that's the site's job. The site has to be inviting and encourage visitors to see more pages and spend more time searching around. So make sure that your site is in order and properly reflects the brand before your campaign gets off the ground.

# Q: HAS WEB 2.0 FORCED BRANDS TO BE MORE TRANSPARENT AS TO WHAT THEY'RE REALLY ABOUT?

**GENEVIEVE SMITH**
**THE BRAND PERSPECTIVE**

I believe it has, but I asked my resident expert, Rick Starbuck, to add his comments and thoughts to this answer. Here's what he said.

### GUEST PERSPECTIVE: RICK STARBUCK

Absolutely, although I think it's more nuanced than that. I think the public-facing parts of brands—their products, services, and people (to the extent that they interact with the public)—have been forced to be more transparent and consistent by, essentially, exposure and pressure from the public via the Web.

But, the lens doesn't go too deep, as the general public is not likely to closely examine the back-office processes or business model of a company that it interacts with on the Web. They will ruthlessly examine the stuff they can see, of course, but as long as that passes the sniff test, they are unlikely to go beyond it.

The level of delving can go deeper for industries that are traditionally vilified (chemical companies, military, and now banks), as subcultures can spring up around criticizing these companies.

**JASON MILETSKY**
**THE AGENCY PERSPECTIVE**

Web 2.0 has transformed the Web into a global conversation. Through social networks, blogs, and other tools, people can communicate and interact in ways that they never could before. People can express themselves and their ideas, their artwork, opinions, and insights, giving them a voice and a spotlight in a public and sometimes very popular forum.

But they're not just talking about sports, movies, and politics. They're voicing their opinions on brands as well—what they like, what they don't like, etc. In fact, leaving reviews about products they've tried has become part of the shopping process for many people—indeed, some shoppers don't feel like their purchase is complete until they've written an online review, be it positive or negative. Getting the run-around from the billing department at your cell service provider? (Sorry, I'm having flashbacks to an awful experience with the thankfully now-defunct Cingular Wireless.) You don't have to suffer in silence anymore. You can leave an online review or write about it in a blog entry. Really love a new restaurant you just went to? Then you can post an online review before the taste of the food disappears.

Brands shouldn't assume that people aren't reading these reviews, or that the blogosphere consists of only a few isolated individuals who are too geeky to matter. There are hundreds of millions of blogs on the Web—and with sites like Digg, Technorati, and others, a well-written blog can be picked up and read by a significant portion of the online audience. And while many people end their purchases by writing online reviews, just as many start the process by researching brands online before they buy—especially looking to read about other people's experiences.

Whether all this makes a brand more transparent, I really don't know. There is no question that consumers and media have greater access to information than ever before, and in a frenzied quest for attention (by media looking for increased ratings and consumers looking for their share of the spotlight), there probably isn't much that's going to stay secret for very long. But what I am sure of is that as Web 2.0 continues to mature, brands will necessarily become more careful. It's taken me four months to write this book. It'll take someone 10 seconds to jump online and give it a bad review. That's the world we live in, and the reality of that world should keep all brands and marketers on their toes and tapped into user sentiment.

Breaking the brand promise a few decades ago might not have been too terrible. It would have taken awhile for word to get out that your brand should be avoided. Break the brand promise now—or give consumers a negative experience in any way—and brands risk immediate and aggressive retribution by a marketplace that is tapped in to the entire world.

Q: • What Changes First:
  • the Brand or the Market?

What's your perspective on this question?
Let us know at PerspectivesOnBranding.com.

**Genevieve Smith**
**The Brand Perspective**

Both! The market is constantly changing. So this question is a bit "chicken or egg." A brand must stay true to its vision no matter what, while constantly evolving and taking risks to put new things on the market. Sometimes the brand will change the market; sometimes the market will change the brand.

On the one hand, people don't stand still, and as a result, the culture and, by extension, the market don't either. Consumers are constantly listening to each other and to buzz generated online and elsewhere more than ever before. And they're fickle. They will change on a dime. On the other hand, brands often look inside to see if they can anticipate and launch a disruptive new product or enhancement before consumers even know they want it. The goal is to stand out, to be unique, to capture consumers' attention, and drive their purchase behavior.

Of course, even as they seek to launch the next disruptive product, brands use research to track consumer trends and measure the impact of those trends on their position or products. As we've discussed, putting a great, new, innovative product on the market is not necessarily a shot in the dark, but rather involves both the art and the science of marketing.

This represents yet another opportunity to reinforce how important it is to actively manage your brand. Your customer expects new things from you; at the same time, you must constantly be focused on attracting new customers. While managing this can be tricky, you don't want the brand to become irrelevant or stale.

JASON MILETSKY

THE AGENCY PERSPECTIVE

It's never that cut and dried. I believe that both brands and markets evolve slowly over time in relation to each other, so in the ongoing, aerial view of brand/market interaction, I think there's no definitive answer. There are, however, instances when massive shifts take place, and in the majority of these cases I believe that the market changes first and that brands then make adjustments in accordance with those changes. Brands, however, do play some part in helping ignite that initial shift.

Musically, the 1980s was known for its lasting wave of hair bands: rock bands with wild, teased-out hair that played pop metal with catchy hooks. Bands like Poison, Ratt, Bon Jovi, and Cinderella were all topping the charts and dominating MTV (which still played videos back then). But the entire industry was turned on its head in 1991 when Nirvana's *Nevermind* debuted and ran over scores of better-known contenders on its rapid (and totally unexpected) rise to the number-six position on Billboard's Hot 100 list.

Seemingly overnight, hair bands left the stage, abandoned the tour bus, and moved back in with their parents while a new era of grunge rock (better known as alternative rock) took over. Heavier-sounding bands like Pearl Jam and Soundgarden mixed metal and punk to change not only music but also pop culture. MTV's video lineup adjusted to reflect the new wave of popular music, as did the play lists of many radio stations. But it was more than just a new offering of bands. Alternative music changed the attitude of the market. Suddenly kids weren't wearing their hair teased up and they put away their neon-colored shirts in favor of darker hues and a just-got-out-of-bed hairstyle. Companies that wanted to reach this audience—in categories from clothing and food to cars and skateboards—would have been shit out of luck if their brand personality had continued to reflect Max Headroom and *Saved by the Bell*; the audience had changed, and brands had to change with them.

Of course, Nirvana wasn't the first alternative band; alternative music had been around since long before 1991. But they were the one credited for popularizing the movement. And MTV needs to be recognized for giving Nirvana's first single the necessary airtime to reach wide-scale audiences in the first place. But even though MTV played an early role by facilitating the introduction of music to market, it was still the market that most radically changed, and the brands that followed suit.

This same kind of shift can happen based on general market conditions. As banks and the housing markets collapsed in 2008, gas prices soared over the summer, and people became increasingly fearful of losing their jobs, brands reacted by changing their approach. Many focused their messages on cost-savings and low prices; others tried to play up their long history and the fact that they were a solid company that consumers could count on. People needed some good news, and brands made the shift to try to fill that need.

# Q: • WHEN THE MARKET LOSES TRUST IN THE • BRAND, CAN IT EVER BE REGAINED?

GENEVIEVE SMITH

THE BRAND PERSPECTIVE

"Trust" is a big word when it comes to branding. In fact, the word is frequently used in advertising, as in "a brand you can trust." Trust is a fundamental requirement; it's the price of entry. If consumers lose trust in a brand, they won't consider purchase. Period, end of subject.

So the question is, can trust, once lost, be regained? It depends. Here are a few points to ponder:

■ Did the brand intend to say, do, or produce something that was less than trustworthy? If not, and if this can be made clear to consumers, then the fix may simply be a matter of producing the facts and stating how the brand will ensure that the mistake never happens again.

> I talked about this a bit in my answer to Question #65, "Can You Brand Yourself Out of a PR Crisis?" using Tylenol as the example.

■ Was what happened a result of incompetence or bad business practices? Alaska Airlines, who I fly frequently up and down the West Coast, lost a plane a few years back in the Pacific Ocean off the coast of Mexico. They didn't intend to lose that plane, but questions lingered about their safety and maintenance practices for quite some time after the accident. Ultimately, the facts exonerated the airline, but they had to work hard to regain their share of travelers who stopped flying them because they had lost trust in the safety of the planes.

■ Does the problem appear to be systemic, such that people will question how deep and widespread the issues are? In other words, is the brand a house of cards? I look at what I'll call "Brand USA"—the brand of the United States of America—and the financial crisis that began in 2008 as a good example of this. Can our political and business leaders be trusted to lead us out of this economic situation? Or will it only get worse?

To answer the question directly, I believe trust *can* be regained—but the brand must be willing to be transparent with the market and must be ruthless with itself in correcting whatever issues caused the loss of trust in the first place.

JASON MILETSKY

THE AGENCY PERSPECTIVE

Get caught cheating on your wife or husband, and what do you think is going to happen? Will he or she come running to you with open arms, telling you how wonderful you are and professing undying love for you? Probably not. Cheating is usually one of those one-strike-and-you're-out offenses. If the relationship does manage to make it through, it's not going to get back to normal anytime soon. There will be months or years of life on shaky ground with the phrase "How can I ever trust you again?" wailed over and over again until it sticks in your head like a bad song.

Brands are a lot like that, just without all the melodrama. Once trust is lost, it can be hard if not impossible to regain. Depending on the brand, how long it's been around, and how much trust equity (years of building trust by successfully fulfilling its promise) has been accumulated, it can be tough to get to that point, but once a consumer loses trust, that may be all she wrote.

I'll illustrate the point with a personal story—one that I am always looking for an opportunity to tell. In general, I tend to trust easily, and I'm pretty loyal to brands I believe in, but I recently lost faith in one brand after years of being a regular consumer. Because I'm usually running around, I often find myself eating in my car or having to throw down a quick meal between meetings, so over the years I've become a fan of Wendy's. As far as fast food goes, it always seemed like the better choice. In fact, although they've never (to my knowledge) come out and said it publicly, part of their promise as far as I'm concerned is that they're a step above McDonald's and Burger King—not just in terms of the food, but in the whole consumer experience.

So one day I stopped in at the Wendy's near my house (in Nutley, New Jersey) and ordered my usual: a number five (grilled chicken sandwich), plain but with cheese, and a Diet Coke with no ice. The girl behind the counter asked, "Medium or large?" My first reaction was a brief relief that they were no longer annoyingly asking me if I wanted to "Biggie Size" it, but that relief subsided quickly when I thought for a second about her question. She didn't ask if I'd like a small, medium, or large, nor did she ask if I'd like to increase my order to medium or large. She just simply asked "Medium or large?" as if those were my only two options. No big deal—probably just a mistake on her part. Poor phrasing of the question. So I asked her, "Is there a small size I can get?" She said yes, put the order in, and that was that. I went off, ate my food, and left, still a fan of the brand—until about two weeks later, when I was in Los Angeles on business. I was running from one meeting to another, and in between I stopped at a Wendy's and ordered my usual number five. And once again, I was asked, "Medium or large?" in a very matter-of-fact, these-are-the-only-two-options-we-offer kind of way. This time it really stood out. It would have been strange for two people in different parts of the country to make that same mistake.

Long story short, this happened about a dozen more times over the next few months—each and every time I went to Wendy's, in every single location, and with every single cashier. I actually started going simply to see if any Wendy's employee, in any location, would offer the small size of my meal. They didn't. Eventually, I went to one location I had been to before (I won't say which one, because I don't want to get anybody fired), ordered my meal, and asked to speak to the manager when I was once again not offered a small size. I explained to the manager that what they were doing was stealing money from people. Personally, I don't care about an extra 35 cents. I go to Wendy's for convenience, not price. But there are a lot of people who can't afford to eat anywhere else, and that extra 35 cents might mean something to them. She pointed out that the menu shows that each item comes in a small size; I told her that was crap, and she knows it. Most people who come to Wendy's know what they're getting already and don't spend time looking at the menu. When the cashiers ask "Medium or large?" they're doing it because they know people will assume that medium is the smallest size they have, and ask for that—automatically incurring a higher fee for something they may not have wanted. After all, we live in a Starbucks world, where the smallest size is often called "medium" or something in Italian that we can't pronounce. Further, I told her that the cashiers made about $7 per hour. They couldn't care less about trying to up-sell, so clearly they were being trained that way, and it's no less than outright theft as far as I'm concerned. We went back and forth a bit, with her arguments getting weaker with each round, until she finally admitted to me that asking "Medium or large" is a corporate directive. She said she didn't agree with it, that she has fielded other complaints about it, and that she has protested the practice to her regional manager, but nothing has changed.

I thanked her for her honesty, and I have tried to contact Wendy's on the corporate level but so far the only response has been to offer me free meals. No, thanks. They've lost my trust. They're not the decent, consumer-oriented company they painted themselves to be. And I am no longer a loyal customer, and doubt I ever will be again. (For the record—I did call Wendy's consumer relations coordinator to give her a chance to comment before I wrote and published this, but never heard back.)

# Q: • Does the Brand Evolve Over Time, • at Specific Points in Time, or Never?

**Genevieve Smith**

**The Brand Perspective**

If the brand is going to endure as a long-term and relevant one, it will be constantly evolving with the marketplace. The world doesn't stand still, and neither should the brand. That doesn't mean the brand should chase the latest and greatest trend; that's not what I mean by "evolve." A dash of buzz does not make for long-lasting relevance.

When a brand is on top of the world and profits are rolling in—especially in a large corporate environment—it's really hard to find the risk-taker who's willing to say, "Let's move this thing forward." Why? Because it's working the way it is! But while the appetite to fiddle around with success may be low, it's important to keep pushing that boulder up the mountain.

One of my favorite books on branding is *Chasing Cool*, by Noah Kerner and Gene Pressman. The book, which includes interviews with some of today's most respected brand innovators and icons, is worth the read for anyone serious about really standing out through branding. One of the interviews is with Bob Pittman, co-founder of MTV; in it, he talks about being faced with a big decision: Should MTV grow old with its audience, or strive to remain the voice of young America? He notes, "We made the decision to be the voice of young America, which meant we had to let people grow out of MTV. You just have to give it up and keep moving." He adds, "It goes against human nature—which is that you find a formula that works and stick to it. At MTV, they constantly throw away perfectly good ideas that are working just fine because they have to come up with new ideas for the next generation."

You may not be courting upcoming generations in your business, but clearly, the only way for a brand to really win—to really differentiate—is to keep reaching for the next big idea. I can promise you that Steve Jobs isn't sitting around trying to figure out how to copy someone else's product or idea; he's moving his own next big idea forward.

Jason Miletsky

The Agency Perspective

↳ I like to look at brands as a three-lane highway, with a slow lane, a medium lane, and a fast lane.

The slow lane always has a steady line of cars in it, each making progress toward its destination, but moving at meandering pace. Looking down at it from the traffic copter flying overhead, you can kind of see that they're moving, but you really have to be paying attention to notice it. This lane represents the ongoing evolution of the brand—the small changes that need to take place over time. Each of these can help move the brand forward slowly at a steady pace, might be noticeable to consumers who are paying attention, but won't overwhelm anybody. Usually these are small changes like adding new but complementary colors to the secondary or accent color palette or swapping out older, dated images and photographs for newer, more modern ones. These should happen as new marketing material is produced; development should always happen with an eye toward improving the brand.

The middle lane has some activity, but considerably less than the slow lane. There are fewer cars there, but each one is moving faster and is more noticeable from any vantage point (although not interesting enough to make you watch them for very long). In terms of brand evolution, the middle lane represents the fewer—but perhaps bolder—changes that you'll make over time. These will happen less often and will be more noticeable by the market, and if done properly, will be seen as a positive step forward—not thought of as alarming or radical change. Updating the Web site with a completely new layout would qualify as a middle-lane evolution, as would a new ad campaign, trade-show booth, or brochure design. These types of changes, depending on what they are or their expense, should happen about every 12–24 months.

And now we're in the fast lane, which seems so empty and stays so empty for so long that you almost forget it's there. But then, seemingly out of nowhere, a car speeds down it, startling you and commanding your attention. It races away, leaving the lane empty again for another good long time, while the other two lanes continue to work as usual. This lane represents the totally infrequent but very attention-getting major evolution that brands sometimes go through. This isn't a "complete makeover" (see Question #79, "When Is It Time to Give the Brand a Complete Makeover?" for a full definition), but still a radical change such as re-writing the tagline or modifying the logo or selecting a new font for the brand name. These types of changes can come as a surprise to consumers;

indeed, they may initially recoil from the change. But they may also—assuming the right research was done prior to launch—ultimately accept and embrace it. These changes shouldn't happen often: Once every three to five years will be fine. Just enough to keep up with the times and let the market know you're not sitting still, but are continuing to grow and mature.

# Q: SHOULD YOUR BRAND CHANGE IN REACTION TO ACTIONS YOUR COMPETITORS HAVE TAKEN?

**GENEVIEVE SMITH**
**THE BRAND PERSPECTIVE**

The previous question is a perfect lead-in to this one, and I'm going to start my answer by asking you to ask yourself a question: Would you change who you are because of external influences, or do you stay true to you? Of course not. You are who you are and you must stay true to that. It's the same with a brand; I think it's a bad idea to allow the brand to change in reaction to competitors. If you've got a great brand, who cares what the competition does? If you do what you do best, if you flawlessly execute the business model, the brand will continue to thrive and grow.

I *do* think you must constantly strive to innovate. The company's products and services must perpetually improve in order to differentiate the brand and keep it fresh. But that activity comes from *inside* the company. It comes from having an environment in which bright people think about the business and push it forward—perhaps to places no one would have thought of. You don't get that by copying the competition.

It's important to listen to the consumer and to watch where the marketplace is moving and how it is changing. But even then, do consumers necessarily always know what they will buy next? Great research and consumer insight is a key to success, but so is the gut of the company that really knows itself and its market and is constantly looking inside to find a better way to run the brand.

**JASON MILETSKY**
**THE AGENCY PERSPECTIVE**

There are going to be some people who *strongly* disagree with me on this, but I've never cared all that much about the competition. Sure, you should keep an eye on them, get a sense of what they're up to, and generally stay on top of things. But I think brands are better off concentrating on who they are and what they do best than worrying too much about what the competition is up to. I'd much rather be seen as proactive than reactive.

What I'm about to say could either make me look brilliant or like a complete idiot, and I may update my thoughts on this question on the *Perspectives* blog, but here goes. Most of this book was written in the back half of 2008, right in the middle of Microsoft's "I'm a PC" campaign. The little bit of research I've done so far hasn't given me any insight into whether or not the campaign is delivering the desired results; that may be more clear by the time you read this. Maybe the campaign will sell more computers, but I'd bet money that ultimately, it's not going to do what it intended to do: clean up Micrsosoft's damaged reputation.

The campaign is in response to Apple's wildly popular "I'm a Mac" ad campaign, which shows a hip, young guy playing the role of the Mac and a nerdy, accountant type playing the role of a PC. Through conversation, PC usually ends up looking pretty dorky compared to his cooler Mac counterpart. Finally tired of being berated by Apple, Microsoft developed a counter attack, showing video snippets of their own engineers and PC users saying "I'm a PC" while doing something cool, like scuba diving, to show that people who use PCs are both cool and diverse. (They also really pander to the liberal environmentalist crowd, as more than a few snippets have to do with PC users doing something to save the environment.)

I know I'm an Apple fan—I've made that abundantly clear in this book—but that doesn't change my opinion about this campaign. Microsoft has, like, what— 90 percent market share? 95 percent? As far as I'm concerned, all the "I'm a PC" campaign does is legitimize Apple. It tells the audience that Apple can play in Microsoft's league, that Microsoft can be injured, that they're not cool enough to take a joke. It doesn't say anything positive about Microsoft at all. Worse, it heightens consumer interest in the Apple campaign. (On that note, if you *are* going to do a campaign in response to another brand's advertising, make sure yours is hands-down better. Microsoft's isn't. When the one guys says, "I'm a PC and a human being. Not a human doing. Not a human thinking. A human being," I was *more* than happy that I am *not* a PC. Seriously, what does all the "human being" shit even mean? I guess somebody thought it was deep….)

Personally, I think Microsoft would have been much better served taking their far-larger marketing budget and coming up with something totally new, totally creative, totally proactive, and totally their own. Make your brand look cool on your own terms—not someone else's. Make it seem that you've never even heard of the Apple campaign—that it's so insignificant you couldn't care less. By reacting to Apple, Microsoft may still own more market share, but in terms of brand perception, they've allowed David to take down Goliath.

# Q: WHAT WOULD BE CONSIDERED SMALL, INCREMENTAL STEPS IN EVOLVING A BRAND (AS OPPOSED TO LARGE SWEEPING CHANGES)?

**GENEVIEVE SMITH**
**THE BRAND PERSPECTIVE**

Early on, I spoke about four broad areas to focus on in brand management: people, products, communications, and experience. The branding strategies that take the longest to implement—things like ensuring your internal operations are true to the brand promise across these four areas or determining what the company could be doing to improve in each quadrant—are by their very nature the least glamorous, and require evolution rather than revolution.

Drawing from my WaMu experience, once we decided simplify our processes in order to create a meaningful sense of ease of interaction for our customers, I had to quickly accept that operationalizing this promise meant taking small, incremental steps along an evolutionary path. Yes, consumers place a huge value on greater simplicity and ease—in fact, this is one of the biggest things happening in brands today. (If you think about it, this makes sense; our lives are increasingly complex, so anything that makes life a bit simpler or easier is going to be a good thing.) But you cannot just wave a magic want and implement something like simplicity in a large, bureaucratic, corporate environment.

But just because a step is incremental doesn't mean it's not worthwhile. Although chipping away at items like legal language or processes or employee communications are truly small, evolutionary steps, in the aggregate they can be very meaningful.

JASON MILETSKY
THE AGENCY PERSPECTIVE

 With any evolution of the brand, you have to consider how everything else will be affected. For example, changing the logo even a little bit—the colors, or even a small design modification—means changing anything that has the logo on it, including printed material, advertising pieces, building signage, etc. This can involve a huge expense, so make sure the change is worthwhile. Similarly, any significant change will be picked up by the audience, who may not necessarily react positively to the change. (People in general don't always take change very well.) So again, make sure the change will ultimately be worth any short-term hiccups the change may cause in overall growth.

Personally, I prefer smaller changes that happen over time over wide, sweeping changes (unless wide, sweeping changes are absolutely necessary). Smaller evolutionary steps can include things like playing up secondary colors that appear in the brand guide but may not be used all that often, and from there starting to add completely new colors to the mix. Try updating images and photography—not just the subject matter, but the style. Play with different angles and lighting—but do so carefully and in such a way that any new photography clearly looks like forward progress but doesn't compete with existing imagery that may represent the brand elsewhere. For example, if you change the images on the Web site but don't want to incur the expense of reprinting brochures just yet, use images that work on their own but won't seem out of place to customers who also look at your brochures. For an even more visible change, consider updating the layout of the Web site and any brochures or sell sheets that may be used.

For companies that can afford to spend megabucks on re-branding but still want to continue a slow evolution of change, then a small, subtle alteration to the logo of the corporate font may be all that's needed. Look at the new Pepsi logo released in 2008. Personally, I'm not a fan (maybe it'll grow on me), but it still uses their red, white, and blue circle—just with a slightly different wave pattern. Noticeable, but not a huge departure. The same goes for the 2005 evolution of the AT&T logo (which I do like quite a bit), which gave their blue-and-white striped globe more dimension and rotated it just slightly so that the northern pole of the globe is visible. Noticeably more modern, but really not that much different. These kinds of changes let the market know you're changing with the times and that you're not stagnating. They keep your brand moving forward without shaking everything up and potentially scaring everyone away.

# Q: THE OLD BRAND MANAGER IS OUT AND THE NEW BRAND MANAGER IS IN. IS THAT A GOOD ENOUGH REASON TO RADICALLY CHANGE THE BRAND?

**GENEVIEVE SMITH**
**THE BRAND PERSPECTIVE**

↳ In a word: no.

Look, if a company was dissatisfied with the outgoing brand manager, then that company might use the changing of the guard as an opportunity to take a fresh look at the brand. And even if the company *wasn't* dissatisfied, a new manager will bring another perspective that could be additive. But the brand is not "owned" by any one manager, so a management change isn't likely to trigger a radical change in the brand—unless the company is bringing in the new brand manager for the specific purpose of overseeing a radical change for other reasons, in which case he or she would be on point to manage the work.

JASON MILETSKY
THE AGENCY PERSPECTIVE

No! I've seen this time and time again: A new brand manager or CMO takes office and wants to make his or her mark by turning the brand upside down and reshaping it in their own image. (This is especially true for smaller brands. Global consumer brands, like Burger King, Tropicana, and Windex, are way too large to be re-branded on whim.)

Bad bad *bad* idea. If the new person comes in with really great vision and can make a strong case for why the brand should change, then fine. Just make sure this new person is going to stick around awhile, and that the general consensus is that the brand is changing for a reason—not just for the new dude's ego. But the chances of someone from outside the company stepping into the role and knowing enough to make a radical change to the brand out of the gate are slim. Earlier in this book we discussed the importance of living the brand. Living the brand doesn't happen overnight. It takes awhile, and to lead effectively, any new brand manager needs to immerse himself or herself in it—get to know it, feel it, and live it. Only after accomplishing that can he or she really be ready to make the decision to completely revamp the brand.

A really good brand manager will do what's right for the brand—not for themselves. (Incidentally, this goes for really good agencies, too.) He or she will look at the market, the brand's place in it, determine what's working and what's not, set realistic goals, and help put a strategy in place to move the brand forward. A brand should never be changed for the sake of someone's ego or for lack of anything better to work on. (I've even seen one instance where a brand manager decided to undergo a complete re-brand simply for job security. Layoffs were coming, but he knew full well that it'd be hard if not impossible for a company to let him go while he was in the middle of a major brand overhaul. He never came out and said this, but it was pretty obvious.)

Branding is serious business, and shouldn't be taken lightly. It's what your market sees and how they know who you are. Your brand is your reputation. Don't give it up or put it in danger to save your job or make yourself the hero. There's simply too much at stake.

# Q: • WHEN IS IT TIME TO GIVE THE
# • BRAND A COMPLETE MAKEOVER?

**GENEVIEVE SMITH**
**THE BRAND PERSPECTIVE**

As I've mentioned, a brand must be constantly managed to be ahead of the market. Sometimes, however, companies fail to place refreshing the brand on the agenda for any number of reasons—for example, if the company has historically enjoyed a lot of success with the status quo. The best time to give the brand a complete makeover is when the company, having been lax and having failed to focus on managing the brand, discovers that the position it believed it held has eroded or that the brand itself is no longer relevant.

When I worked at WaMu, we did completely make over the brand—which, by the way, was neither easy nor cheap. In retrospect, I feel that we waited too long to do so. While the effort itself brought a lot of energy and positive momentum to the brand (and, I might add, to the employees), the company was too entrenched in the attitude of sticking to the tried and true. Even with new leadership and support for the makeover, we still could never really do what we said: make banking simpler and make our customers smile. Many things we did were revolutionary to banking and additive to the position, but from my vantage point today, I can see that we did not have the stomach for true innovation, nor were we able to eliminate the bureaucracy in order to really get the job done.

As a counterpoint to this, consider the case of Gucci and Tom Ford. Gucci, formerly a (stodgy) luxury brand mostly noted for manufacturing loafers for the old guard, had the guts to bring on Tom Ford and completely reinvent the brand for today's customer. Gucci still stands for quality and fashion, but in a whole new way. Now *that* was a makeover!

JASON MILETSKY
THE AGENCY PERSPECTIVE

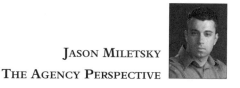

 I think I need to break this question down a little bit before answering it. It's not that I'm OCD (well, maybe a little...); it's that I want to make sure we're all on the same page so my responses make sense. I've never been big on ambiguity.

A "complete makeover" is pretty extreme. It's Michael Jackson, I'm-going-to-look-nothing-like-my-former-self extreme (except with a brand, the new results have a shot at being an improvement). To me, a complete makeover means that everything changes—the name of company, the logo, everything. Maybe the products and services stay pretty much the same, but all the elements that represent the brand will be different.

If this is what we're talking about, then the answer is simple: Avoid a complete makeover at all costs. Building a brand takes time and consistency. It requires ongoing communication to get the name and promise of your brand into the minds of the market. Over time, your audience will get to know you and trust you (assuming you're fulfilling the brand promise). They'll come to understand the promise and personality, products, services, and benefits you offer, so that as soon as they see your logo or hear your name, they'll make an immediate connection with what your brand is all about. That's brand equity, and it's important. A complete makeover pretty much erases that brand equity and can confuse the market. It'll take a lot of positive PR to keep consumers up to date with the changes.

There are really only a few reasons for a brand to go through a complete makeover:

- The company has merged with or has been acquired by another company. In this case, a total revamp of the name and brand may be considered in order to better transition the two companies into a cohesive corporate environment and to approach the market as a single unit. Ordinarily, the new brand name is a combination of the two names, especially in a merger situation, such as JP Morgan Chase.

- A persistently negative perception in the marketplace about a particular brand forces that brand to re-emerge as something else. For example, in 2003, Phillip Morris re-branded its holding company's name to Altria in order to distance itself from the ongoing negative news associated with tobacco.

- The current name is holding the brand back from further growth or otherwise confusing markets. WebMD is a good example of this. Although WebMD is widely known as a Web site where people can look up medical information and research symptoms, the Web site only accounts for a relatively small percentage of its revenue. The company's main focus is facilitating transactions between payers, providers, and patients—a B2B service that has little to do with the popular Web site. But as the site grew in popularity, the name began to hold the rest of the company back—until they changed the corporate name to Emdeon. (They still own the WebMD site.)

Maybe I'm missing something, but I really can't think of any other compelling reason to go through something as dramatic as a complete brand overhaul. There are, of course, evolutions and changes that are massive in scope but stop short of being complete makeovers. Changing the logo completely but leaving the name intact, for example, can be a huge change, but isn't likely to cause the same short-term collateral damage to brand equity that a complete makeover would.

But even this type of change needs to be considered very carefully. Large changes to the brand can cost a great deal of time and money—and still cause confusion in the market among consumers who have gotten to know your brand in its current incarnation. Smaller, more subtle evolutionary changes are usually better for keeping consumers tied to your brand (I talked about this more in Question #77, "What Would Be Considered Small, Incremental Steps in Evolving a Brand [as Opposed to Large, Sweeping Changes]?" so I'll skip that discussion here), but there are reasons for taking more drastic approaches. Negativity about your brand in the news may have injured the brand's reputation, and new logo design shortly after the news has been quelled is often a good idea. Alternatively, if your logo looks dated, an overhaul of the look and feel might be necessary to get you back up to speed. (Again, I'd personally recommend more subtle evolutionary changes in either of these cases, but I can see how they could be the basis of an argument for more dramatic changes in brand look and feel.) Large-scale brand alterations may be needed if the product mix changes or the target market shifts considerably. Regardless of the reason, brand managers need to do a full assessment to feel comfortable that changing the look, feel, personality, or whatever is really in the best interest of the brand and its market and will produce positive returns.

# Q: • WHEN IS IT TOO LATE TO GIVE THE • BRAND A COMPLETE MAKEOVER?

**GENEVIEVE SMITH**

**THE BRAND PERSPECTIVE**

⮑ If the business is going to fail due to the company's business practices, then it is too late. If you can't make money, then hang it up; a rebrand won't help. Let's use Circuit City as an example. Circuit City operated in an extremely competitive market with heavy pressure from other electronics retailers like Best Buy as well as general retailers such as Wal-Mart. In 2008, facing mounting losses, Circuit City hired Goldman Sachs and developed a plan to sell themselves to the only interested party: Blockbuster (although Blockbuster was itself a struggling brand, affected by the advent of movie-rental channels like Netflix and Apple downloads).

Part of the perceived benefit for both Circuit City and Blockbuster in merging was the opportunity to make over both of these brands by joining them together—for example, cross-merchandising in-store or cross-selling electronics with movie and digital subscriptions. Blockbuster CEO Jim Keyes, quoted in a *Business Week* article about the potential deal, called it a "game-changing entertainment retail concept."

Needless to say, this sale never happened—and in January of 2009, Circuit City filed for bankruptcy. As we've discussed already in Question #33, "Is a Good Brand Enough To Keep A Brand Alive? Is There Anything the Brand Manager Can Do to Fix a Failing Company?" a brand makeover cannot fix fundamental weaknesses in a company's operating model.

In this case, it was simply too late for Circuit City. Maybe a combined Blockbuster/Circuit City would have been able to tough it out and, through a merger, develop a strong new brand. Personally? I don't think so, given the competitive pressure and changing consumer preferences that have caused both brands to struggle.

JASON MILETSKY

THE AGENCY PERSPECTIVE

You know Lehman Brothers? Linens-n-Things? KB Toys? It's a bit too late for them.

Obviously, this question is referring to companies that are struggling for survival, companies that are the focus of some crushingly negative news that is severely damaging the brand's reputation within the marketplace. But as long as you're still in business and it looks like you'll be able to stay in business for the foreseeable future, there's always a case to be made for a complete re-branding.

But there are rules. For instance, even if your company is going to survive whatever problems it's gotten itself into, any significant re-branding really needs to wait until after the storm has subsided and the spotlight is off your company for a while. If you re-brand while bad news is still circulating, the negativity will simply overtake the new brand. If you re-brand immediately after, bad market sentiment may still be strong and the re-brand will look like little more than using a vase of flowers to mask the scent of rotting garbage.

There are other instances when a complete makeover—however badly needed—may be too late. For example, it's possible for a brand to become so strong and so well known that it simply can't keep up with the changing market. This is mostly the fault of brand managers who are likely so enamored with how strong their brand is that they can't see that it's that very strength that will ultimately do them in. That's why it's important to keep an eye on the market, see how audiences and the industry are changing, and continually evolve the brand to keep up.

Probably the most fabled instance of a brand that reacted to market changes too late was GM's Oldsmobile line of cars. When it became clear that the cars weren't reaching a younger generation and that the middle-class values that the brand stood for were, by the 1980s, outdated, they did an about-face and introduced that now-infamous tag, "This is not your father's Oldsmobile," simultaneously shutting out their core market of loyal consumers and having no real impact on younger consumers.

Another good example, though not nearly as well-known, was Foxton's Realty. Still a premier brand in England, Foxton's came to the U.S. promising to charge commission's of only 2 percent—far less than the industry-standard 6 percent.

They weren't much help in finding you a place, but they had a stellar Web site that did a lot of the work for you. They created a very strong brand as a discount realtor, but when the housing market was falling, they weren't able to shift to being a more high-end realtor. (They tried, but their discount brand was just too strong.) Eventually, 2 percent of really low housing prices did them in.

I guess a basic rule of thumb is, if you find yourself asking "Is it too late to completely re-brand?" then it probably is.

# Q: • THE DECISION HAS BEEN MADE TO REDO
# • THE BRAND COMPLETELY. WHAT'S NEXT?

**GENEVIEVE SMITH**
**THE BRAND PERSPECTIVE**

 Now the fun begins!

This question says, "The decision has been made to redo the brand completely," so let's start from there. What went into the decision? Was it dissatisfaction with the brand position based on results, research, management, or a fundamental change in company direction? It could be that one or more of these have triggered this decision. Regardless of which one(s) it was, what happens next is a fundamental re-examination of the brand position. This exercise will result in either a gentle update or a major re-articulation.

This examination should include the following:

- Evaluation of where the brand has been positioned, including what is good and relevant and can be evolved versus what is no longer valuable

- Clear articulation of the business goals that have prompted the decision to redo the brand

- Insights into the current position through research with executives, management, and employees

- Insights into the hopes and dreams for the brand from these same employees

- Consumer research about the brand's position

- An exploration of the territories that could be ownable and distinctive based on the company's business model, the competition, and the internal gut for risk

- Vetting of the candidate territories with employees and consumers

- Final position testing through consumer research

Once the new brand position has been determined, a company will go through all the practical steps we have discussed previously to communicate this internally and externally and to implement it into business practices.

The way I have described these steps may seem somewhat cut and dry; it's important to remember, however, that the brand is the heart and soul of the company. The decision to redo the brand marks the beginning of a journey. So take your time on this. Don't succumb to pressure to produce before you are sure—from the gut of the company—that you have it right.

**Jason Miletsky**
**The Agency Perspective**

↳ Call my agency, ask for me, and we'll get started. (If only all sales were that simple!)

Okay. You've decided to redo the brand completely. Take a deep breath, say good-bye to your family for the next few months, and roll up your sleeves. It's time to go to work! The first thing you'll need to do is hire an agency. You don't want to go this alone. There's just way too much to do, and you're going to need the extra hands (creative minds, strategists, project managers, graphic designers, copywriters, programmers, and other professionals that the brand probably won't have on staff) and the outside point of view to get it done quickly, professionally, and in such a way that it really resonates with your market. You're also going to need people who've gone through the re-branding process before (whether in your industry or not); they'll know in advance the steps to take and how to best keep all the balls in the air.

Don't assume your current marketing agency will be able to re-brand your company. Re-branding is tricky work and might not be one of your marketing agency's core competencies. While we're on the topic of agencies, let me also point out that there are three distinct areas in any re-branding effort. While it's possible that one agency could handle all three areas, you might also consider dividing the work among different agencies:

- **Developing the name:** If your complete re-brand will include a name change, this will be the single most important part of the re-branding process. The name you decide on will stay with you for a long, long time. You need to make sure that all key executives are happy with the name and are satisfied that the market will react to it positively. I recommend finding an agency that specializes in brand-name development. This one area can be intense, expensive, and time-consuming, but ultimately one of the most important.

- **Developing the brand guide and Web site:** Compile a list of each and every brand identifier (colors, fonts, logos, tags, etc.) and each page of the brand guide that needs to be written, as well as definitions that need to be developed (such as adjectives to describe the brand personality). Then put together a full project plan that outlines the order in which everything needs to be done (including market research and legal sign-off) and the due dates for each item. (There will likely be parallel efforts.) There'll be a lot of creative development throughout this process, which should culminate in the publication of a completed brand guide, the launch of a new Web site (this needs to happen when the re-brand is made public), and a kick-off brochure, sales sheet, and/or PowerPoint template and presentation. There will also need to be a communications component, where the brand is announced to clients, employees, and the public. All of this could be completed by the same agency that develops the name, but doesn't have to be. It could be done by another agency or, if they're qualified, your marketing agency of record.

- **Creating all additional collateral material and marketing the brand:** Part of the re-branding process should be assembling a list of all collateral material, presentations, videos, etc. that need to be redone within the new brand guidelines. New marketing campaigns will also need to be created to announce and promote the brand. Most likely, some small changes will need to be made to the brand guide at this time, and maybe a few holes filled in. Your marketing agency of record can handle all these responsibilities.

---

Whatever agency you do hire (your current marketing agency or a new firm), make sure you pay for the re-branding on a project basis, not using an ongoing retainer. You don't want this to go on forever. Brands may evolve over time, but initial development should have a completion date.

---

If you haven't gone through the process, there really is a lot to it. Don't go it alone. Take the first step and get the right agency (or mix of agencies).

# Q: THE BRAND HAS A BAD REPUTATION IN THE MARKETPLACE. IS THAT THE CLIENT'S FAULT OR THE AGENCY'S?

**GENEVIEVE SMITH**

**THE BRAND PERSPECTIVE**

It is totally on the client. A bad reputation is the result of much more than a bad ad campaign, a PR flop, or inappropriate graphics. It is about the company. You cannot outsource your company's reputation. The client owns their own fate when it comes to this.

Can you see hiring an agency and telling them they are accountable for the firm's reputation? If that were so, you would be hiring the agency to manage the company's financial results, the company's ethics, the quality of the company's products and services, its compliance with regulatory requirements, its human-resource practices, its legal department, and much more.

I don't even think you can fault an agency for bad creative work. Internal talent owns the results of brand expressions and communications as well. Many firms choose to outsource the majority of their creative thinking and, in some cases, a majority of their strategic work to agencies or to consultants. I think that is a mistake. No doubt it is beneficial to outsource some functions, and no doubt in many cases the best talent will be found working at agencies. But how can you outsource your brand?

If you employ people who are innovative, in touch, and inspired by the brand, they will naturally move the brand forward—and they will intuitively work with agency partners to put creative work in the market that is true to the spirit of the brand.

JASON MILETSKY

THE AGENCY PERSPECTIVE

I don't know how to write this without sounding like I'm passing the buck or trying to shield agencies from the real pressure of accepting responsibility, but if the brand has a bad reputation, that's the brand's fault.

Out of curiosity, I Googled the term "worst customer service companies" and clicked on the first link that I saw, which was a 2007 list compiled by MSN of the companies with the worst customer service, based on consumer submissions. It didn't surprise me that Sprint was ranked in the top spot by 40 percent of all respondents. I was once a Sprint customer myself; it was only after years of intense therapy that I finally recovered from the mental anguish their customer-service department put me through (until I signed up with Cingular, which made Sprint look like they actually had their act together).

I don't remember exactly why I entered the Sprint store and signed a contract with the company. I'm not ashamed to say, however, that on some level, it was because I was responding to their advertising—probably not any one specific ad, but their overall marketing effort, which kept their brand name in my mind, which in turn built trust. The marketing got me through the door, and it obviously got a lot of other people through the door, too. So the agency did a good job—but that's where their work ended. That's where Sprint should have taken over and done what they needed to do to make sure that they fulfilled their promise and that their customers had a good experience—and that's where Sprint dropped the ball. And that's why I didn't just abandon Sprint; I go out of my way to tell people about my bad experiences with the company. It's also why enough people responded to the MSN call for entries to put Sprint at the top of the list of companies with the worst customer service.

Ask yourself this: If you were shopping for a wireless provider, how much marketing would Sprint have to do to make you forget about seeing their name as the worst company for customer service? There isn't any amount of brand advertising that's going to make you forget that list. The only thing that's going to make you consider using Sprint is for Sprint to improve the consumer experience—to get themselves on a list of companies with most-improved customer service or, even better, a list of companies with the best customer service.

An agency can spread good news. Agencies can even cover up bad news for a short while. But they can't be held responsible when the brand doesn't fulfill its end of the bargain and keep their customers happy.

# Q: CAN CREATING A NEW BRAND NAME AND IMAGE ERASE NEGATIVE CONSUMER IMPRESSIONS ABOUT A BRAND?

**GENEVIEVE SMITH**

**THE BRAND PERSPECTIVE**

↳ I don't know how a brand that is fundamentally the same can repackage itself and expect consumers to change their opinions as a result. In the first place, consumers probably didn't develop this negative opinion because of the brand name. As Shakespeare said, "A rose by any other name...." And as we've said repeatedly in this book, the brand is about much more than the name or the expressions. It is fundamentally what the company stands for and who it is.

---

Changing opinions about the brand's image—that's doable. For more on that, I'd refer you to the discussion about Tylenol in my answer to Question #65, "Can You Brand Yourself Out of a PR Crisis?" While that is an extreme example, it illustrates of the type of effort that is involved with re-imaging a brand.

---

A brand's image in the marketplace is developed over time across multiple dimensions such as quality, honesty, trust, appeal, coolness, and many more attributes. The importance of these are of course informed by consumer opinion. So, just like a public figure or celebrity can, through his or her own actions or through the media, sully his or her image, so too can a brand.

But at the end of the day, although consumers are fickle and can easily abandon a brand or switch favorites, they also can be forgiving. If a brand is in touch with its core customers and with the consumer groups it wants to develop, it will find a way to repair its image—but that won't come about via a new graphics package.

JASON MILETSKY
THE AGENCY PERSPECTIVE

If negative consumer sentiment is strong enough, then a name change isn't likely to change the opinions of consumers. Consumers might not have long attention spans, but they're not stupid.

A better plan of attack is to hold off on the name change until any major negative buzz dies down. In the meantime, combat negative impressions through the media with an aggressive public-relations campaign in an attempt to spin negative news into something more positive. When bad news is affecting consumer sentiment, your brand doesn't need a mask, it needs a voice. Make knowledgeable, eloquent spokespeople available for interviews to get the brand's side of the story out there.

During this time, serious work also needs to be done within the brand to tackle the issues that are doing it damage. This will likely not a be a branding job at all; it could fall to finance, operations, customer service, distribution, or some other department to fix the problem. Upper management must pinpoint the root of the problem and make the necessary adjustments to get the company back on track and start building positive sentiment back up. Any major internal problem that can negatively affect the consumer experience needs to be addressed and smoothed out so that the brand can start to rebuild its reputation.

After all of this is done and the negative news has subsided (assuming that the news wasn't so poisonous that it crippled the company beyond repair and the company is still in business), the brand manager can assess whether a name change is in order. If the negative news—even after it has subsided—has left a lingering aftertaste in people's mouths, a new name might be what's needed to jump-start positive brand sentiment. But it's not going to happen overnight—and it's not guaranteed to happen at all.

# PART FIVE
# Just for Fun

# Q: • Are You Loyal to Any
# • Particular Brands? Why?

Jason Miletsky
The Agency Perspective

If you've read more than 10 pages of this book, you're probably pretty sick of hearing me talk about Apple and Diet Pepsi. Clearly, I'm a fan of those brands. I've probably touted them so much that you've wondered if they're paying me to endorse them. (They're not—but I'd be open to discussing it with them....)

I promise I won't bore you anymore by talking about those brands. I think I've made my feelings on each pretty clear. Instead, I'll toss out some other brands I'm loyal to (now that I think about it, even I'm a little surprised by how many there are) and why:

■ **Fox News:** My guess is that simply because I included Fox News in this list, many of you concluded that I must be a Republican. Talk about branding! (Actually, I lean to the left on social issues, but I vote based on my views on foreign affairs and the economy, which lean right.) Regardless of their claims of being "Fair and Balanced," most people see Fox as a very right-leaning media source. Personally, I think that they actually are pretty middle-of-the-road and do a good job of giving both sides of an issues. (Well, maybe they're a bit to the right, but not as much as their reputation would suggest.) Anyway, even though CNN and MSNBC are only a click of the remote away, Fox News is always my choice when I want to get caught up with what's happening in the world or if something big is going on (like an election). Part of this is because I'm not crazy impressed with the competing networks. CNN just seems a bit old and stodgy to me (maybe that will change after Larry King retires), and MSNBC is just so extremely to the left that I can't watch it for more than a few minutes at a time. (The best part about the Obama presidency is that it may make Keith Olbermann a little less necessary.) But the bigger part is that I just think Fox News really knows how to run a network. They have a good balance of news shows and editorial shows, and they're innovative, entertaining, and informative. They're also hipper—but without seeming to obviously pander to a younger crowd.

■ **BMW:** In my answer to Question #42, "What Role Does the Brand Have in Enforcing Service Standards and Customer Interaction Models?" I talked about my experiences with BMW—and I hope you'll forgive me, but I'm going to repeat in this answer what I said in that one. I've driven BMWs for about seven years and I have no interest in switching to anything else. It's not because they're better-made cars (they might be, but I wouldn't know—all I know about cars is where the cup holders are and that I like driving around with the top down), but because I like the way their vehicles look and because BMW provides outstanding service. When the headlight of my X3 SUV blew out 30 miles before the warranty expired, not only did the dealership fix the headlight, they also installed new brakes and shocks—not because I needed them, but because they wanted to make sure everything was good before my warranty expired. Treat me well, and you'll have a customer for life.

■ **Verizon Wireless:** I won't go into the litany of truly awful experiences I've had with other wireless providers (the list is long). It's not that I don't think you'd be interested; it just irritates me to think about it, and why stress myself out? Verizon Wireless has it all put together: They've got a huge network (the TV spots are right!), and I haven't dropped a call in the four years I've been using them. I can even pick up signals in elevators far below street level. Verizon's plans are fair and easy to understand, the people at their stores are helpful, and any billing issues (there haven't been many) have been handled quickly by a friendly and knowledgeable customer-service representative. (Apparently those still exist! Who knew?) They've not only gained my loyalty, but they've made me into an advocate.

■ **The *New York Post*:** The *New York Post* is just a great paper. What other paper can you read from front to back and still have absolutely no idea what's going on in the world? (I mean, how can you *not* love a paper that, in mid-April, 2005—while other papers were reporting the nationwide sweep of 10,000 fugitives, the Lebanese Prime Minister stepping down, and the body of a missing Florida girl finally being found—led with a story about a man arrested for painting a yellow brick road outside of a midget's house, with the headline "HI HO HI HO…IT'S OFF TO COURT HE GOES"? Classic news reporting.) But that doesn't really matter. Their style of writing works for me, as does the layout and organization. Plus, between them and the *New York Daily News*, I think the *Post* comes up with *waaaaay* better headlines. (Case in point: the "HOLY SHIITE" headline for a story about *Newsweek* retracting its deadly toilet tale.) Their editorials work, as does the balance of copy to pictures—and everything seems to have just a little bit of a sardonic edge to it, which I like.

**GENEVIEVE SMITH**

**THE BRAND PERSPECTIVE**

↳ I hate this question—my answers will say too much about me and my taste—but I'll answer it:

- **Apple:** I love the products, the stores, and the advertising.

- **Harley-Davidson:** I'm a dyed-in-the-wool Harley owner. I love the ride.

- **Mini:** Just the right car for me—it's distinctive and it makes me smile.

- **Bumble:** They're the best hair products I've found.

- **Whole Foods:** If you have to shop for groceries, why not enjoy the experience?

- **Facebook:** It's far and away the best way to stay in touch—even with people you'd forgotten about.

# Q: WHICH BRANDS JUST SEEM TO GET IT?

What's your perspective on this question? Let us know at
PerspectivesOnBranding.com.

JASON MILETSKY

THE AGENCY PERSPECTIVE

I know—in my answer to the last question, I promised I wouldn't mention Apple again. But it goes without saying that I'd put them on my list in this answer. But they're not the only ones. There are a good number of brands that just seem to get it. Over the years, I've tried to make a mental note of it when I come across a brand that I really think has figured out how to establish themselves and connect with their market. In fact, there's a pretty long list of brands I could write about—not necessarily brands that I use or care about, but brands that consistently seem to do the right thing. To keep from droning on and on, I'll just present my top five:

- **M&M's:** I hate to include this one because my agency does Internet development work for Hershey's, but I think anybody in marketing has to admire the work that's been done with the M&M's brand. By personifying each of the colors and maintaining their characteristics over time, they've broadened their appeal and really connected with their audience. They're fun, they're lively, they maintain an edge, and they continue to get their message out there through a variety of avenues. They connect with their audience through clever movie tie-ins that allow them to have some fun with the M&M's characters (I particularly liked their tie-ins with the fourth installment of the Indiana Jones franchise), and they periodically get consumers directly involved with the brand by asking them to vote for a new color or giving them the chance to send personalized messages to people printed right on the candy. It's just a very organized, well-established brand that continues to evolve in all the right ways.

245

- **Budweiser:** I'll be really interested to see what happens with Bud once the InBev takeover has been in effect for awhile, but up to now, Bud has managed to associate themselves with the heart of America and create an indelible connection with the blue-collar worker. Most amazingly, they've done this without alienating or shutting out white-collar execs. The bright red and the iconic eagle in their logo make the brand unabashedly American, tapping into a sense of patriotism, while their marketing campaigns have reached people through humor, drama, sports, and nostalgia. And somehow, they've been able to manage their growth and evolve their brand without ever losing touch with the spirit that's engaged their massive market.

- **VH1:** *Such* a smart brand! I'm not a huge fan of MTV anymore. I think they've really fumbled the ball, going from being the standard-bearer for pop culture to being somewhat of a joke. But they've made a really good move with VH1. Clearly aiming for a slightly older audience, VH1 constantly cranks out a mix of reality shows, videos, and commentary-type shows that never seem to take themselves too seriously. It's almost as though every show on that network is connected by the fact that they know they're being silly without coming right out and being silly. Where other networks run pseudo-serious reality shows that manufacture drama, like *Survivor* or *The Bachelor*, VH1 produces reality shows where Sharon Osbourne teaches charm school or an 80s hair-band rocker searches for love among a gaggle of bimbos. Their commentary shows (for lack of a better phrase) on pop culture, current events, best videos, and more parade out obscure personalities spanning the last four decades, giving the audience a sense of nostalgia and the opportunity to say "I remember that guy!" And through it all, everyone on every show seems to be sharing the same inside joke: that they couldn't care less if anyone is watching. They're just having fun! It's that attitude that makes the network so watchable.

- **Cheerios:** Personally, I'm not a big fan of Cheerios. I mean, I suppose they're okay, but to me they're just kind of bland. Then again, I'm staring down 40 and still like to eat the marshmallows out of the box of Lucky Charms. But Cheerios have tremendous appeal for both health-conscious adults and small children. (The best part of my college waitering days was sweeping up the endless piles of Cheerios underneath the tables where kids had been sitting.) But I don't need to personally be a fan of the cereal to recognize that they have consistently done a wonderful job of maintaining their connection to the market and keeping their brand prominent in the media. Their marketing plays up the nutritional benefits of the cereal. More importantly, it does so by highlighting the connections between people—parents and kids, husbands and wives—all while maintaining an image that clearly sets Cheerios up as a brand that doesn't just care about your family's health, it has for generations.

- **Marvel:** As a kid, when you read comic books, you were either a DC Comics reader or a Marvel Comics reader—and I was always on the DC side. And although I haven't picked up a comic book since I was 12, to this day I believe that between the two, DC has the better characters: Superman, Batman, Flash, Green Lantern, Wonder Woman.... (Lynda Carter didn't exactly hurt Wonder Woman's appeal. When I was young, my biggest crush was on Lynda Carter—at least until I saw the girl in Billy Idol's "Cradle of Love" video. But I digress.) My point is that while I think DC has got the better overall characters, Marvel has *way* out-branded DC. How is it that the three Spiderman movies (Marvel) are among the highest-grossing films of all time, but DC's *Superman Returns* (which, in my opinion, was a truly awful movie) fell way short of expectations? Granted, 2008's Batman movie, *The Dark Knight*, scored *huge* at the box office, but that's not the point. The point is that Marvel has created an entire universe of characters that don't necessarily inhabit the world together or at the same time, but somehow still seem to be interconnected in odd ways. They all embody a certain "screw you" kind of angst. The brand is organized and edgy. It's not afraid to take chances, to show the more personal, darker side of the characters. They just seem as though they have a plan—and DC doesn't. DC has fans, absolutely. But Marvel has fanatics. It might be geeky to be into superheroes, but Marvel has somehow made it cool to be geeky.

- **Jimmy Buffet:** Anybody who can parlay a couple of three-minute songs that are mediocre at best into an empire that includes a tequila brand, an island resort, multiple books, concert tours, a restaurant chain, legions of fans worldwide, and God knows what else because I've stopped paying attention, gets my vote as a brand that just gets it.

There are way more brands that get it that I haven't gone into: Ikea, Target, Dunkin' Donuts, and others. Some brands and brand managers just really understand how to reach their market.

GENEVIEVE SMITH
THE BRAND PERSPECTIVE

Well, obviously I think the brands I am loyal to "get it!" But beyond that, I do think there are brands that are notable on the "get it" front that I don't necessarily use. Target comes to mind, especially as a marketing person, purely from the marketing perspective. They have been absolutely genius in building and managing that brand. I don't think the in-store experience necessarily feels like the communications, but you cannot argue with success. I also think Costco has done a great job of managing their brand and of putting the products together in the warehouse in such a way that is appealing to both consumers and small businesses. And even though some folks are trashing eBay a bit these days, I think eBay has done a good job of cornering the online shopping market and creating ubiquitous brand presence.

I think applying the term "gets it" really involves personal taste to some degree. That said, there are certain companies that are used over and over again as examples of outstanding brands; some of my favorites—and possibly some of yours—are in that category. I'd wager the brands on your list of favorites seem to you to "get it" because they are relevant to you, but when whole segments of the population feel that same way, then you know a brand *really* gets it!

# Q: ARE THERE ANY BRANDS THAT YOU JUST DON'T LIKE, STRICTLY BASED ON THE BRAND PERSONALITY?

JASON MILETSKY

THE AGENCY PERSPECTIVE

↳ I do find certain brands irritating based on their personality, and as a result refuse to give them a chance. Surprisingly, though, there really aren't a lot…at least, only a few quickly come to mind. (Maybe I'm mellowing out as I get older.)

- **FreeCreditReport.com:** Do I really need to explain this? By now, every-body on the planet has seen the singing guy in a pirate suit, on a bike, in a crappy car, as a rap artist, etc. And I have to be honest: I think he becomes more unlikable with each new commercial. I've never been to the site, but I can pretty much guarantee that there's nothing "free" about it. (Somewhere in each spot it says something—in, like, eight-point font for about two seconds—about needing to be enrolled in a triple advantage thing in order to get the "free" credit report. Screw that.) The whole thing comes off as a scam. Even if I *were* interested in getting a copy of my credit report, I'd certainly find a company more serious—and more up front about the costs—than FreeCreditReport.com.

- **MSNBC:** I briefly mentioned MSNBC in my answer to Question #84, "Are You Loyal to Any Particular Brands? Why?" as one of the reasons I like Fox News so much. MSNBC, in my opinion, has assembled some of the most contemptible personalities on television to create an extremely stand-offish, over-the-top liberal station that somehow finds ways to twist even the most benign information into an outrageous right-wing conspiracy orchestrated by Bill O'Reilly. I'm sure all their hosts are fine people away from the camera, but on air I just don't find any of them—or the station as a whole—even remotely watchable. (Rachel Maddow may be the one exception; somehow, I can take her more on TV than I can on her AirAmerica show.)

And before anyone jumps to conclusions, this has nothing to do with MSNBC having a different political point of view than mine—it's how they present it. I enjoy a good debate (I'm the one came up with the concept of offering two different opinions through the *Perspectives* series, after all), but I think Keith Olbermann looking directly into the camera and telling Bush to "shut the hell up" pretty much paints the personality of the entire network.

■ **Bob's Discount Furniture:** If you live anywhere between New Jersey and Maine, you've undoubtedly been subject to these awful, obnoxious commercials starring Bob and one or two of his cronies (either in real life or claymation), a talking mattress, or other pieces of furniture chatting with each other about how Bob has "busted" the competition. The spots are crude, low-class, and—based on the growth of the company—clearly working. Nonetheless, it's a brand personality that severely turns me off.

■ **Vonage:** In hindsight, I'm thinking we should have asked a question in this book about the value of running deliberately annoying ads to get your brand to be remembered. Maybe I'll add it to the blog. Personally, I'm not a fan. I've never liked the idea of trying to bother people as a means of getting a point across. On the one hand, it's practically impossible to forget Vonage—that awful "WooHoo" song has gotten stuck in my head some nights and literally made it impossible for me to sleep. On the other hand, I don't want to work with a brand that's trying to irritate me. That's not going to make me feel close to the brand at all; it makes me feel contemptuous, and the only interaction I'll have with Vonage at this point is to race for the remote control to hit the Mute button before the song starts to play. In fact, I find this brand personality so irritating that when the company was experiencing financial problems, I was actually happy about it.

Before anybody writes me a bad review or sends me hate mail, let me just mention that my comments have nothing to do with the success of these brands. Some or all of them may be wildly successful, and some or all of that success could be based on their brand personality. But this isn't about whether or not they're successful—this is about the brand personalities that repel me as an individual. It's also possible that I could be misjudging some of these brand personalities because I'm basing my opinions entirely on their TV advertising (except for MSNBC). But in all these cases, I think that's enough.

## Genevieve Smith
## The Brand Perspective

Whenever I am asked this question, the one that comes to mind is Wal-Mart. I despise everything about this brand, *especially* the brand persona—which in my mind feels like the opposite of quality, value, community, and humanity. My impression of Wal-Mart is that it's a huge corporation that crushes both suppliers and local competition. And if that's not bad enough, they build the biggest, ugliest stores I've ever seen, and run people through them like cattle.

So that's my personal take on Wal-Mart. It's a reaction to the company's brand persona as I perceive it through multiple inputs. To tie into the previous question, in my book, Wal-Mart doesn't "get it"—yet they sell more than most any other brand in the world. So I'm obviously not voting with the vast majority in this case.

# Q: WHICH BRANDS CURRENTLY ARE IN NEED OF A SEVERE MAKEOVER?

JASON MILETSKY

THE AGENCY PERSPECTIVE

⤶ The problem with this question is that in most cases, by the time a brand is in need of a severe makeover, they're largely out of the public eye and forgotten about. But there was one brand that did immediately come to mind when I looked at this question: the NBA.

Let me start out by saying that I am not a sports fan. I kinda sorta follow the Yankees enough to have a semi-intelligent conversation about them, but not because I actually care. It's just that living in the New York metro area, you find yourself left out of a lot of conversations if you don't know what's up with that team. I understand the rules for most sports and I like to play (I played rugby in college and still try to grab a tennis racquet when I can). But in terms of being a fan? My thought is that when the players on some team come to my office to cheer me on while I do my work, then I'll be happy to reciprocate by cheering for them to do theirs. Until then, I'm not really that interested. But I actually believe that not being a sports fan makes me more qualified to comment on the NBA because I can express a completely unbiased opinion.

The NBA has basically become a league filled with thugs. Players getting arrested on gun charges, accused of rape, assault, drugs—you name it. You could argue that the NBA is no different from any other league; football's had its share of problems as well, and baseball is only a news report away from being embroiled in the steroids scandal again. But there are a few key differences between the NBA and these other leagues:

- The NBA has never enjoyed the type of popularity that MLB and the NFL have had. According to a 2008 poll by Harris Interactive, the closest the NBA ever came was in 1998, when 13 percent of adults named pro basketball as their favorite sport, compared to 26 percent for pro football and 18 percent for pro baseball. That's just not a strong enough fan base to withstand the impact of continued negative press.

- Crimes by NFL and MLB players are more interesting. Michael Vick was arrested for promoting dog fights; some dude on the New York Giants got arrested on gun charges after shooting himself (nice job). Baseball is over-run with steroids, which people don't come across every day. The crimes committed by NBA players, however—at least, the crimes that are widely reported—are more common...and more violent. It's a lot easier to cheer on a guy using steroids and harming himself than it is to cheer on a guy who was just arrested for rape or assault.

- The players in the NBA are a lot more visible—literally. Baseball players wear uniforms from neck to toe; the only parts of their bodies not covered are their faces and hands. Football players are even more concealed behind their helmets. Basketball players, though, have their legs, shoulders, and arms exposed to the fans—and many are covered in large, imposing tattoos. Argue with me all you want, but there is a negative association with a lot of tattoos on the part of the general public, and given the players' less-than-Boy Scout antics off the court, the tattoos aren't helping the image.

- The NBA's past popularity is based largely on the extreme popularity of a single individual: Michael Jordan (and to a lesser extent the Chicago Bulls franchise) and other scattered individuals like Larry Bird, Magic Johnson, Charles Barkley, Reggie Miller, Shaquille O'Neal, Karl Malone, and so on. When these guys retired, many fans didn't find much left in the league worth sticking around for.

The NBA has to make some serious changes—and in my opinion, the changes it needs to make are pretty clear. First, it needs to very publicly institute and enforce a Stop the Bullshit policy. Commit any crime worse than a moving violation just once, and that's it—you're done. It must be a zero-tolerance policy—I mean, really, how hard is to not do drugs or own a gun? The NBA also has to aggressively use their players in community-service type activities way more often during the off season and be really public about it. They need to show the softer side of the NBA, focusing on players who are well spoken and are poised in front of the camera. Finally (well, there's more, but I don't want to write a book on the NBA), the league has got to stop trying to turn every player into the next Michael Jordan. I can understand why they'd want to—the same Harris Interactive poll that I referenced earlier that showed the league's popularity peaking at 13 percent in 1998 (the year before Jordan retired) now, 10 years later, shows that only 4 percent of adults named pro basketball as their favorite sport. But Jordan wasn't as huge as he was based on skill alone. Granted, he was arguably the best athlete of his generation (maybe ever), but it was more than that. He came off as a gentleman. He spoke intelligently and he had a look and a smile tailor-made for the camera. He was able to transcend race and socio-economic classes. It was just hard not to like him. LeBron James may be a great player, but even if he broke every one of Jordan's records, he doesn't have all those other qualities that made Michael Jordan Michael Jordan. Stop looking for his replacement, clean up the rosters, and build the brand on the basis of the game itself.

GENEVIEVE SMITH
THE BRAND PERSPECTIVE

This may seem like a strange answer, but I think the United States of America, which I will call "Brand USA," is the number-one brand in need of a severe makeover. We are neither trusted nor admired in many places around the world. We are the root cause of a huge economic disaster. We went into a country on false pretenses, bombed their citizens, and ruined a society for absolutely no reason. We don't take care of the health and education of our citizens very well. We pollute.

On the other hand, we are the richest and most powerful nation. We are a country full of fabulous diversity and limitless opportunity. I don't mean in any way for this to be a political statement; it is not. I'm simply discussing the United States as a brand. And it pains me to see where we find ourselves and the damage we have done to our image and reputation both inside and outside the country.

# Q: • What's Your Best Personal
# • Experience in Building a Brand?

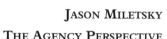

Jason Miletsky

The Agency Perspective

Since I started PFS, I've been involved in a number of brands of different sizes and in various stages of development. But there is one that stands out in my mind because of a very simple—but very memorable—compliment I received.

We had been the agency of record for Ceridian Corp (the second-largest HR-management and payroll provider in the industry) for about three years when we tackled a major re-branding initiative for them. The name wasn't changing, but everything else was—the logo, colors, fonts, images. The plan was to redevelop the company's personality to be more approachable and friendly after learning through intensive research that the market found Ceridian to be too large, difficult to work with, and unapproachable.

It took months to develop new logos and brochures, with endless nights brainstorming over just the right wording and what the best imagery would be to convey the appropriate brand message. It was exhausting, but exhilarating—a rush to see it all come together. We completed the brand and immediately launched a new print ad campaign, called "Freedom," to promote it. Each ad in the Freedom campaign showed an HR director having fun in the office because Ceridian had freed them from the stress and burden of endless paperwork associated with their daily routine. (The first ad featured a woman using a hula-hoop near her desk.) They were cool ads, especially for that industry and for HR publications.

About six months into the campaign, I went to HR World—one of the industry's trade shows in New York City. When I arrived, I discovered that the people running the show had made a mistake when they printed my badge; instead of putting my title as CEO of PFS Marketwyse, they had me as a journalist for some trade pub. This didn't bother me; I figured if nothing else, more people would talk to me if they thought I was a journalist than if they knew I was with an agency. So I wandered around the show, chatting it up with people, and ended up talking to a guy who worked for one of Ceridian's smaller competitors in the marketing department. Thinking I was a journalist, he told me how difficult it was to find a good agency. He felt that most agencies that were creative didn't understand the HR market and therefore couldn't develop good ads for it, and that the agencies that *did* understand the market just didn't seem to be very creative. But then he said—and this has stayed in my mind ever since—"Have you seen the new Ceridian ads? I don't know what agency they use, but that agency really gets it. They've changed their whole brand around. There's this one ad with a girl using a hula-hoop that I ripped out of a magazine and keep on my desk as an example of how to advertise this stuff the right way."

I *so* wanted to tell him that I was the guy who came up with that ad, but I didn't. It didn't feel like the right thing to do, and anyway, it wasn't like I could retain his company as a new account as long as we were already working for Ceridian. Later that year we won a few awards for our work on that brand, but none of those meant as much to me as that single compliment from a guy who had no idea he was even complimenting me.

GENEVIEVE SMITH

THE BRAND PERSPECTIVE

Hands down, my best experience was with WaMu, building the "Simpler Banking and More Smiles" brand. We had support from the very top, we had unbelievable employee and management engagement, and we got to start with a clean slate and build from scratch. We worked with some of the best agencies I have ever had the pleasure of collaborating with: Ave A/Razorfish, TBWA/Chiat Day Los Angeles, and Wolff Olins. We had a disruptive idea and worked for a company that was willing to take the risk and make the investment. We worked in an environment where all ideas were considered and where the best idea for the brand won out over bureaucracy and bias. And I got to work with the best team I've ever had the pleasure of associating with. But in the end...as a result of declining consumer and investor confidence in the midst of the global financial crisis, the FDIC seized the bank in and sold it to JPMorgan Chase. The brand supported the business, but ultimately the business failed the brand.

# Q: WHAT'S YOUR WORST PERSONAL EXPERIENCE IN BUILDING A BRAND?

JASON MILETSKY
THE AGENCY PERSPECTIVE

I'm not just saying this: I really haven't had a lot of bad experiences building a brand. They're all hard work and can drive you nuts, but I've always found that building brands is one of the most rewarding challenges I ever face. But of course you don't want to read that. You want to read about my worst experience—after all, everyone likes a train wreck.

My worst experience might not be on the level of twisted metal, but here it goes: In 2007, Cardinal Health, which we had done some spot projects for, sold one of its divisions to a holding company that basically allowed it to function as is. The only thing was, it needed to re-brand. It couldn't still function under the Cardinal name. Fortunately, the part of Cardinal we were working for was the part that got sold. Unfortunately, we didn't get the nod to develop the brand elements and assemble the brand guide—an agency in New York City that the holding company had worked with numerous times in the past got that. (When the parent company already has a relationship with an agency, there's not a lot another agency can do to take work away from them.) We did, however, get agency-of-record status for all their non-PR marketing needs after the brand was developed.

A few months later, the new company, now named Catalent, was ready to be introduced to the world. There was a lot to do: more than 60 brochures for five divisions of the company, a zillion PowerPoint presentations, trade-show marketing and booth design, advertising campaigns—the list went on. It was great stuff—the billing was good, there was a lot to juggle, and it was exciting to be working with what was, in essence, a $2 billion startup. The only problem was when we got the brand guide from the agency in New York, it was a well over 150 pages long—which was fine (a little long for a new brand, but fine)—but it was so detailed and exacting that we were branded into a corner. The agency had put together a certain crosshatch design that looked nice, but was a nightmare for printers to work with due to tight registration issues and left absolutely no room for creativity or marketing innovation. Worse yet, the Catalent brand manager (we worked directly for the director of marketing) was an absolutely by-the-book individual who refused to allow the internal marketing department and my agency any room to work outside the guide, even in instances where the pre-set brand rules hindered forward marketing progress. (Somewhere in this book I mention that I believe the guide to be just that—a guide—and that people involved with marketing should be expected to work within the spirit of the brand, not handcuffed to the rules.) In the end, the only thing left that made it worthwhile were the invoices that went out. The account was never fun for me or the creative staff at my agency to work on, and the marketing overall was, in my opinion, bland, boring, and fell far below its potential. As an agency guy, there's nothing more frustrating than seeing an opportunity to do some great marketing—but not be able to actually do any of it.

GENEVIEVE SMITH

THE BRAND PERSPECTIVE

⮑ My worst personal experience was also at WaMu. Early on, when I was the CMO of the mortgage division, we developed the position "The Power of Yes"—as in yes, the loan is approved. This position was developed when the company was what's known as a portfolio lender, meaning they held all loans originated on the books and did not sell them to the secondary market. Because the company held all the risk, it was able to develop its own underwriting rules, which meant it could "say yes" to a wider variety of loan types beyond simply a 15- or 30-year fixed.

This brand position was wildly successful with employees, consumers, realtors, and B2B companies (third-party originators like mortgage brokers). We put together some great advertising, which won a bunch of awards, and we led the way for the company in entering significant new markets like New York, Chicago, and Florida. So what happened? WaMu became number-one in U.S. market share for new loans, and number-one in U.S. market share for loan servicing. All good, right? Unfortunately, the company had expanded far beyond the reach of a portfolio lender over the years and gotten itself in financial trouble through these practices. When this happened, "The Power of Yes" quickly became verbal shortcut for everything that was wrong in the mortgage division—internally throughout the company and even to some degree externally. That was a fairly humiliating experience.

# Q: IF YOU COULD TAKE THE HELM OF ANY BRAND IN THE MARKET, WHICH WOULD YOU CHOOSE AND WHY?

JASON MILETSKY
THE AGENCY PERSPECTIVE

There are so many brands that I'd love to take over that I'm almost hesitant to name only one. I would definitely want it to be a company that's not currently at the top of their category or even on an obvious rise. I'd want to run a brand that clearly has potential and that once owned greater market share but has since fallen from their peak. I wouldn't want them to be the leader in their industry; I'd prefer to work with the number-two or three brand because it just makes for a more interesting challenge. I'd also choose a consumer brand because as interesting and challenging as working on a B2B brand can be, I think consumer brands have more marketing vehicles at their disposal and it would just make the branding process that much more exciting.

In my answer to Question #85, "Which Brands Just Seem to Get It?" I included Marvel in my list even though I personally believe that their rivals at DC have far better characters. Part of me thinks that I'd choose DC as the brand I'd like to run, because it frustrates me to see them squander what I believe to be an amazing stable of characters at their disposal (and by "squander" I mean that even if they're making money, I think they could be making more—*lots* more).

Midway Games would be another good choice. At one time, you couldn't go into an arcade or even shop for a video game without seeing the Midway name everywhere; they were the undisputed king of gaming. But over the years, they've given up market share to others, and their stock (which I own some of) has been battered down to about 18 cents a share at the time of this writing. Still, they have a rich history behind them (*Joust*, *Defender*, *Spy Hunter*—the classic games that got everything started) and some great games in their current lineup (including *Mortal Kombat*, one of the best fighting games ever made, and coincidentally just released in a new version using DC characters).

I would love to take the reins there and make some wide-sweeping changes:

- I'd get rid of the lesser-performing games, concentrating on core titles to both reduce costs and allocate more money to marketing titles with greater potential.

- I'd completely redo their online gaming site, which in my opinion is sub-par and clearly not performing well. (Alexa.com, a site that ranks other sites by traffic, recently ranked Midwayarcade.com as the 859,751 most visited site. Another gaming site, Bubblebox.com, was ranked 4,314. Bubblebox,com? Seriously, how does Midway Games lose to a site called Bubblebox.com? Actually, it's pretty obvious how—Bubblebox.com has its act together in the online world; Midway doesn't.)

- I'd restore some innovative spirit to the brand. Their *Mortal Kombat* game with DC characters looks really cool (although I personally haven't played it yet), but my guess is that it's probably way cooler than their advertising shows it off to be. The trailers and TV spots looked well-produced, but you're dealing with characters everyone knows and a completely new twist on a 15-year-old game. Do something really cool with it! Where is the viral component? Where is the larger-than-life aspect to the title? Where is the edge? A billboard showing a Batman logo with the Superman symbol in it appears for three seconds in the movie *I Am Legend*, and droves of people scour the Web for information about the Superman-versus-Batman movie that has been rumored to be coming out for the better part of a decade. People want to see these characters fight! Play up on that—do something different and get people's attention. Look for other cool ways to get games into the public eye. They've got the bait; I just think they need to do a better job casting the reel.

I'd also like to see what I could do with the Saladworks chain—although I'd probably only do it if I had control over more than just the brand. (For anyone who doesn't know, Saladworks is a fast-food–style chain that lets people choose the ingredients to make their own salad. It looks like a buffet, but someone who works there actually makes it for you.) Every time I walk into a Saladworks store, it's pretty much empty—at least compared to the Panera Bread place right next door. Why? I mean, the concept is a good one. The ingredients seem fresh, the food is good, and there's a lot of emphasis in the media on staying health conscious. (Okay, not all of the ingredients are healthy, but for most people, the word "salad" equates to "it's good for you.") Then you get to the cash register and find out why the store is pretty empty: A salad and soda will put you back $11. But aside from lowering the price, there's a lot that could be done. For one thing, you'd need to really make the case that salads can be a meal on their own—especially for dinner, when the stores seem particularly empty. People are happy to have a salad for lunch, but when it comes to dinner, they see salads as something you have *before* the meal—not as the meal itself. Saladworks needs to change that assumption and get more people in their stores during evening hours. I'd also play up some of the paninis and other non-salad foods that not only might bring people in at night, but might bring them back more often. The first step toward this goal would be to change the name of the chain to Saladworks Plus—the addition of that single word lets people know there's more going on than just salad. I'd also completely revamp their advertising, which from what I've seen seems to heavily rely on roadside billboards. I'd add some TV and radio to the mix, playing up the health aspect and freshness of ingredients. I'd also try to run some joint marketing efforts with health-club chains like Curves, and to remove any billboards that exist on some random highway and reposition them to appear near the parking lots of more fatty chains, like Fuddruckers, laying the guilt on nice and thick. The list goes on—I think Saladworks is a great chain, but that they're missing the boat in terms of branding and marketing. (By the way, this chain might be wildly successful overall. I'm just basing my opinions on the fact that the stores are nearly empty every time I go.)

There are so many brands I'd love to get my hands on! But I guess the real answer for me is that I'd be excited to take the helm of any brand that allowed me to take some chances and really do something exciting!

**GENEVIEVE SMITH**

**THE BRAND PERSPECTIVE**

I would be interested in taking the helm of a brand that intends to make a difference for humanity and the planet. Like Red, as an example. Here's a brand that levers commerce and people's consciousness. If someone is going to buy a shirt, why not purchase the one that'll make a difference to someone in Africa? I think this is a brand idea that has all the necessary components: vision, purpose, promise, and intent. And, it's supported by mass brands, big business, and star power. Moreover, it is relevant to *today*. People are finally facing the fact that we have to fix our problems. We cannot sit around a wait for government to do it for us. As Bono put it, "If people are jaded or cynical...or genuinely not interested, then we fail. But we've tried. I think we've come up with a sexy, smart, savvy idea that will save people's lives." He continues, "It is sexy to want to change the world, not to leave it as it is."

I would choose Red because I think it is tremendously smart to use people's buying power in this way, and I believe the opportunities are unlimited. I would find it rewarding, challenging, and gratifying to be involved with Red.

# CLOSING REMARKS

### JASON MILETSKY

As the creator and series editor of the *Perspectives* series, I've had a hand in the development of each of the first four books: this one along with ones on marketing, increasing sales, and managing employees. Somehow, though, this book seemed a little different. For awhile, I couldn't figure out why—until it finally dawned on me: Branding is at the very heart of all of these books. It's at the heart of any business relationship, between product and audience, salesperson and customer, manager and employee.

It's amazing how a concept as vague as "branding" can play such an integral part in defining what a company is about. It goes well beyond the logo, deep into consumers' subconscious where trust, conviction, and loyalty reside. A well-branded company doesn't just sell to consumers; it creates advocates who will remain loyal and even pass their dedication on to others.

In presenting the agency perspective of this book, I tried to give real and honest answers based on my own experiences working with and studying a wide variety of brands. The thought process, politics, strategies, and expectations—not to mention the sheer creativity—that exist in and around every brand is simply remarkable. Without understanding what a brand really is and how it speaks to audiences, marketers are doomed to communicate in a vacuum, sending lifeless messages that will ultimately fail to sway consumers to take action. Branding correctly takes time, patience, research, creativity, strategy, and an ability to measure success while also keeping one's mind open to recognizing potential failure and making adjustments before it's too late.

I appreciate the time you've taken to read this book. Sincerely, thank you. It was a lot of hard work to put together, and involved many long, introspective nights trying to figure out what I really believe (not just what I've gotten used to saying at pitch meetings). I set out to teach, and ended up learning a lot myself. I hope you did as well.

### GENEVIEVE SMITH

I hope you've enjoyed reading our perspectives on brand-building and that some of what you've found in this book will be of use to you. A brand is is the very soul of the entity or individual it represents. It's a precious asset.

In this book, we've talked about some of the world's best brands and noted that behind these icons are people willing to take risks, be disruptive, and change with the consumer gestalt that is itself constantly changing. My "outside in" view is that these visionaries respect and apply the science of branding, but at the end of the day they lead with their gut and intuition, and they show respect for what's genuine to the brand idea instead of chasing after the latest flash in the marketplace. These brand leaders are never satisfied; they are always seeking the next evolution of their brand, as risky as that may be to the status quo.

I've discovered through this writing that there are probably a million and one ways to approach branding—and that you could spend a million and one days trying them out to hit on just the right one. But there is no one right approach! Each brand has its own true north, and finding it is the secret to effective branding. You may lead or you may react, but the winners are completely in tune with their brand and with the consumer.

Thank you for taking the time to read this book.

# INDEX

public, brand introductions to general, 103
publishing blogs, 181. *See also* blogs
purple, 31
purpose of campaigns based on brand stages, 163–165

## Q

quality, 17–18
    brainstorming, 166
    effect on repeat business, 6
    sacrificing for speed, 75

## R

Ralph Lauren, 90
Ratt, 214
reactionary management, 78
reactions to brands, 222–223
reasons
    for brand makeovers, 229–230
    for building brands, 52
    for loyalty, 71–73, 242–244
re-branding, 27, 38, 107, 234–236. *See also* brands
recognition of brands, 3
Red, 261
Red, White, and Blue, 116
Red Bull, 166
red (color), 31
Redit, 186
Reebok, 13
reflection of brand personalities, 21–22, 107–109
relationships, management, 137
relevancy of blog content, 183
reliability, 114
repeat business, 6
representation on blogs, 182
reputations, 3
    brands, 237–238
    trust, losing, 12
research, 43. *See also* test-markets
    brand management mistakes, 78
    Internet, 147
    Nielson, 173
    positioning, 151
    tiger teams, 102
responsibilities, departments, 125–126
retail banking, 95
retaining agencies, 195

return on investment (ROI), 140, 160, 205
    measuring, 206–207
return on marketing investment (ROMI), 154
reviews, online, 173
risk
    of not using brands, 24
    taking calculated, 75
rogue offenders, reining in, 112–113
role of PR, 185–187
rollouts, phased, 107–109
royalties, images, 34
RSS (really simple syndication), 185
rules, breaking the, 105–106

## S

Saladworks, 260
sales, determination of success, 200–203
salespeople
    communication with, 108
    operationalizing, 112–113
sales tax on the Internet, 174
sales videos, 38
Sans-serif fonts, 31
*Saved by the Bell,* 214
screen savers, 133
Script fonts, 31
selection of goods on the Internet, 174
select retailers, limited test runs, 49
sell sheets, 38
Serif fonts, 31
services
    associations, 24
    consideration and preference for, 7
    decline of, 201
    standards, 119–121
Sharapova, Maria, 156
sharing video, 186
Sharp, 87
shipping payments, 174
Shoprite, 161
short-term goals, 204–205
short-term revenue gains, 7
signs, 107–109
Simpler Banking and More Smiles (WaMu), 14, 60
slogans, 207
social-media releases (SMRs), 186
social networking, 185
Sony PlayStation, 93

Here is a preview of five
questions from another book
in the *Perspectives On...* series

Now available!

# PERSPECTIVES™ ON
# MARKETING

- Exciting new information to help you become a more successful marketer
- Topics include getting the most from the client/agency relationship, messaging, strategy, ROI analysis, and more
- Hear what the agency and the client have to say—authors have not collaborated

**THE AGENCY PERSPECTIVE**
**JASON I. MILETSKY**

**THE CLIENT PERSPECTIVE**
**MICHAEL HAND**

# Q: WHAT MAKES AN AGENCY A GOOD AGENCY?

**JASON MILETSKY**
**THE AGENCY PERSPECTIVE**

↳ Any time this question comes up, the knee-jerk answer is "creativity." But saying that creativity defines an agency is like saying a logo defines a brand—it's too simplistic, it's too obvious, and it doesn't paint the complete picture.

That's not to say that creativity isn't a key ingredient, because it absolutely is. But there's a world of difference between creative and *smart* creative. Smart creative involves defining a concept with a marketing purpose—specifically related to the client and its needs. At least once a week, I remind our art directors and designers that we are not creating art for the sake of art, and we're not designing for the refrigerator door. Everything we do, every idea, every design, every brush stroke—all of it has to have a sound and reasonable marketing rationale behind it. Aesthetics alone don't cut it; neither do wild, out-of-the-box ideas that may raise eyebrows but not the bottom line. Creativity provides true value to the client only if it can send an effective message to the intended audience and has the potential to generate a positive ROI. Agencies may be jam-packed with creative, artistic people, but this is a business, not an art school. Our job is to market effectively, not just beautifully.

Smart creative is only part of the story, though. Good agencies are also insightful strategists that understand who and where the audience is and how it can be reached. More often than not, good agencies do this with minimal research and limited time, as clients are almost always under ridiculous pressure to get creative launched quickly and show results immediately. Timelines usually don't leave a lot of room for doing the amount of research that's really necessary, and data compiled by the client is often spotty and questionable at best. A good agency will be able to think just as creatively when it comes to outlining strategy (based on little or no data and within specific budgets) as it does when developing concept and design. What avenues work best? How long should we wait between touch points? Which marketing methods are worth the expense? How do we expect the audience to respond? A good agency will consider all of these issues—and about a million more—when developing effective marketing strategies.

Service, of course, is another key factor—one that I can't emphasize strongly enough. Perhaps more than any other client/vendor situation, agencies form true relationships with the companies they represent. Agencies act as their clients' outside perspective, representing the eyes and ears that gauge how people outside a client's walls perceive their brand. It's the agency's job to give clients new insights into their audience and feed them new ideas. At the same time, agencies need to accept criticism when clients don't like our ideas or agree with our strategic approach. Once again, this is a business; good agencies don't take criticism personally, complain internally that the client is "stupid," or consider a client's negative reaction as an affront to their art.

We need to communicate our thoughts clearly and often, letting clients know that we're on the case, that we care about their needs, and that yes, we are staying on schedule. Strong project management on the part of the agency will often be the determining factor in whether the relationship with the client works or falls apart; as such, a good agency will put an equal amount of resources into its project-management department as it puts into its creative department. Most marketing efforts, regardless of the creative concept and strategic plan, will involve numerous moving parts, all of which need to be organized and accounted for by the agency in order to build client confidence.

Finally, really good agencies look out for their clients' best interests before looking out for their own. This is actually pretty rare, no matter what the agency says in its sales pitch. It's common for agencies to push designs that may work for the client but will work for the agency's own portfolio a little more, or to develop strategies that may allow them to bill a little extra or extend billing a few more months. Similarly, we may turn into yes-men, agreeing to everything the client wants to do, even when we know it's a mistake, because we don't want to risk losing the account. The best agencies promote ideas that may be better for the client than for the agency, are willing to speak up for what's best for the brand, and are confident that making selfless decisions will result in a more successful, profitable relationship in the long run.

MICHAEL HAND
THE CLIENT PERSPECTIVE

 If you look up the word "agency" in the dictionary, you would see a definition somewhat like the following: "An organization, company, or bureau that provides some service for another." (This one's from *Dictionary.com v1.1*.) You can find little to argue with in that definition—an agency certainly does provide some "service." The definition, however, tells you nothing about what makes one of these organizations, companies, or bureaus better than the next.

When answering the "good agency" question, most client folk tend to fall into one of two camps. The first camp focuses its answers around great creative idea development; the second focuses on superior account/customer service. I, however, am of the belief that truly great agencies supply that special mix of both. (I know, great answer, I'm really going out on a limb with that one.) Strong creative without a great account team to manage the delivery of the idea and the expectations of the client will fail every time. Likewise, the strong account team that is not balanced with sound creative thinking will be left with no programs to execute and support.

In fact, I'd take this notion further to assert that the very best agencies demonstrate strong interaction across multiple disciplines:

- **Account service:** Every client wants good chemistry with its agency, and that has to start at the account level. Indeed, I believe *everything* starts with strong account service. The account team—the group that plays the ever-important roles of telephone operator and office psychologist—represents the front line of defense and acts as the face of every agency-client interaction. This group must make sure everything that is discussed with the client is speedily conveyed to the home office, lands in the right hands, and is communicated accurately and in detail. (This last point is the key to avoiding questions from the associate design director like, "Did they not like green, or simply that *shade* of green?") In addition, this group must be able to talk the client off the ledge when things are not really as bad as they seem (or as bad as the client wants to make things out to be). While most clients expect the creative team to be a bit odd in demeanor and character, that's not the case with the account team. Clients rarely expect the creative team to stand up in their wedding or attend the funeral for a loved one, but you damn well better believe that clients want an account team whose company they enjoy enough to share dinner, drinks, and the occasional weekend activity. When you have the wrong person as your point of contact with the client, the relationship is doomed from the start.

- **Strategic planning and development:** Most clients will tell you that not only do they have all the research they need to build rock-solid plans, they actually have everything planned out. I can tell you first-hand, however, that they are typically wrong. Most clients have great product data and can tell you more than you ever need to know about the ingredient content and how best to run production lines. What most clients don't have is a truly unbiased look at who their consumer is and how they should go to market. Don't get me wrong—clients have a very good idea who they want to talk to and what message they want to communicate, but they could always use a little help to make sure their information is accurate and their assumptions work beyond the walls of the corporate headquarters building. For this reason, agencies should be solid in strategic planning and development.

The best strategic-planning groups are not only gurus in their chosen field (advertising, promotion, interactive, etc.), they also bring cross-category exposure to the best-in-class model. That is, they can present unique ways of looking at data that they gathered while working with another client. In this way, they can serve as a conduit for, say, clients that are giants in consumer packaged goods to learn from telecommunications brands, clients that are automotive manufacturers to learn from soft-drink peddlers, and so on.

- **Creative:** Creative is always crucial to an agency's DNA. Every client wants to hear big ideas and talk about super-creative ways to go to market— even when a good number of those ideas will likely scare a client and won't get executed as originally intended. Let's be clear: No agency has ever lost an account because it was *too* creative. The issue here is reality. Most clients come to the table with their own ideas and simply want somebody to agree with those ideas and then execute them with excellence. The best creatives I have encountered are those teams that can tightly tie the brand insights/ strategy work into an idea, making it appear obvious to the client (and ultimately the consumer). These strong creative teams can also embrace an idea that is not their own and find ways to make it better before it ends up in the market. The worst creatives, on the other hand, are either so arrogant that they will fight over every copy point and utterly disregard constructive feedback or totally unimaginative, taking everything at face value and simply executing what they are handed. Creative teams need to be left alone to conceptualize and ideate, but they also need to find ways to get the client involved in this process. Clients will support and fight for ideas with much greater passion if they are part of the development phase.

- **Project managers and production staff:** Typically, this is the most overlooked group at agencies. It doesn't always get highlighted in mid-year reviews, and rarely drives the agency's compensation model. But this group more than earns its pay in that it is behind every good agency-client link. Nobody thanks these guys for getting work out the door on time and within budget, but they get raked over the coals if they run up the bills and start missing deadlines. The best agency teams have rock-solid people who make sure things get done behind the scenes. When the phone rings at 4:30 p.m. on a Friday afternoon, they're usually the ones who get stuck working over the weekend to get a project out the door. They do it without a direct thank you, and they do it without complaint (some of the time).

- **Accounting and legal:** In order for any client-agency relationship to work, these two groups must stay on top of things. I personally know this area is going well if I (as the client) never hear a word from them or from my finance team. The legal guys need to keep everybody out of trouble and make sure that every contract-negotiation period runs smoothly, and the accounting guys must ensure that billing is always clean and easy. With respect to billing issues, clients hate the phone calls and time it takes to clear these up. Submit bills in a timely fashion, make sure purchase-order numbers are written on the top of each one, and don't wait until a year after a project shuts down to send the final invoice. By then, most clients have moved the money and closed the accounting line; you are only going to piss people off. How much trouble do you want to stir up over a $525 fee for photocopies and shipping charges 12 months after the fact?

- **Leadership:** Leadership at the agency's highest level needs to be involved in client interaction. Every client wants to feel that their business is important to an agency. It's a fact: The team at the top needs to spend a little time each quarter massaging clients' egos. They need to do more than just pop in for the Christmas party (even if they plan to pick up the bar tab) or casually sit through the annual review; there needs to be some real dialogue on the state of the business. More than likely, the client has selected the agency due in part to expertise of this leadership group. And while clients anticipate that the executives who pitched on behalf of the agency will eventually exit the relationship to move on to the next pitch, it helps if you don't make it so obvious.

As you can see, a lot goes into answering this question. But to sum up, the best of the best recognize these unique functional areas and worry more about personal relationships than made-up acronyms for a proprietary process developed to track ROI.

# Q: What Makes a Client a Good Client?

**Jason Miletsky**
**The Agency Perspective**

⤶ I think this might be more easily answered by considering the opposite: What makes a client a bad client. The truth is that in any relationship, issues are going to come up. There are going to be times when agencies and clients don't see eye-to-eye. But a client would have to display egregiously poor behavior for an agency to sever the relationship.

The biggest issue is the abuse of anyone who works at the agency, outside of key executives. Yes, we are the agency, and yes, the client pays the bills—but no, that does not give any client the right to berate anyone on the account team. In the years since I founded my agency, I've thankfully run into this issue, where a client verbally abused one of the project managers to the point the project manager was brought to tears, only twice. As far as I'm concerned, no matter what the reason is, the first time you make one of my employees cry is the last time we do business together. There's just no reason for it. As the CEO, I have no problem with an angry client letting loose on me—vent all you want, call me every name in the book, and then we'll figure out a solution to whatever problem we face. But never *ever* attack one of the managers who has dedicated himself or herself to your account, no matter what the reason.

Obviously, those are extreme cases. But lack of respect can manifest itself in other ways besides boorishness. Bad clients tend to forget that this is a relationship, and that they hired the agency for a reason—not to be their lackeys, but to provide insight, consultation, and a different point of view. Maybe it's ego, or maybe they've never learned to let go of the reins, but bad clients will forget that the agency has something valuable to add, setting the strategy and creative themselves and leaving us with little more to do than micromanaged execution.

Another trait that makes a client a bad client (and I apologize if my answer to this question is turning into a bitch session, but I have to admit, it is somewhat cathartic) is when the client doesn't "get it." This is especially true of small companies or companies where the person heading up marketing efforts also happens to own the company. Very often, these people think they understand marketing, but the truth is they don't. They don't really get the need for planning in advance, for understanding the audience, or for setting a strategy. They think negative space in marketing material is a waste, and that every free inch of paper presents an opportunity to add more copy or make their logo larger. They don't see a difference between their target market and their barber, and they seek out feedback on everything marketing-related from everyone they come across and then urgently pass that feedback on to the agency as though it held any sort of relevance. And worst of all, these non-marketing marketers have no sense of how long it takes or how hard it is to execute a successful campaign, are more demanding, require more hand-holding than true marketing professionals, keep a stranglehold on the budget, and typically will have no ability to pull the trigger on even the smallest decision without a monumental struggle.

Finally, bad clients forget that they have to put personal feelings aside and do what's best for the account. Tell us the truth; we can take it. I'd rather you tell me point-blank you don't like an idea, or aren't happy with a strategy we're proposing, than have you smile and tell us how great everything is only to find out later that the account is suddenly up for review. As long as you're smiling, we'll think you're happy. In dealing with my own employees, I've always believed that if I don't tell them what's wrong, it's not fair of me to expect them to fix whatever issues I may have with them. They're not mind-readers. The same rule holds true for clients and agencies. There will be problems—we accept that. And there will be times you're not happy with our ideas. But good clients will tell us how they feel and respect us enough to handle it. Bad clients will spare our feelings at the risk of injuring the relationship.

Agencies are bound to run into bad clients now and then, but fortunately those clients make up the minority. For agencies hungry to grow and anxious to produce quality work, any client that doesn't fit into any of the aforementioned descriptions can be considered a "good" client—and these do, in fact, comprise the majority in the marketing landscape.

↳ Although being a good client always ends up being more difficult than it needs to be, I think it comes down to one simple principle: no bullshit. Let's face it, people just want to know where they stand. They want clear direction that they can believe in. This is a job, not a hobby; agency teams don't enjoy spending countless hours of fruitless labor chasing ideas that will never see the light of day. Agency teams also want to be treated like equals. Just because you are the client does not mean that your time is more valuable or that you are more important.

Here are a few keys to being a good client:

- **Communicate and focus:** Right from the start, you need to have a plan. It may be a scope of work, it may be a calendar of activities, or it may be something else. Regardless of what it is, clients need to stay on task. Relationship struggles pop up when the workload gets too intense and when proposed projects get erased from the board for a whole new set of priorities. Business is always in a state of flux, but rarely do you get *really* big surprises. Keep the agency team informed of changes in overall direction and corporate strategy from the start. When you get that first call that the Chief Marketing Officer (CMO) is not quite sure where the big idea is headed, loop your partners in. They will appreciate the fact that they were able to see changes coming rather than having a new direction pop up out of nowhere (because that will inevitably require folks to work weekends and start the process over again). Just as the biggest issue facing married couples is communication, so, too, is communication key to any successful long-term client-agency partnership.

- **Objectives:** Don't just talk about objectives; set them. It's not much more complicated than that. When expectations are established and people know how they are going to be judged, it takes the unknowns out of the equation. Do you want to sell more widgets? Do you want to distribute more samples or simply drive more awareness? Whatever it is, do your best to quantify what you want to deliver and then measure against it.

- **Senior leadership:** The client's senior leadership can make or break any client-agency relationship. Corporate leaders should be exposed to the agency and should have a clear connection to the plan you are trying to implement through the agency's work. This group needs to provide stability. It needs to be able to motivate people and provide sound strategic anchoring. Most folks (not all, but most) in these chairs have paid their dues; people tend to forget that. They have worked their own way up through the ranks and they demand a bit of respect; they feel they have earned it. Also, every good client must remind their leadership team that nothing happens overnight. (Actually, many things happen overnight, but hopefully you get my point.) Keeping expectations in check is critical.

- **Agency reviews:** You need to get these on the schedule, and they should be held on a regular basis. Nothing is worse for an agency than thinking everything is going fine and then finding out it is not. The best clients conduct and provide regular feedback sessions (and remain open to feedback in return). If your agency touches multiple parts of your business, don't just have the marketing team take a survey. Instead, share the review criteria in advance and obtain feedback from employees company-wide. For example, talk with sales and/or customer teams to get a sense of their interactions. If these interactions are limited, then at least hear what they think of the work outputs they have seen and find out whether they think those outputs are helping to make a difference in the outside world. If the feedback dialogue is slow to occur and nothing is getting accomplished, consider bringing in a third-party consultant to counsel and spark the conversation. I personally believe you can get this organized by yourselves (just lock the client and agency teams in a room and make them talk to each other), but then again, this is too critical a step to take chances on. If you place a real value in the long-term relationship with a client, placing this in the budget—perhaps as a shared expense—is critical.

- **Celebrate the wins:** Things will go bad (or at least get stressed) at some point, and when they do, most clients will find some fault in the work of the agency roster. I can't explain why; it just happens. In some cases, this "blame" will be justified, but in other cases, it will not be. This is not, however, the point I want to make here. Rather, my point is to celebrate the victories with as much passion as when you analyze the missteps. A simple cocktail hour near the agency's office or a Friday-morning bagel delivery to say thank you goes a really long way. People want to feel like part of a team. The best clients have a way of embracing even the team who handles the agency's FedEx deliveries from the mailroom (and if the client doesn't, well, they should not expect their advertising boards in the morning delivery pouch on the day of the "big" meeting).

# Q: • THE CREATIVE BRIEF: WHO WRITES IT, AND • WHAT'S NEEDED TO MAKE IT USEFUL?

**MICHAEL HAND**

**THE CLIENT PERSPECTIVE**

One of the biggest mistakes made by marketers at companies across the country is allowing advertising/media/consumer promotion/interactive agencies to write their own creative briefs. This practice must stop ASAP. Clients will never truly take ownership of the end product unless they play a strategic role in the development of the concepts and plans involved—and writing the creative brief is the best way for the client to do that.

What should a creative brief contain to make sure it is useful? Every good brief will consist of the following information, regardless of what marketing discipline is developing the work:

- **Business situation:** What's happening in the marketplace that has required this work to be produced? This is the section to share information on usage behavior, brand perceptions (both internally and externally), category dynamics, and competitive threats. It's also where you should include any charts or graphs that convey important data points as well as research findings to date and current brand health measures. The strategic planning team will refer to this section of the brief more than any other area.

- **Marketing/communication objectives:** What is this project looking to achieve? What exact action do you want the consumer to take? How will success be measured upon completion? This is the section to lay out share gain and volume goals, key competitive measures, and marketing challenges with both customers and consumers. Leave no room for ambiguity. This is the section to which the client's senior management will refer during the creative selection. They will probe to confirm whether the measures can realistically be achieved by the recommended action. As an agency, do not try to "re-interpret" these objectives. You can seek clarity, but do not look to rephrase for your purposes. Objectives must be lifted verbatim from the brief.

Use the S.M.A.R.T. approach outlined in the answer to Question #40, "What Are the Best Objectives Based On? Who Ultimately Determines Specific Goals?" to establish both how success will be measured and strong criteria for making the creative selection.

- **Assignment description:** To help you avoid overdeveloping a concept, this section of the brief should clearly define what tactics are required and establish what the final creative review will (or will not) include. The "will not" portion is equally important here; if you have an agency that specializes in interactive work on retainer and you are briefing for a consumer promotions concept with your CP agency, be clear that you do not expect to see Web extensions in their final presentation. This level of clarity will save everybody time and effort, while also forcing a more focused deliverable. This section is also where you should specify exactly what the client expects to be presented and which products/line extensions/models are to be included. I beg the agency: During the review of the brief document, spend extra time on this section and ask as many clarifying questions as you need.

- **Target audience profile:** Who are you trying to reach? Is the program focused on the end user or on the person actually making the purchase at retail? This section should include as much demographic and psychographic/attitudinal information that is available on the audience you want to reach with your message. It should also include any insights not shared in the "Business Situation" section that relate to the user's lifestyle and behavior. It may also include a primary and secondary target for the program at hand. (You should be clear on how big a priority these alternative audiences are.)

- **Positioning statement:** This section serves to ensure that nothing created falls outside of the brand character. It provides a frame of reference for the brand in general, and should highlight the brand's unique point of difference that will need to be reinforced in the development process.

- **Geographic/seasonal/class-of-trade priorities:** Not every brief will need this, but if you work in a business or with a brand that skews more heavily based on a particular factor, it must be added. Geographic skews come into play when you compete in a segment that includes many small regional players or if you want to tailor your message to a particular retail location. Seasonal considerations must be articulated for products that see big fluctuations in consumption or purchase behavior depending on the time of year. For example, the auto industry often sees lower sales volume in January and February, and the beer business typically experiences big spikes during the summer (from Memorial Day to Labor Day). Class of trade is of great interest for brands with different shoppers who may be in the market at the same time. Creative teams need to know if they need to alter a message going to young adult males at the convenience store for the 35–44-year-old female who is the primary grocery-store shopper for her family. Some program overlay may occur, but you need to be careful to avoid alienating the user base. In the confection arena, I personally faced the issue of whether to select a spring movie property that worked very well for young adult males and promised great revenue gains at convenience stores but could also be deemed too violent for mom in the grocery store. The brief should help you choose the correct path on tough issues like that.

■ **Budget:** How much do you really have to spend? As the client, you must be realistic. I myself have been guilty of writing a brief that requests $2–3 million ideas when I knew full well going into the project that my budget was $1.5 million. Yes, it's always exciting to see what more money can get you, and it's tempting to hold onto the idea that if the idea is big enough, you'll find the money. But the reality is that funding is usually hard to come by, and too many ideas fall apart when you start stripping elements to hit your lower (read: more reasonable) dollar figure. Be realistic from the start and manage expectations. Ask the agency to bring some ideas for what they might change/add if more money were to become available—not the other way around.

■ **Timing/critical path:** When will you sit down to review the concepts, and when will the program be executed in market? Be very direct about when you need to see the first round of ideas and lock the date on your calendar from the start. Things may change a bit along the way, but two dates should never move: the first review date and the in-market execution date. Make sure the timeline includes enough time for approvals, legal reviews, and contract negotiations if third parties are involved. This can be more complicated than you ever imagined. Dealing with multiple members of a band or an entire cast on a film extends the time needed to get things signed off. Plan accordingly to avoid surprises and rush charges.

---

To establish the timeline, look at the end date and work backward.

---

■ **Creative Mandatories:** Is there anything that absolutely *must* be included in the final work? This is the section where you should include your trademark guidelines, talent requirements, color palette demands, POS specifications, etc. If you have specific tactical or executional considerations, they should be listed here.

- **Signatures:** After the briefing process is complete, make sure you have an agreed-upon document to work from, signed by the individual(s) who will be driving the selection process. If a VP gets the final vote, that person should sign the brief so he or she knows what to expect and does not change the direction at the eleventh hour. I would like to avoid going up the chain of command on the brief development process, but I can swear by the fact it will save you time in the end. Creating ownership and a commitment by agreeing to the brief will only help you down the road.

---

The creative brief should be altered to reflect any changes made during the review. This document needs to be 100-percent accurate before you commit to the assignment. A major stretch, I know, but you cannot change the brief after the work gets started.

---

I mentioned that clients should write the brief—and I believe they should. That said, if the agency *does* take the lead in writing the brief—perhaps due to time factors or a shortage of human resources on the client side—the document must be approved by the client before the creative juices start flowing. More so than any other file you exchange between parties, you *must* have agreement on this document. The brief-review process also requires solid conversation; it can't be a simple "We e-mailed the brief for your review." Take time to get on the phone or, better yet, get in a room together and discuss the deliverables.

JASON MILETSKY
THE AGENCY PERSPECTIVE

I've worked on some accounts where the client writes the brief and others where we write it. I've even worked with clients that couldn't have cared less whether or not there *was* a creative brief—but that really should never be the case, so I'm not going to spend time discussing that.

It's an interesting situation: Creative briefs can be a pain in the ass to write, so it's always a relief when the client takes on that responsibility. (Plus, it gives them the opportunity to put their thoughts and needs into writing.) But even though it can be a chore, I honestly believe that creative briefs should be written by the agency, because that way the agency can prove to the client that the agency understands their needs. Typically, we have one or two meetings with the client to discuss the purpose of an upcoming project or campaign, what it should entail, who we're trying to reach, etc. Then we'll put together the creative brief as a detailed review of these meetings. We submit the creative brief to the client to ensure that we're all on the same page and that we took from the meetings the directives they were giving; their sign-off on the brief is their seal of approval—acknowledgment that we did, in fact, understand everything correctly.

I don't know that there is a single best way to write a brief; I think every brief will be a little different depending on the client, their brand, and their needs. But there are some elements that every brief should include in order to be effective:

- **Contact names and account information:** After the first brief for a client, this can usually be copied and pasted from one brief to another, but should still be present. Just standard info like the main contact names on both the client and agency side, phone numbers, e-mail addresses, project or account numbers (usually assigned by the agency for organizational purposes), and who prepared the brief.

- **The project or campaign and its primary objectives:** Obviously, there needs to be a review of the project or campaign in question, what's being worked on, and what the deliverables will be. These should be accompanied by the objectives of the effort—not necessarily numeric goals (although you can use 'em if you've got 'em) but at the very least a more general statement like "To build awareness of XYZ's west coast capabilities" or "To increase weekday traffic in ABC's retail outlets."

- **Competition:** A list of potential competitors that the brand is up against. Agencies should be aware of what these competitors are doing and saying in the market to make sure that similar efforts being undertaken are both starkly different and markedly better.

- **Target market and audience insights:** The specific demo you'll be trying to reach and any insights (statistical or otherwise) that might be helpful to keep in mind during development.

- **Desired message:** A description of what you'll be trying to get across. This is the most likely point of disagreement between agency and client, and should be reviewed by both sides to guard against subtle differences that might change the scope of the project or affect the outcome.

- **Communication tone:** The tone of the messaging as it'll be related through copy, image, script, design, or something else. This is usually already determined by the brand guidelines, most likely in reference to the brand personality.

- **The brand promise:** Another brand guideline issue. It's helpful to reiterate what the brand promise is, even if it won't specifically be referenced in the campaign or project in question.

- **The brand's USP and support for the USP:** Specifics about what makes the brand unique among it competitors and evidence that supports these claims. Again, these may not be specifically mentioned in a given effort, but they should be included in the creative brief for any subtle references they might inspire.

- **Specifications:** Depending on the effort, there may be specifications that need to be considered such as the size of a print ad or how long a commercial or other video should be.

- **Mandatories:** Unless these are standard and can be copied and pasted from one brief to the other, this section is one that almost always needs to be completed by the client. It includes information such as which phone number or URL to promote, any legal language that should be included (like copyright or trademark info), etc.

Like I said, each client will have a different setup and might require information I haven't listed here, but you'll never go wrong having at least this information included in every brief.

One more thing: At the start of this answer, I mentioned that some clients couldn't care less about creative briefs. On the other extreme are clients who are brief-happy, requiring one for every single project—even simple sales sheets or PowerPoint decks. My personal theory is that if the creative brief is going to take at least half as long as the project will take to complete, then you shouldn't bother writing it. The creative brief should be helpful in getting the project done right, not an exercise in how to waste time.

# Q: • IS "GOING GREEN" FOR REAL?
# • OR IS IT JUST A FAD?

What's your perspective on this question?
Let us know at PerspectivesOnMarketing.com.

**JASON MILETSKY**
**THE AGENCY PERSPECTIVE**

Okay, I know I'm going catch some real shit for at least part of my answer to this question, but screw it, I'm going to write what I believe. Actually, considering the extreme political differences between me and my lovely and remarkably brilliant editor (hello Kate), I'll be surprised if this answer even gets printed. So here is it, plain and simple: There are two camps when it comes to global warming and the environment. There's the one camp that's really loud about "going green" and uses scientific evidence in an attempt to prove that man is wreaking havoc on the Earth and if we don't change our ways now we're headed for imminent doom. Me? I'm in the other camp—the much quieter group that finds more credibility in scientific reports that prove humans have had no measurable effect on the environment. But the other guys are way better organized; under the leadership of Al Gore, this group has used the media to market its stance incredibly effectively. If you don't believe me, check out the commercial on YouTube starring that dude from *ER*, speaking on behalf of the World Wildlife Fund. It shows two polar bears (one of them is a baby, of course, because what's cuter than a baby polar bear?) standing on a small piece of ice and then diving into the water in search of, well, a *bigger* piece of ice. It all seems very sad, sure to elicit endless "awwws." But it's the *music*, folks! Replace the sad background from the "Songs to Die By" CD with something out of a Peter Sellers flick, and you've got yourself a couple of much happier looking polar bears. But you gotta hand it to them—it's great marketing!

But this is a marketing book, not a treatise on climate change. I'm not a scientist, and I'm not going to waste pages here reprinting scientific analyses that support my beliefs. (Be happy! I'm saving trees!) I'm here to give the agency's perspective on marketing issues. So even though I think all this climate-change stuff is a bunch of bullshit, the "go green" movement has taught me a valuable lesson: Going green is going nowhere. It's here to stay.

I used to believe the whole going-green thing was a fad—that it would go away as soon as we had something else to think about. I figured the environment would be fine as soon as it was no longer in the spotlight. The real solution, I used to joke, was to use federal money to encourage Britney Spears to start partying again. If only our Hollywood actors would keep behaving badly, we'd get tired of talking about polar bears and carbon dioxide and leave the world alone to spin through space in peace. Well, apparently I was wrong. Watching the housing and financial markets collapse in 2008 might not have been as entertaining as watching Lindsay Lohan's career spiral out of control, but those stories did dominate headlines—and still this damned go-green thing wouldn't go away.

And it's not going to, because going green is the perfect issue. It's more personal than, say, giving money to a cause that helps homeless people. Climate change is everywhere and affects all of us—our kids, our grandkids, our pets, and the *future of the whole freaking universe*. It's also easy for people to do next to nothing (like buy a product that is eco-friendly) and fool themselves they're actually making a contribution. Plus, it's got a powerful, organized movement behind it.

I do think, though, it'll die down. Eventually we'll have some major legislation aimed at saving the planet, and people will think they don't have to think so much about it, which will open the door for the next great cause. (Sorry PETA, it won't be you. Fish won't be called "sea kittens," and we'll still eat veal.) But we're still a ways away from that—and going green will never vanish completely. So for brands looking to connect with consumers: Like it or not, it's time to start the office-recycling program and slap a "We're Green" sticker on your packaging or you, too, could end up on the endangered species list.

**Michael Hand**
**The Client Perspective**

⌐ I was one of the biggest skeptics out there. I never thought this "green" thing was really going to amount to much. Yeah, the world would always have a bunch of "tree huggers" who ran around and stood in front of bulldozers in

Birkenstocks to save their neighborhood forest or who floated around the world's oceans in rafts trying to stop oil drilling and prevent large fishing boats from dropping their nets near dolphins. But in my mind, they were the minority. They were the "crazy" ones. As it turns out, I was wrong. Those particular tactics certainly were a bit extreme, but the world has definitely taken notice of the "green movement;" albeit in a less dramatic way. When a former Vice President of the United States (Al Gore) adapts a PowerPoint presentation into a movie (and wins an Academy Award) about global warming that nets almost $50 million at the box office, you can be sure the issue is here to stay. I am not going to say that I am a card-carrying "greenie" myself, but from a marketing perspective, you need to take this group seriously.

Every marketer is jumping on the bandwagon and touting themselves as "environmentally friendly" and made with more "sustainable" materials/ingredients. Those marketers who don't make the jump will be left behind as consumers across the globe worry about helping to "save the world" one plastic bottle and recycled package at a time. It has also become a fashion statement to show your environmental friendliness by sporting bold, iconic markings on your eco-friendly garb to show off to your peers. More and more consumers are shopping at their local grocers with canvas bags, and celebrities are showing up on awards show red carpets stepping out from a Prius rather than a stretch Hummer Limousine.

What started as a simple mantra to "Reduce, Reuse, Recycle" is now backed by governmental regulation. Stronger enforcement that ranges from elimination of plastic bag usage at grocery stores in San Francisco to emissions controls on automobiles across the United States is now commonplace. Think about it: The United States alone uses approximately 100 billion plastic bags annually, and petroleum based plastics are not biodegradable. This means that not one plastic bag will ever decompose. That is a serious problem. If you thought that paper bag usage was much better, guess again. According to the *Washington Post*, the production of paper bags generates 70 percent more air pollutants and 50 times more water pollutants than the production of plastic bags. I guess we are screwed either way.

Honda continues to stand out as one of the top eco-friendly brands in the world. For decades they have been seeking ways to help the environment through advanced technology and innovative new products. These products range from one of the first hybrids on the market (Insight) to the newest generation of emissions-free vehicles (FCX Clarity). The American Council for an Energy-Efficient Economy has recognized Honda for having the "greenest" vehicle on the planet (Civic GX) and placed three additional vehicles on their most environmentally conscious list. This has become just another deficit the US automakers are facing in the long uphill battle to regain market share.

Another great example is footwear manufacturer Timberland, who is placing "nutritional labels" on each shoe box that includes information about where the shoes were made and the manpower it took to produce them. On the inside of each box Timberland challenges the purchaser with a simple question, "What kind of footprint will you leave?" The reason this type of message is so effective is that it puts the decision back in the consumer's hands and gets them to take an active role in change. They point out that the purchase is only half of the equation.

As a marketing person I can tell you that we in the industry are thinking harder about how we produce our materials and keeping a tighter watch on waste from the client side. Major corporations have instituted waste measures in packaging runs and work with third parties to re-purpose all their scrap for other production needs. They are using more recycled materials in the development of point of sale displays at the printing stage and trying to limit their use of coatings and varnish to cut back on pollutants. These are all positive steps, but most marketers also know that about one-third of consumers don't relate to environmental messages. Marketers will make continued changes, but don't expect an overnight shift to screaming about the topic.

# Q: • WHAT IS THE BEST SINGLE
# • AD EVER PRODUCED?

**JASON MILETSKY**
**THE AGENCY PERSPECTIVE**

↳ I'm going to admit something that nobody in advertising is supposed to admit—at least, not out loud. I didn't like Apple's *1984* spot. I know it put them on the map, and I know all the stats that prove how effective it was, and I know that it's sacrilegious to say anything negative about it. After all, there are certain things you're supposed to just accept in life: Led Zeppelin's *Stairway to Heaven* is the greatest song ever written, *The Godfather* is the greatest movie ever made, and Apple's *1984* is the single greatest commercial ever produced. But I'm sorry, I just don't dig it. It's good and well-produced for its time, but it just isn't what everyone seems to make it out to be.

So what *do* I consider the best single ad to be? I came up with two that I had a hard time deciding between, but finally decided that I had to name one the winner. So first, the runner up: Honda's "Cog" spot. I'm not going to spend a lot of time describing this spot. I can't do it justice. But I definitely recommend you check it out on YouTube. Basically, it's like the old game of Mousetrap or a series of dominoes set up to fall over. Starting with a simple gear rolling down a plank, a chain reaction made up of car parts is set in motion until the reveal at the end shows a fully assembled Honda, accompanied by a voiceover that asks, "Isn't it nice when things just…work?" It's a full two minutes, and it's addicting to watch—there's just no way to watch it only halfway through. It's fun, engaging, and well worth the payoff at the end.

I know I didn't do the "Cog" spot enough credit, but if you think I undersold that, there is absolutely no way I can do justice to what I consider to be the best ad ever made: Campbell Soup's "Foster Child" spot. It's been a long time since I've seen it, so I may have some of the details wrong, but basically the spot opens with a social worker standing with a small girl on the porch of what will be the girl's new home. The child, clutching a teddy bear, looks sad and scared. The foster mother answers the door and tries to talk to the girl, but the child won't respond. Before leaving, the social worker tries to reassure the dispirited foster mom that the little girl will come around; she just needs time. So the foster mom goes to the kitchen and makes a bowl of Campbell's soup, which she takes to the little girl in her room, hoping to create some sort of connection. But the little girl still won't look at her; she just clings to her teddy bear even more tightly. Completely dejected, the foster mom turns to leave. She's one foot out the door when the little girl says, "My mommy used to fix me this soup."

Are they fucking *kidding* me? Seriously—I didn't shed a tear at the end of *Love Story*. In fact, the only time I've ever gotten teary at a movie was at the end of *Rudy*. But there I was, all watery-eyed at the end of a 30-second commercial. Unreal. Campbell's did an amazing job tapping into a powerful emotion. (By the way, if the spot sounds depressing, it really isn't. There's a nice payoff at the very end, where the foster mother, fighting back tears, answers, "My mother used to make it for me, too," and the foster mom and little girl bond. But my eyes stop being dry as soon as the little girl delivers her line.) My hat goes off to anybody who can evoke an emotion out of me in only 30 seconds.

### Michael Hand
### The Client Perspective

**⌐** Most of the best known advertising critics will say without any hesitation that the best television ad ever produced was "1984," which introduced Americans to the Apple Macintosh computer for the first time. It had everything that a big ad needs to get your attention: it was in the Super Bowl, it was directed by a high-powered Hollywood movie team (led by Ridley Scott), and it had both tremendous drama and hype. To make this ad even more special, it never appeared on television again after this event.

The storyline provided depth of character with its direct link to the George Orwell novel of the same name, where Big Brother is watching every move and forcing (practically celebrating) social conformity. The overcast industrial setting set the tone as the heroine of the spot—an Olympian-like female runner—entered the scene carrying an oversized hammer. While she is chased by faceless people in black uniforms, Big Brother rambles on about the need to stick with the status quo—until she launches her hammer into the Big Brother master screen and destroys it. Peace is restored and people are free to express themselves openly.

The commercial concludes with an introduction date on the screen and the phrase "You'll see why 1984 won't be like 1984." Powerful stuff. I can imagine the guys around the chips and dip looking up and saying "Holy Crap!" while another turns to his buddy with a glazed look and says, "What just happened?" Not many ads can get that type of reaction. Unlike the critics, I will not call it the best ever; but I will give it mention on my short list.

As I thought harder about this question, a few favorites came to my mind:

- **"Aaron Burr"—Got Milk? campaign.** How great is this ad? As a functional message it portrays the product (milk) as hero that is just out of reach. You watch in pain (granted you are laughing through the pain) for this guy surrounded by the contest trivia answer and unable to speak. I guess we should all have milk on hand for such an occasion.

- **"Frogs"—Budweiser.** I am not the biggest fan of the product portfolio coming out of the St. Louis brewery (my Milwaukee connection runs deep), but you need to hand it to these guys. They have made some classic ads and this is one of the best. All young adult male consumers (and even some awkward older ones) were croaking their brand name in bars across the globe. It is a smart ad, and high on my list next to the first two Bud Bowl events.

- **"When I Grow Up"—Monster.** Every day people go home from work and feel sorry for themselves because aspects of their jobs suck. This ad took all the inner thoughts running through their heads and made them public. It was suddenly OK to be looking for more than "middle management." Best part, they used kids to tell the story of what they had to look forward to. Very funny, but also a very powerful statement.

- **"If You Let Me Play"—Nike.** This is another great use of kids to tell a story, albeit a more emotional one. I'm not sure I truly appreciated this ad before I had a daughter of my own, but it certainly hits home now. For all the testosterone that Nike throws around and athlete endorsement money they spend, this is the best I have seen from the Portland office.

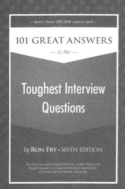
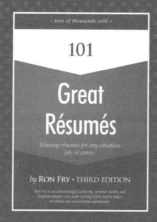
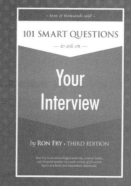